ETHNIC POLITICS AND LTTE IN SRI LANKA

ETHNIC POLITICS AND LTTE IN SRI LANKA

Rajkumar Singh

KALPAZ

Ethnic Politics and LTTE in Sri Lanka

ISBN: 978-81-7835-919-9

Published in 2012 in India by
Kalpaz Publishing House
23, Main Ansari Road
New Delhi-110002
Phones : 23282060, 23261060
Fax : 011-23285914
E-mail: kalpaz@hotmail.com

Laser Typesetting : Quick Media, Delhi
Printed at : Chawla Offset Printers, Delhi

Dedicated to

Dr. Hemlata Singh
Wife

Contents

Preface

Ethnic Politics and LTTE in Sri Lanka makes a deep dent on the aspects of ethnicity in Sri Lanka right from the days when the Sinhalese and the Tamils first became acquainted with each other in the periods before Christ. Except historical wars they both lived harmoniously. It, however, took an alarming proportion when the Britishers invited and encouraged a large number of Indian origin people to come in the island nation as plantation workers. On the eve of Independence and soon thereafter the issue of ethnicity was politicised as the Sinhalese are the sole majority community of the country. Several laws favouring the Sinhalese were enacted in order to achieve political gains at the cost of the interest of minorities, the Tamil, in particular. The Tamil political parties of the time failed to make a bridge and the Tamil leadership was passed on to the Tamil extremist group – the Liberation Tigers of Tamil Eelam, a deadly dominant terrorist organisation, whose single avowed aim was to achieve a separate homeland for the Tamils called 'Eelam'.

As a result of the violence escalated due to LTTE's attacks and activities, the Government of Sri Lanka initiated dialogue for peace process, mostly by foreign collaboration in 1985, 1987 and lastly in February 2002. On the other hand, the LTTE, since its formation in May 1976, had established and strengthened its terror networks in Sri Lanka and in dozens of foreign countries of the world. Many of the foreign governments and peoples were sympathetic to Tamils' cause and they helped them through Tamil diasporas. Large scale violent activities were carried out by the LTTE in the Eighties and Nineties causing an immense loss to political values and economic development.

After decades of violence, the end of the terror commenced with the assumption of Mahinda Rajapaksa as the new President of Sri Lanka in November 2005, who declared a fight to finish the LTTE militarily. The actual war between the LTTE cadres and the Sri Lankan security force started in August 2006 but as the war prolonged and advanced, the Tamil Tigers proved weak. Their strongholds – one by one, were recaptured by the Sri Lankan forces. Deadly decisive wars were fought in the first half of the year 2009 that ultimately decimated the LTTE and smashed its military power totally with the death of its sole, all powerful leader Velupillai Prabakaran on May 18, 2009. With the end of LTTE and the ethnic war, a fresh chapter has begun in the history of Sri Lanka. President Rajapaksa in his second term of office which started on November 19, 2010, has laid emphasis on resettlement of internally displaced persons and assured the development of all sections of society with equal treatment and without any discrimination.

I wish to thank the institutions and individuals for their encouragement, cooperation and good wishes that I received and staff of the central libraries at New Delhi and other places where I got a lot of information and analytical/critical views of different subject experts. They all concerned deserve cordial thanks.

I am deeply grateful to several persons and colleagues. Among teachers Dr. D.N. Mallik, Dr. Kirtyanand Singh, Dr. R.N. Kumar and Dr. M.R. Kazami, retired Professors of the University Department of Political Science, BRA Bihar University, Muzaffarpur, have been constant source of guide and encouragement at every stage. Colleagues Dr. Dhirendra Narayan Singh, Department of Political Science MLT College, Saharsa, Dr. Chandra Prakash Singh, Department of History, Dr. Kumar Jyotivardhan, Dr. Usha Sinha, Department of Hindi, Dr. Ram Naresh Singh, Department of Maithili, West Campus P.G Centre, Saharsa and departmental colleagues, Dr. Bijay Kumar Verma and Dr. Pawan Kumar are thankful for their cooperation and goodwishes. My eldest brother, late Suryanath Singh, my second elder brother, Bhuvneshwar Prasad Singh, father-in-law Shri Ramanand Singh, retired Professor and Head, University Department of Physics, BRA Bihar University, Muzaffarpur, deserve deep sense of gratitude for their sincere goodwishes. I am no less grateful to Rajeev Ranjan who performed the painful task of composing the book, and to colleagues and staff of the B.N. Mandal University, West Campus, P.G. Centre, Saharsa.

I would be failing in my duty if I do not record my honest goodwishes and gratitude to the family members including my wife Dr. Hemlata Singh, son Aditya Priyadarshi and Apurv Adarsh in the completion of the book.

However, for the facts, analysis, views and misjudgements contained in the book I alone am responsible.

7th December 2010 **Rajkumar Singh**

List of Abbreviations

ACD	–	Asia Cooperation Dialogue
AD	–	Annie Domini
AIADMK	–	All-India Anna Dravida Munnetra Kzhagam
ANC	–	Autonomous Zonal Council
APC	–	All Parties Committee
APC	–	All Party Conference
APRC	–	All Party Representative Committee
BC	–	Before Christ
B-C	–	Bandaranaike – Chelvanayakam
CA	–	Competent Authority
CAAT	–	Campaign Against Arms Trade
CFA	–	Cease Fire Agreement
CNC	–	Ceylon National Congress
CP	–	Communist Party
CPA	–	Centre for Policy Alternatives
CRM	–	Civil Rights Movement
CWC	–	Ceylon Workers Congress
DDC	–	District Development Council
DoD	–	Department of Defence
DWC	–	Democratic Workers' Congress
ENLF	–	The Eelam National Liberation Front
EP	–	Elephant Pass
EPC	–	Eastern Provincial Council

EPDP	–	Eelam People's Democratic Party
EPRLF	–	The Eelam People's Revolutionary Liberation Front
EROS	–	The Eelam Revolutionary Organisation of Students
EU	–	European Union
FBI	–	Federal Bureau of Investigation
FDLs	–	Forward Defence Lines
FP	–	Federal Party
GDP	–	Gross Domestic Product
GOC	–	Government Office in Command
IDPs	–	Internally Displaced Persons
ICG	–	International Crisis Group
ICRC	–	International Committee of Red Cross
IIC	–	India International Centre
IPKF	–	Indian Peace-keeping Force
ISGA	–	Interim Self-Governing Authority
ITCC	–	Indian Tamil Cultural Council
JSS	–	Jatika Sevaka Sangamaya
JVP	–	Janatha Vimukti Peramuna
LLRC	–	Lessons Learnt and Reconciliation Commission
LSSP	–	Lanka Sama Samaja Party
LTTE	–	Liberation Tigers of Tamil Eelam
MCNS	–	Media Centre for National Security
MEP	–	Mahajana Eksath Peramuna
MoU	–	Memorandum of Understanding
MSR	–	Main Supply Route
NAM	–	Non-Aligned Movement
NFZ	–	No-Fire Zone
NGO	–	Non-Governmental Organisation
NMAT	–	National Movement Against Terrorism
PA	–	People's Alliance

PDS	–	Planning and Development Secretariat
PLO	–	Palestinian Liberation Organisation
PLOTE	–	People's Liberation Organisation of Tamil Eelam.
PPC	–	Political Parties Conference
PSC	–	Parliamentary Select Committee
PTA	–	Prevention of Terrorism Act
P-TOMS	–	Post-Tsunami Operational Management Structure
RAW	–	Research and Analysis Wing
RNG	–	Royal Norwegian Government
SAARC	–	South Asian Association for Regional Cooperation
SCOPP	–	Secretariat for Coordinating the Peace Process
SFG	–	Strategic Foresight Group
SLA	–	Sri Lankan Army
SLAF	–	Sri Lanka Air Force
SLFP	–	Sri Lankan Freedom Party
SLMC	–	Sri Lankan Muslim Congress
SLMM	–	Sri Lankan Monitoring Mission
SLNP	–	Sri Lankan National Police
SMS	–	Sinhala Maha Sabha
STF	–	Special Task Force
TC	–	Tamil Congress
TELA	–	Tamil Eelam Liberation Army
TELO	–	Tamil Eelam Liberation Organisation
TEM	–	Tamil Eelam Movement
TMVP	–	Tamil Makkal Viduthalai Puligal
TNA	–	Tamil National Alliance
TNT	–	Tamil New Tigers
TUF	–	Tamil United Front
TULF	–	Tamil United Liberation Front
UF	–	United Front

UFPA	–	United Progressive Freedom Alliance
UNP	–	United National Party
UPFA	–	United People's Freedom Alliance
UTHR	–	United Teachers for Human Rights
WFLT	–	Women's Front of the Liberation Tigers

1

GENESIS OF LTTE

On solid grounds of sociological theory we feel and assert that today Sri Lanka has to recognise its patriotic identity built upon a confederative principle that recognises the existence of several communities as well as three nations within the entity Lanka (Ceylon). The three nations are the Sinhalese, the Tamils and the Muslims. The communities are the Malays, Burghers, indigenous Vaddas, Colombo Chetties, Borahs, Sindhis, Parsees and Memons. Identities together have enough potential to strengthen patriotism and nationalism in the island nation.

Early Inhabitants

The earliest known inhabitants with any living descendants of modern Sri Lanka are the Wanniyala-Aetto, commonly known as Vaddah, Nagas and Yakkhas. It is generally believed that these aboriginal inhabitants of the island have migrated from the south India in the remote past when the two countries—India and Sri Lanka are supposed to have formed a single landmass. Historians – A.L. Basham, G.C. Mendis and others are of the view that a people of Dravidian stock were the earliest settlers. Basham opines that Dravidian infiltration into Ceylon must have been going on from the earliest historical times and probably before. It is a proven fact that a pre-Aryan aboriginal tribe of hunters called Vaddah lived in certain parts of the island before the arrival of the Vijayan band.[1] G.C. Mendis, the Ceylonese historian also supports this theory and writes in this connection that it is possible that like the wild animals that came from south India to Ceylon, the Vaddah occupied this island at a time when it was not separated from India by a stretch of sea. Then waves rolled and ages passed, and the continental drift came to separate Sri Lanka with her pre-Aryan inhabitants from the Deccan plateau by a stretch of water which in course of time, received such geographic names as Bay of Bengal, Arabian sea, Indian Ocean, Gulf of Mannar and Palk Strait.[2] Most of the early inhabitants have lived as villagers for some time. A few tribes have until recently continued to live the hunter-gatherer lifestyle, but although attitudes are influx, the government has made this increasingly difficult.

Being strategically located in the Indian Ocean and separated from the Indian sub-continent by a narrow strip of shallow water called the Palk Strait, it could not, however, snap its links with India and shares common race, language and history with the Indian mainland. The country is multi-ethnic in nature with varied racial and religious groups inhabiting the island. It is also an interesting part of the history of Sri Lanka that the two principal communities, Sinhala and Tamil, originated from India. The first to come in the island were the Sinhala. Later, the Tamils attacked the Sinhala and ruled a part of Sri Lanka and maintained there supremacy in the northern part of the country. The rivalry between these two communities has not died out yet and has an important bearing on the political life and history of the country.[3] Despite the linguistic and religious differences, the two communities have strong cultural and racial similarities. Physically the Sinhalese and Tamils cannot be differentiated. Though the initial Sinhalese migrants were probably Indo-European language speakers who arrived over 2500 years ago, Practically, all later arrivals were South Indians, mostly Tamil speakers, who were assimilated into the Sinhalese – Buddhist community.[4] Kinship and marriage patterns among the Sinhalese are also part of a larger Dravidian pattern. It is these cultural and subdoctrinal similarities that permitted the assimilation of South Indians over centuries into the Sinhalese Buddhist social structure.

Sinhalese

Most historians believe that the Sinhalese came to Sri Lanka from northern India, near Bengal, during the 6th century B.C. and Vijaya Singha was believed to be the legendary ancestor of the major race of the island, namely, the Aryan Sinhalese race. He was described historically the first king of Sri Lanka and honoured as the founder-hero of the Sinhalese (Lion) race. Vijaya Singha when reached the island with his band of 700 followers at Tambapani on the north-west coast of Sri Lanka on the day of Lord Buddha's Parinirvans', he found the country in the occupation of the Yakkhas, the earliest inhabitants of the territory. The new comer defeated them easily with the help of Yakkhini whom he married. Soon thereafter, Vijaya established an extensive settlements throughout the island, giving the name of Sinhala and making himself the eponymous hero of the Sinhalese race, he, however, was not willing to declare the Yakkhini, his wife, as the queen of the kingdom. He searched out a maiden of a noble house and for the purpose sent envoys to Madhura in the Pandu country. Identified as the Pandya territory in

South India to request its king to give his daughter in marriage to Vijaya Singha. The envoys piloted the mission successfully and came back not only with king's daughter but also many other maidens of good birth for marriage with Vijaya's followers together with craftsmen and a thousand families of the eighteen guilds. Following the custom of the time, the Pandya princess was consecrated by Vijaya Singha as his queen and now formally called himself the king of Lanka. Thus the Aryan kingdom came to be established in Sri Lanka, but even today it is a point of dissent — whether the eponymous founder of the Sinhalese race hailed from the east coast of northern India or from its west coast.

King Vijaya Singha ruled Sri Lanka for nearly forty years (543 – 505 B.C.) but died leaving no son from the Pandya Princess to succeed. After one year of his death the throne was offered to Pandu Vasdeva, his nephew, who arrived at Sri Lanka from Vijaya's ancestral homeland. If Vijaya typified the man of action, Pandu Vasdeva typified the man of thought. These two Aryan types together with the Dravidian and aboriginal elements produced the great civilisation of Sri Lanka. Devanampiya Tissa (247-207 B.C.) was the next important king of the kingdom who was the contemporary of Mauryan emperor Asoka. Devanampiya Tissa was succeeded by his three younger brothers each of whom ruled for ten years, one after the other and during the reign of Suratissa, the youngest of the three brothers, two South Indian adventures of Tamil extraction introduced and seized the kingdom for twenty two years. About the middle of the second century again Elara, a prince from the Chola Kingdom of South India ruled over the Sinhalese Kingdom for forty four years. Later on invasions on the part of Chola dynasty of South India became frequent and they acquired sovereignty in Sri Lanka over Sinhalese kings with intervals. However, for most part of the history the island was ruled by the Sinhalese kings and Parakramabahu VI was the last Sinhalese king who could be said to have ruled the whole of Sri Lanka (1412 – 67 A.D.). Parakramabahu VIII ruled the small kingdom of Kotte, near Colombo when in November 1505 some Portuguese ships anchored at Colombo and registered the entry of westerners in the island nation.

Vijaya Singha, the first Sinhalese King of Sri Lanka had settled in the northern plain. The other invaders and settlers probably arrived from both the east and west coasts of north and central India. These people spoke an Indo-Aryan language and settled by the shores of rivers in the northern, south-eastern and western parts of the island. They were originally engaged in pastoral occupations but in course of time they took to agriculture and spread into the interior where they developed Anuradhapura in the north, and Magama in the south, into great cities. The developed Anuradhapura was made the capital of Sinhalese kingdom for a long time but later in the A.D. 900, it was moved to Polonnaruva where it remained for about 400 years. Further, Tamil attacks saw another withdrawal of the Sinhalese Kingdom to the hills and ultimately to Kandy.[5]

In the period of Sinhalese kingship for over a thousand years, Anuradhapura was the centre of Sinhalese civilization. The core of the Sinhalese identity was Buddhism : the destiny of the ethnic group and that of the religion were inseparable. Myths and historical events confirmed the twin facets of this identity. Buddhism was first introduced to the island when Asoka was the Maurya Emperor of India in the 3rd century B.C. and his counterpart in Sri Lanka was Devanampiya Tissa, a king renowned for his piety and good deeds. Asoka's son Mahinda came to Sri Lanka to spread the gospel of Buddhism. Before that, the religious beliefs of the islanders were by and large of a primitive and animistic kind. There were, besides, small groups practising various forms of Brahmanism, Jainism and Saivism. Then Buddhism made a strong foothold and became the State religion while spreading farther, to other countries. Most of the sects of religion, in course of time, adopted into Buddhism and Sri Lanka evolved a kind of *theravada* Buddhism for which it has acquired a reputation among the Buddhist countries of south and south-east Asia.[6] Especially, the reign of King Tissa saw a spurt in building a large number of Buddhist temples in Anuradhapura and elsewhere.

Buddhism and a sophisticated system of irrigation became the pillars of classical Sinhalese civilization that flourished in the north-central part of the island with capitals at Anuradhapura (200 B.C. – A.D. 1000) and Polonnaruva (AD 1070 – 1200). The building of great religious edifices dedicated to the promotion of Buddhism, the construction of irrigation facilities to ensure a regular supply of water and the guarding or freeing of the country from south Indian invaders as occasion demanded were the main preoccupation of Sinhalese kings in ancient times. In addition, the social as well as the cultural life of the Sinhalese have also been determined by the geographical stand-point. The Sinhalese are categorised as Low-Country and Up-Country or Kandyan Sinhalese. The Low-Country Sinhalese are mostly concentrated in the west and in the south of the island. They experienced significant changes through the 400 years of European rule with many of them taking to Christianity and English education. The Up-Country or Kandyan Sinhalese have maintained their independence for a long time in comparison with other kingdoms and were late in coming under European influence. They preserved their social pattern which was feudal, hierarchial and conservative in nature. They considered themselves the repository of pure Sinhalese tradition and have emphasised traditional Buddhist education rather than English education. As we all are aware opposing the Sinhalese – Buddhist identity was the Tamil Hindu identity.

Tamils

The origins of Tamil presence on the island are not clear. But due to the country's close proximity to the mainland, it is very likely that the people have travelled back and forth throughout human history. Island's first inhabitants, the Sinhalese, migrated from India and the Tamils followed a couple of centuries later. The Sinhalese origin story describes their first men taking 100 wives from South India. Historians conclude that during King Tissa's reign a large number of Hindu Brahmins came to Sri Lanka and the Sinhalese named them Bamilas from which the word 'Tamil' is derived. It is also evident from the excavations made so far and particularly by the German scholars that Tamils had been living in the northern and eastern parts of the island from time immemorial. Several small fragments of pottery with a few Tamil Brahmi letters scratched on them have been found from the Jaffna region. According to an excavation conducted at Tissamaharama, a pottery inscription has been found on the Southeastern coast of Sri Lanka. In it a fragment of a high-quality black and redware flat dish inscribed in Tamil in the Tamil-Brahmi script was found in the earliest layer which was provisionally dated back to around 200 B.C.[7] The inscriptions also bear a testimony to the presence in southern Sri Lanka a local Tamil mercantile community organised in a guild to conduct inland and maritime trade as early as at the close of the 3rd century B.C.[8] Around the period and even earlier, Tamils ruled Sri Lanka and their fight with Sinhalese Kingdoms also took place occasionally.

The systematic history of Tamil's rule in Sri Lanka starts, about the middle of the 2nd century B.C., under the spell of the rule of prince Elara from the Chola Kingdom in South India. The prince Elara seized the northern Sinhalese Kingdom and ruled it for forty-four years. The Tamil King Elara tried his best to unite the two races, Tamils and the Sri Lankans, into one. His Tamil Kingdom extended to the south till it reached the kingdom of Gamini's father. The two kings coexisted peacefully. However, the Tamil invaders generated national solidarity among the Sinhalese and ultimately King Elara was dislodged by the Sinhalese warrior from the southern sector of the island, Dutthagamani, who succeeded in bringing the entire island under his sway. Dutthagamani made Anuradhapura the centre of his rule, turned deeply religious and built monasteries and temples. He made it known to all that Sri Lanka is for the Sinhalese and is the home of the Sinhalese and the Sinhalese only.

The occasional fights between the Tamils and the Sinhalese weakened the Sinhalese and years afterwards the island relapsed into Chola rule. The Chola King Rajaraja I (A.D. 985-1016), acquired sovereignty over northern Sri Lanka and founded a new capital at Polonnaruva, situated on the south east of Anuradhapura. Another Chola King of Sri Lanka was Rajendra Choladeva I (A.D. 1016 -1044), during whose reign the south Indian invasion of Sri Lanka reached a new height as he conquered most of the island in A.D. 1017. In this period Sri Lanka ceased to be an independent kingdom and remained a mere province of the mighty Chola Empire of India till the island regained her independence in A.D. 1070. However, during the long years of Chola occupation, Buddhism and the Sinhalese suffered a great deal from neglect and oppression. It witnessed the end of Anuradhapura, the centre of Sinhalese civilization and thereafter Sinhalese history followed a chequered course. Especially, after the reign of Parakrama Bahu the Great (1153 – 86), a brief decade of peace and stability remained but it signalled the end of a great and ancient civilization.

As the Parakrama Bahu the Great, had no son to succeed, the confusion which followed his death ultimately led to the establishment of a separate Tamil Kingdom at Jaffna in the northern extremity of Sri Lanka in the thirteenth century. The Sinhalese rulers had, therefore, to retreat southward to keep off the Tamil invaders, abandoning the ancient centres of civilization like Anuradhapura and Polonnaruva and moving their Headquarters from one place to another. In general, the country being disordered split into several ruling factions, some Sinhalese, others Tamils. But the internal strifes between the Sinhalese and the Tamils did not affect the religious creeds which flourished side by side. The Tamil Kingdom of Jaffna had ceased to be an independent unit when in 1618 it was subjugated by the Portuguese. At the time, the Portuguese arrived in the island country in 1505, it comprised of three kingdoms – Jaffna in the north, Maha Nuwara or Kandy in the central highlands, and Kotte in the south-west maritime districts. In the rivalry and struggle for sovereignty over the island, among the Portuguese, the Dutch and the British the the last one succeeded in capturing the island in 1815 by defeating, the king of Kandy, the last of the native rulers and created the Crown Colony of Ceylon.

Effects of British Occupation

The economy, society and politics as well began to take a turn with the coming of the Britishers in Sri Lanka and their occupation of Kandy in 1815. They established plantation economy based on tea, rubber and coconuts. The Industrial Revolution that raised its heads in West Europe affected much the political, social and economic set-up of the then England and accumulation of access capital in private hands motivated them to invest the capital in developing countries like Sri Lanka, India and others. The British capitalists exported their cash to the colonies abroad for investment in railways, mines and plantations and Sri Lanka appeared to be the country where their capital could be employed profitably in plantation economy. However, the cultivation of coffee was in practice before the British came to the island nation and it assumed special significance with their entry and Kandyan Highlands offered an ideal soil and a congenial climate for the cultivation of coffee. All classes of the British people and a handful of Ceylonese citizens became the planters in Sri Lanka and established their estates in different parts of the country.

The culture of the plantation crops required an adequate supply of labourers ready to be employed on estate work and willing to reside on estate areas. Although the work on coffee estate was seasonal, the plantation of tea required a regular supply of labour, both male and female, throughout the year. The available Sinhalese and Kandyan labourers were ready to work but unwilling to stay on the plantation areas permanently. To the Sinhalese labourers the employment in plantation work was only subsidiary to the cultivation of their paternal lands which supplied most of their economic needs. In the other hand, most of the Sinhalese labourers belonged to peasant class. According to the Ceylon Census Report of 1891, nearly 92 per cent of the entire agricultural class were cultivators and agricultural labourers. Moreover, the Sinhalese labourers preferred to call themselves cultivators, as agriculture was looked upon by them as an occupation dignified in Buddhism and entirely in accord with the natural inclinations of the people.[9] The idea of procuring plantation labourers from China and importing African slaves as labourers was also not congenial for the estate owners of Sri Lanka and was abandoned finally.

Under the circumstances and on the recommendation of Emmerson Tennent, the Officiating Lt-Governor of Sri Lanka, the only resort then left to the planters was the South Indian labour. In his dispatch of 21 April 1847 Tennent wrote to Lord Grey, the Colonial Secretary, "The great object of the colonial government should be to create a permanent and indigenous supply of labour within the island and, if this is not to be effected by stimulating the inert and contended Sinhalese, another expedient is still open by holding out such encouragement as may induce the Indian labourers to settle permanently in Ceylon. Such a settlement should be encouraged on the estates."[10] As a result, the South Indian Tamil labourers was, in course of time, followed by middle-class migrants. In a nutshell, the poverty and social handicaps of the low-caste Tamil agricultural labourers, on the one hand, and, on the other the British capitalists' investment of private capital in the plantation economy of Sri Lanka, necessitated the import of labour from abroad. The migration of middle class to Sri Lanka was due to introduction of trade and industry. Sri Lanka not only provided the large masses of indigent population of the Tamil South with a way to escape from the pinch of poverty and the tyranny of caste but also opened up before the Indian industrialists, businessmen and bankers, tempering avenues for their economic interprises.[11] However, they went there with no desire to settle permanently but to stay there as the holders of temporary residence permits, renewable from time to time.

The employment of the Kandy by the British had paved the way for the developmental projects of the island nation in almost all walks of life. The new ruler stressed the need of adequate and suitably skilled and semi-skilled labourers for reclamation and development works. It compelled the Colonial Government to form, in 1821, a semi-military organisation, known as the Pioneer Labour Force and the South Indian labourers, thus recruited as members of the Pioneer Labour Force. Within a decade or two of the formation of the Pioneer Labour Force, the recruitment of Tamil labourers for the coffee estates started through the Kangani system and the first batch of Tamil labourers had reached the island in 1837. Initially there was no law prevailing on migration between India and Sri Lanka. If however met some restrictions in 1847 through the Act XIII passed by India. The majority of the estate labourers hailed from the Tamil speaking areas but it also included the labourers of Malayalam speaking and Telugu – speaking, though very small in number.

Thus broadly speaking, the Indian Tamils residing in Sri Lanka have been divided into two distinct groups – (i) The Ceylon Tamils and (ii) The Indian Tamils. The Ceylon Tamils are also called indigenous Tamils and are the descendants of those Tamils who reached Sri Lanka in the wake of the Chola invasions beginning with the Chola prince Elara or even earlier. The Ceylon Tamils ultimately settled in Northern and Eastern provinces which constitute the dry zone of Sri Lanka as opposed to the wet zone inhabited by the Sinhalese. In a sense, the Ceylon Tamils are both Ceylonese and Tamils – Ceylonese because they enjoy Ceylonese citizenship, and Tamils because they have cultural affinity to the Tamils of South India. The Ceylon Tamil group is important both politically and economically. They are well represented in commerce, professions, academia and government service.[12]

Traditionally, the Tamils of the east coast and the parts of the North Central Province owed suzerainty to Sinhalese Kings of Kandy and the trade routes connected the east coast with the Kingdom of Kandy. Sinhalese - Tamil intermarriage, exceptional in the north, was accepted and practised on the east coast until the recent times. But a certain amount of nostalgia in both the Tamils and Sinhalese about the past history makes the Tamils aware that at one time they had ruled portions of the island. The Sinhalese have not forgotten that the Tamils had occupied parts of their country and had to be driven away.[13] Another significant fact is that the Jaffna area near Tamilnadu in India has been the traditional home of a heavy Tamil population. There are many Hindu temples in this area.

In comparison to the Ceylon Tamils, the Indian Tamils immigrated into Sri Lanka recently especially in the 19th and early 20th centuries from the Tamil-speaking areas of South India. They included (i) estate labourers (ii) non-estate workers, and (iii) traders and business men. All these three categories of Tamils and their descendants came to be known as Indian Tamils. The majority of estate labourers are concentrated in the plantation districts and were assisted with advance and passage money to immigrate into Sri Lanka. Most of them were recruited labourers or labourers recruited by licensed Kanganies. Some of the estate labourers were non-recruited who were composed mainly of old labourers. In addition, the labour force employed on estates was composed not only of the Indian Tamils but also of other social groups such as the low-country Sinhalese, Kandyan Sinhalese, Ceylon Tamils, Ceylon Moors, Indian Moors, Europeans, Burghers and Eurasians, but the Indian Tamils on estates formed a predominant social group in the total estate population of Sri Lanka. The occupation of estate labourers was limited mainly to the work connected with plantation.

The estate Tamil labourers who immigrated during the British colonial days led a full social life in which the caste rigidity of South India was almost non-existent. They formed a society of their own in the estate areas where they were employed. The Tamil estate labourers in Sri Lanka normally maintained the social tradition in which their ancestors grew up in South India but no caste prejudices have affected the Tamil life on estates. High-caste labourers do not scruple about serving under low-born Kanganies. High and low castes live quite agreeably side by side. It was observed by T.L.R. Chandran, Agent to the Government of India in Sri Lanka that the rigidity of caste system which prevails among the peasantry or agricultural labourers in South India stands modified and overlaid with new and liberal ideas of social relationship in Sri Lanka. Differentiation between high and low castes is no doubt, recognised but intermarriages between the members of different sub-castes are quite common. The term untouchability is almost unknown among the Tamil estate labourers in Ceylon.[14] Although somewhat liberal in respect of caste-principles and caste-prejudices, the estate Tamil labourers were fairly conservative in matters of religion.

The Tamil estate labourers of Sri Lanka strictly followed their religious life built upon the religious beliefs and traditions of their ancestors. They had left caste behind in South India but carried their religion with them while immigrating to the island for estate work. To them religion consists in worshipping deities in their crude way, propitiating evil spirits and in observing certain ritualistic festivals. Every large plantation has its little temple or church usually erected by the Tamils themselves. The religious-minded among the estate labourers make annual pilgrimages to Kataragama and Adam's Peak situated on the south-east coast of Sri Lanka. Although the South Indian Tamil estate labourers of Sri Lanka were not without recreational facilities to break the monotony of their routine duties on estates, unfortunately they have a poor health as a consequence of poor diet. In spite of that they are loyal and hard workers, contributing to the economic prosperity of Sri Lanka.

The non-estate labourers of Indian origin in Sri Lanka included manual workers, variously employed as domestic servants, porters, rickshaw-puller, workers in factories, workshops and warehouses, also as workers on roads and alike. Ranganathan, the Indian Agent, confirmed in his report submitted in 1923 that domestic servants in the city of Colombo were of Indian descent until recently.[15] He also mentioned further that in this kind of service it may be said that the Indians have almost displaced the Sinhalese. The Public Works Department, Railways, alongs with other departments were also well-represented by the workers of Indian descent. But Indian workers in Sri Lanka possessed lower posts in the island's Railway where ninety per cent of the skilled workers have been Sinhalese. In the thirties, the Department had strictly followed the government policy of giving preference to the Sinhalese labourers while engaging new hands. Indians who found employment as daily-paid hands were not at all happy. In March 1939, the Ministry of Communications and Works made a proposal for the discontinuance of the system with a view to replacing them by the Ceylonese. The term 'Ceylonese' was defined as a 'person born in Ceylon'.

The Indian business-community in Sri Lanka included, besides those, engaged in general professions, big business men, small traders and boutique-keepers, resorted to by both the Indian settlers and local inhabitants. A certain percentage of the miscellaneous immigrants belonged to the professional class such as lawyers and doctors. There had been many Indian employed as clerks in commercial houses and as teachers in schools. Even before the independence of Sri Lanka in 1948, Indian immigrants were largely figured in the profession of ladies' tailors, barbers, shoe-makers, eating-house keepers, dairymen and of itinerant vendors of food-stuffs. In addition to the aforesaid occupations, there were a few more in which the miscellaneous immigrants were engaged such as the production of gas and electricity, printing, book-binding, fishing, pottery, work in iron and steel, work in precious and other metals bakery, dress-making and construction of carts etc.[16] Although the recent immigrants of Indian origin in Sri Lanka were not indigenous to the island, they had the same legal status as the Sinhalese and the Sri Lankan Tamils during the British rule. It, however, posed a threat to the Sinhalese and rivalry between the two for dominance in Sri Lanka in 1920s and thereafter.

Ethnic Issues Around Independence

Like other societies of the world ethnicity in Sri Lanka emerged on the basis of differentiations prevailent in economic and social classes. With the coming of Westerners, especially the long staying of the British had transformed the traditional agrarian economy into an export-oriented economy based on tea and rubber plantation. This uneven capitalist development created serious socio-economic divisions within the Sri Lankan society. The new plantation agriculture, in due course, formed a legion of new trades and occupations : landowners, planters, transport agents, contractors, and businessmen. Among the Sinhalese, some castes such as the fishermen and cinnamon peelers were also benefitted from the emerging new economic order. On the other hand, the traditional elite – the chiefs and headmen among the Low Country Sinhalese and the Kandyan aristocracy formed a new class. For a long time, the Kandyan Sinhalese boycotted the colonial masters and remained attached to their traditional social pattern. In addition, the Sinhalese are divided by a caste system. The first is that between Low Country and Kandyan Sinhalese. It refers to the part of the island from which one's family originates. The Low Country Sinhalese are from the lowland coastal belt around the entire island which were ruled by the Dutch and the British for three centuries and as a result became far more Westernised than the residents of the hilly Kandyan areas. Consequently, the Kandyan Sinhalese, who remained independent till their occupation by the British in 1815, are seen less urbanised, and less exposed to both the western culture and English language as well. The social divide between the Low Country Sinhalese and Kandyan Sinhalese led to their disparity in the economic spheres and the latter normally faced greater hardships.

Apart from the Ceylonese Tamils who were residing in the country for centuries, the British occupation of Kandy introduced another complexity of Sri Lanka's social life. They brought in large numbers of South Indian tribal and often low status groups as coolie labour on the tea plantation of the central highlands. Thus, Tamil-Hindu number can now be found throughout the island, but they are concentrated in three areas : the Northern Province where they form an overwhelming majority, the Eastern Province where they are predominant in some areas and greater Colombo. Though the outside world in general, see the Tamil problem as one, the internal reality is different. The northern Tamils were much more orthodox Hindus than the Tamils elsewhere and were strongly patrilineal. The east coast Tamils came from Kerala and were divided into matrilineal clans, while the Tamils of the central province were recently introduced groups from South India, alienated from both the groups. They were thrust into the midst of a surrounding Sinhalese population from whom they were also alienated.[17]

The origin of ethnicity can be traced back in the 1920s when the Indian Tamils started first in the form of a cooperative movement and later under the Jaffna Youth Congress, a social movement against caste distinctions in Sri Lanka.[18] It was the result of the reluctance of the Sinhalese to take to the regimented life of the estates. The period also witnessed arising of a political question relating to the representation in legislature. It posed a threat to the Sinhalese who were opposed to giving the large numbers of Indians the right to vote as recommended by the Donoughmore Commission in 1928. From the view point of Sinhalese, it meant (i) a dilution of the electoral strength of the Kandyan Sinhalese in most of the constituencies in the Kandyan areas; (ii) the possibility of Indian Tamils being returned as representatives of Kandyan Sinhalese constituencies in the event of the splitting of the Kandyan Sinhalese vote between rival candidates; and (iii) the likelihood, especially at the time of the Donoughmore reforms of British planters, and /or Indian estate Kanganies herding the Indian vote in favour of the candidate of their choice. Later in 1929, the report of the Commission was debated in the Ceylon Legislative Council and the provision relating to the franchise of the Indian immigrants was modified by imposing several restrictions and the communal character of representation continued even thereafter. Earlier the changes effected in the composition of the Legislative Council in 1909 and 1920 did not go far enough to satisfy the Ceylonese reformers, but in 1923 the Legislative Council was expanded so as to have a majority of Ceylonese unofficial members with a large elective element.[19] At this stage a cleavage occurred between the Sinhalese and the Ceylon Tamils. While the latter with the support from other minority groups, namely the Indians, Muslims, Burghers and Europeans, wished communal representation to be maintained, the Sinhalese reformers asked for the introduction of the territorial principle. Both communities – the Sinhalese and the Tamils became principal rivals in establishing their cultural superiority and administrative hegemony over the other.

By the time the ethnic identities of both the communities became evident, the Buddhist revivalist movement contributed towards the end significantly. Sri Lanka is the only country in the world where Threavada

Buddhism had the largest following. As an opposition to the growing influence of Christian religion and English language in matters of social and cultural living, there was a Sinhala Buddhists cultural movements to assert the rightful place of Buddhism. The movement propounded a theory of cultural nationalism which established a special relationship between Buddhism, the Sinhalese people and the island. According to this, Sinhala Buddhists alone had the original rights to Sinhaladvipa. But, above all, a fear of Indian domination, particularly of being swamped by the Tamils from across the Palk Strait, figured prominently in the Sinhala-Buddhist discourse. The presence of a large number of Indian Tamil estate workers in the heart of the Sinhalese country, as it were, and that too in the island's economically most rewarding sectors posed both a political and an economic threat to the Sinhalese people.

At the start, the Sri Lankan Tamils did not feel threatened by the Sinhalese revivalism. The elites of both the communities worked together for constitutional reforms. In 1919 they came together under the banner of Ceylon National Congress whose first president was a prominent Tamil, Sir Ponnambalam Arunachalam. But the position did not last long and the progressive reforms and gradualism in constitutional development characterised the demands of the Ceylonese nationalists. The differences between the two communities surfaced following the constitutional reforms of 1920 which introduced territorial representation and enlarged the legislature with an unofficial majority. It led to the question of communal representation in which the Sinhalese insisted upon representation according to population strength-wise. The Sri Lankan Tamils wanted representation in excess of their numbers.

Discrimination based on religious differences is much less common than discrimination based on ethnic group or caste. It, however, played significantly while shaping the religious identities of both the communities. The trauma of imperial conquest and the disestablishment of the two major religions produced in the north Tamil-Hindu revival movement headed by Armugam Navalar and in the South a Sinhalese-Buddhist revival headed by Anagarika Dharmapala. Both the reformers rationalised their respective religions, scorned folk beliefs and rituals, affirmed their respective greater traditions. Navalar gave contemporary Hinduism a philosophical base in Saiva Siddantha while Dharmapala affirmed the ascetic and abstract values of doctrinal Buddhism largely influenced by Western commentators on Buddhism.[20] In a nutshell, both provided a philosophy and an ethic for classes that had practically no historical parallel in the past, a bourgeoisie and a proletariat that emerged in the colonial and post-colonial periods. Dharmapala not only affirmed the traditional Sinhalese-Buddhist identity but opposed it to other identities – Muslim, Hindu, Christian.

Related to the whole issue is the concept of ethnic war. It is a large scale violent incident entailing an organised and prolonged military engagement and confrontation between regular government forces and highly mobilised insurgent or militant groups. In this context, the warring parties and their grievances and goals are solely defined in ethnic terms.[21] Winning the war is, therefore, the fundamental objective of the combatants. Compromise is hard to arrive at in negotiations, so long as the asymmetry of power between the ethnic parties is not altered. Thus power assumes an important factor in determing the outcome.[22] Though the internal ethnic wars are serious hostile event, it however, does not develop in vacuum or automatically, but stems from deep rooted socio-economic and political grievances that cannot be redressed by normal political means. In the sense grievance-formation as a principal source of ethnic war is a dynamic process in which each ethnic group with seemingly different ethno-ideological and value structures, try to consolidate and promote its identity and material interests from a threat or invalidating behaviour of other groups.[23] It is deep-rooted in a situation, where one group's core sense of 'self identity' or 'interest' in politico-cultural and economic sense is perceivably or in reality threatened by the demands of, or denial by another group, thereby eliciting the former group's defensive response.

In Pre-Independence phase, the Donoughmore constitution of 1931 was the most important one, because, through, it the Sinhalese desired further change and utilised the power they had obtained to improve the conditions of the Sinhalese electorates while the minority groups, especially the Tamils felt neglected and dominated and at every stage demanded safeguards. Earlier differences between the two potential ethnic groups arose over the question of ratio in communal representation and particularly over the refusal of the Sinhalese to agree to the creation of a separate communal electorate for the Ceylon Tamils of the Western province. Soon thereafter the Sinhalese leadership became more antagonistic to the communal principle and by mid 1920s, the Ceylon Tamil began to consider themselves and the Sinhalese as the two major communities in the country, while referring to the other groups as minorities.[24] The constitution of 1931 ultimately included universal suffrage and territorial representation perhaps as desired by the Sinhalese and with these provisions the notion of communal representation was abandoned. It, however, widened the scope for communal thinking which gathered a new strength and momentum in the following years.

The general elections in Sri Lanka were held in 1936 which followed the formation of the Pan-Sinhalese board of ministers by the State Council, the same year. A further indication of communal thinking in the island was evident from the formation of communal organisations which worsened the prevailing situation. In 1937 the Sinhala Maha Sabha was formed by S.W.R.D. Bandaranaike and the All Ceylon Tamil Congress in 1944. In between the period several other organisations were formed such as the All Ceylon Moors' Association (1935), the Burgher Political Association (1938), and the Ceylon Indian Congress (1939). As the independence of India and Sri Lanka approached representatives of both the Governments met together at a conference at New Delhi in 1940 to find out a satisfactory basis for formal negotiations on all issues of common interest between the two countries, but gained nothing due to difference of opinion with the counterpart delegation. The Ceylonese delegation included D.S. Senanayake and S.W.R.D. Bandaranaike who were poles apart on the issue. While the former favoured the idea of the retaining all the immigrant labourers, the latter could not agree to the policy of retaining the entire body of Indian labourers. D.S. Senanayake was the man who tried from the mid-1930s to stand above all communal conflicts and function as a conciliator.

As their last attempt, to be free from the Sinhalese domination, the Tamils of Ceylon produced the demand for balanced representation and sought 50 per cent of seats in the legislature be reserved for all the minority groups and that statutory provision be made for not more than half of the members of the cabinet to be chosen from any one community. The proposal of Ceylon Tamils was rejected by the Sinhalese political elites and the Soulbury Commission, but the latter had recommended various constitutional safeguards which they hoped might allay the fears of discrimination. Under the new Soulbury Constitution a general election was held in Sri Lanka in August-September 1947 in which the United National Party of D.S. Senanayake formed in September 1946, got the largest number of seats, though not a majority in the House of Representatives. He was appointed Prime Minister of the country by the British Governor, Sir Henry Monck-Mason Moore. In December of that year the British Parliament adopted the Ceylon

Independence Act and with the consent of the new government of Sri Lanka appointed the date 4 February 1948 on which the country was to become a sovereign nation. End of British rule was not the end of the problem of ethnicity in the island nation rather it opened a vast space for indigenous majority Sinhala community dominated government to discriminate and alienate further the Tamils of Sri Lanka in a authoritative way. Thus the independent government of Sri Lanka and the nation as well inherited the problem of ethnicity since its birth.

Years After Independence

Alienating Factors

After the independence of Sri Lanka in February 1948 the internal scene changed against the Tamils. It was based on the ethno-political dominance of the Sinhalese majority and as a result the ethnic divide between the Sinhalese and the Tamils have sharpened and widened in the years following independence. There are at least three aspects : (i) education and employment; (ii) religion and national culture; and (iii) language have dominated the policies of the Sri Lankan governments which have clearly fostered the ethnic divide between the two communities of the island. The Presidential system which was adopted was soon found to be unsuitable to the heterogeneous nature of Sri Lankan society pushing the country into ethnic mess. In fact, the most important factor in antagonism between the Tamils and Sinhalese was British English education that was adopted by the Tamils more widely than Sinhalese. As a result, the former grabbed most of the opportunities generated and provided by the British.[25] This consequently resulted in resentment and jealousy among the Sinhalese. They felt that they have been discriminated in their own country. It led the Sinhalese politicians to bang the drum of ethnic chauvinism. Sinhala became the island's official language and discriminatory laws affecting entry to university and the civil service alienated the moderate Tamils.[26] Even in post-independence years, the Sri Lankan Tamil community was in the perception that from 1948 the Sri Lankan state had been impervious to the pleas of the Tamil community to amend the discriminatory state policies favouring the Sinhala majority.

Education and Employment

Since the introduction of a free education system from 1951, there had been a rapid expansion of educational facilities at all levels in Sri Lanka. The government expenditure on education in about two decades succeeding the freedom of the nation had increased nearly five times. In the year 1950-51 the expenditure on education was Rs. 105.7 million which rose to Rs. 512 million in 1969-70. Similarly, the school enrolement during 1950-51 was 1,336 million which reached 2,679 million in 1969-70. Even the World Bank in its preliminary survey of education prepared in 1966 praised the educational facilities at all levels but observed in the report that the system has expanded without any consideration of the manpower needs of the country or of the financial resources available. the content is heavily weighed in favour of the humanities and the approach is too academic. This is partly responsible for heavy unemployment.[27] The indication of World Bank report was in the light of a change brought in educational system after 1956, when 'Sinhala Only' policy of the government came into force. Earlier the medium of education was English but now it was replaced by Sinhala and Tamil languages, opening the universities to a larger body of applicants. At the same time, the university expansion was also slowed down because of lack of funds and it became impossible to admit the increasing number of qualified candidates and only 20 per cent in 1965 and 11 per cent in 1969 got admission among the aspirants. Of those who were selected often opt the traditional road to bachelor's degree and neither the government nor private enterprises of the time could absorb the glut of graduates. It resulted in larger scale unemployment in the country.

Unemployment in Sri Lanka, at large, was due to defective educational system and the slow economic growth of the island which failed to create sufficient employment opportunities. The educational system of the country has played a negative role in solving the unemployment problem. No attempt was made after independence of the country to redraw the school and college syllabai keeping in view the changing needs of the society. The education never addressed itself to the needs of the planned economic growth. Obviously, the economy of the country has not developed rapidly enough to absorb the annual increase in the population of working age. Faulty investment policies adopted by the past governments are also responsible for creating the problem of unemployment. Instead of imparting training in certain skills useful for economic development, the emphasis remained on degrees and diplomas.[28] Moreover, the existing system of education developed in the youth the attitudes and aspirations that are divorced from the realities of life.

Even in the deteriorating position of education and employment, the

Ceylon Tamils were targetted especially. In the field of higher education between 1942 and 1969, disproportionate numbers of Tamils entered the employment-oriented faculties of science, medicine and engineering in the University of Ceylon, as compared to those of the Sinhalese. A large number of Christians also entered the university than their population warranted.[29] To check the trend in 1970, a pro-Sinhala Minister of Education in United Front government introduced a system of standardisation of marks by language media at the university entrance examination obligating Tamil students to obtain a greater aggregate of marks to enter the employment-oriented faculties. In addition, a district quota basis was implemented in 1975 ostensibly to benefit rural areas but in reality to provide advantages to the Kandyan Sinhalese and Muslims. However, with a view to pacify the Tamils both these provisions were withdrawn in 1977 by the newly elected government of the United National Party.

The position of Ceylon Tamils in the spheres of employment and per capita income was also disappointing and an evidence of clear-cut discrimination. Employment figures clearly indicated a decline in Ceylon Tamil representation in public services and professions. According to a calculation conducted by the Government Tamil Clerical Services, it had been noted that between the years 1956 and 1970, there was a drop from 30 to 5 per cent in the Ceylon Administrative Service, from 50 to 5 in the clerical services, 60 to 10 in professions, such as engineers, doctors and lecturers, 40 to 1 in the armed forces and 40 to 5 in the labour forces. Out of 23000 teachers appointed by the state between 1971 and 1974, 18000 were Sinhalese, 1867 Tamils and 2507 Muslims. In the sphere of per capita income, the two surveys conducted by the Central Bank of Ceylon in 1963 and 1973 provide the evidence of declining economic situation of the Ceylon and Indian Tamils and the gains made by Low Country and Kandyan Sinhalese. In fact the presence of a large number of Indian Tamils in Sri Lanka were looked upon as a threat to the existence of the Sinhalese race. The policies adopted by pro-Sinhala governments to counter it have resulted in a self-fulfilling prophecy.

Religion and National Culture

Sri Lanka is a multi-religious country where Buddhism, Hinduism, Islam and Christianity are practised. The Constitution accords Buddhism the 'foremost place' but it is not recognised as the state religion. The Constitution also provides for the right of members of other faiths to practise their religion freely, and the government generally respects this right in practice. In the island approximately 70 percent of the population are Buddhists, 15 percent are Hindus, 8 percent are Christians and 7 percent are Muslims. Religion is a mandatory subject in the school curriculum. Parents and children may choose whether a child studies Buddhism, Islam, Hinduism, or Christianity. Students of minority religions other than Islam, Hinduism and Christianity must pursue religious instructions outside the public school system. There are no separate syllabi provided for smaller religions. Religion is taught in schools from an academic point of view.

After independence, the first Sinhalese-dominated government took steps to deny citizenship to the Tamils of Indian origin on the ground that even though many of them were born in Sri Lanka, they were only temporary residents of the island and did not have long term ties to the country. The three successive Acts namely, the Ceylon Citizenship Act, No. 18 of 1948, the Indian and Pakistani Residents (Citizenship) Act, No. 3 of 1949 and Ceylon (Parliamentary Elections) Amendment Act No. 48 of 1949 have excluded a large number of persons of Indian origin from Ceylonese citizenship and from exercising the right to franchise or the right to seek election to Legislature. As a protest to the governments policy regarding citizenship and franchise of Indian origin Sri Lankans, the Ceylon Indian Congress launched a Satyagraha movement on the pattern of Mahatma Gandhi's non-violent struggle in South Africa and India in April 1952 and appealed to the country's conscience for a fair and just deal with the people who, though of Indian origin, were born in Sri Lanka and had been living there for generations. The organisation, in a statement had termed the existing citizenship and franchise laws as unjust and as prejudicial to the interests of the Indian community.[30] It pleaded that the citizenship question being a problem in human relation should be approached from that angle. The Satyagraha movement of Indian origin Sri Lankans was withdrawn in September 1953 after an assurance given by the Ceylonese Prime Minister D. Senanayake.

The Sinhalese of Sri Lanka, having got a pro-Sinhala government in the initial years following the independence, attempted to assert and propagate their Buddhist-identity. It was the idea that Sinhalese equals Buddhist and held the view that the nation is a Buddhist one. This Buddhist identity was tempered by a Buddhist conscience which concretised the abstract values of the doctrinal tradition and gave a Buddhist humanism to traditional culture.[31] In the island nation Buddhism was a compulsory subject and parents left the onus of teaching Buddhist values to the school curriculum. The socialisation of the conscience, to be effective, must start in infancy and early childhood. The Buddhist of Sri Lanka felt the gap or absence of this Buddhist conscience and began to ask that religious instruction be imparted to Buddhist children attending schools run by the Roman Catholic and Protestant missionary organisations. When these missionary-run schools did not respond and refused outright, the Sinhalese Buddhists demanded that the schools themselves should be taken over by the state.

From the Sinhalese Buddhist points of view, there was three ways of dealing the situation. First, make the mother tongue the compulsory medium of instruction at all levels in the educational system - in effect from the Kindergarten to the University. Further, it was accomplished by the system of standardisation of marks, introduced in 1970, and admissions on a district quota basis implemented in 1975 respectively. Secondly, declare Sinhalese as the sole official language throughout the country. And it was hoped that this would displace most of the English-educated Sinhalese and Tamils from the position they held in the public services. This was done in 1956 when the Government of Sri Lanka enacted the Sinhala only law and enforced it throughout the country. Thirdly, to nationalise the schools would be of public service. To make the issue a burning pressure, politics was also used and the All Ceylon Buddhist Congress appointed the Unofficial Buddhist Committee of Inquiry in 1953 to require into all aspects of Buddhist questions in Sri Lanka. The Inquiry Committee, in its report of 1955 condemned Section 29 (2) of the Ceylon Constitution which prohibited legislative discrimination on racial or religious grounds. Most of the demands asked by the Committee in its report were met, when Mrs. Bandaranaike's Sri Lankan Freedom Party (SLFP) government assumed power. The new powerful pro-Sinhala government nationalised the majority of schools during 1960-61.

Buddhism in Sri Lanka is the religion of the majority race namely, the Sinhalese and no government of the time dared to overlook this fact. The UNP government of D.S. Senanayake (1948-56) to satisfy the majority group extended a measure of patronage to Buddhism, although knowilling to do it openly. Though the government of Senanayake officially participated in the religious celebrations connected with Buddhism and provided the government of Burma with a sizeable financial subsidy for specific Buddhist activities. It declared in its election manifesto, issued on the eve of general election, 1952, that there was no need to render any special assistance to the great religion of Buddha and further took pride in the fact that it had treated all religions alike. Despite the soft corner for Buddhism, the Party's election manifesto of 1956 also insisted that while it had taken note of the fact that Buddhism was being practised by the vast majority of people, it would be consistent with the true principles of democracy to recognise the policy of non-discrimination on religious grounds which is embodied in our constitution. The UNP lost power in this election and SLFP took over the regimes (1956-65), a more pro-Sinhala Party who took several decisions in favour of the Buddhists and the UNP too when regained power in 1965, showed greater concern for the problems of the Buddhists than it had done in its earlier regimes (1948-56).

Not only on religion but also on the issue of national culture, the Sinhalese community of Sri Lanka was equally emphatic. In this connection the Buddhists of the country were conscious enough to check the religious activities of the Christian missions and mission-run institutions. They were of the opinion that country's religion and culture are being undermined by the process of deracination that had set in, due to westernisaton and activities of Christian proselytising agencies. In the context, the unofficial Buddhist Committee, formed in 1953, had also demanded a ban on Christian activities and more specifically that Ceylon should not be allowed to become 'an eastern outpost of the Vatican'.[32] It also asked the State to follow the traditions of the ancient Sinhalese kingdom, accord Buddhism, adequate recognition on ceremonial occasions, and give it the status of an official religion.

Language

After independence the Sri Lankan government pursued the economic policy which produced great socio-economic discontent among the masses. It was partially able to maintain their support, however, by securing certain political and economic privileges for the Sinhalese majority against the Tamil minority. Under a policy, the then Sri Lankan Government had resettled landless Sinhalese peasants in the Tamil region so as to preempt their rising up against Sinhalese landlords. The next attack was made on Tamil's language by making the 'Sinhala Only Act'. It made the majority language in Sri Lanka, the only official language of the country, allowing for the educated Sinhalese educated bourgeoisie to better secure state and public sector employment, depriving the Tamil speaking employees of their jobs. Tamil students also find themselves disadvantaged, compared to their Sinhalese companions, with regard to higher education quota. In the situation-employment and identity for both the communities became a hot issue revolving round the language problem. Whether Sinhalese or Tamil or both should be treated as the official language engaged the attention of the country's political leaders. In the island nation language is not only an element of culture the people wanted to preserve, but also a medium for competing a number of government jobs.

Unlike India among the Sinhalese, *Jati* can refer to caste, but in most cases it refers principally to the Sinhalese language group, conceived of as a race. Although the Sinhalese are a substantial majority on the island, they tend to see themselves as an endangered minority within the South Asian Region, and their culture as threatened by hundreds of millions of Indians of the north. Sinhalese revivalists emphasise that while Hinduism and Tamil are sure to flourish in South India, Sinhalese is spoken and their brand of Buddhism is practised only in Sri Lanka. Therefore, they held the view that the government has a responsibility to promote Buddhism and Sinhala, irrespective of minority religions and languages.[33] Thus, the demand to make the Sinhalese language the sole official language arose from different motives. Primarily, the motivations was cultural and economic. There was wide-spread anxiety that the process of deracination gaining ground among the middle and upper rungs of Sinhalese society, would ultimately destroy the Sinhalese language, Sinhalese culture and Sinhalese Buddhism.

Debate over the official language in and outside the government started in pre-independence period and the issue was discussed by the State Council in 1944. On 24 May, J.R. Jayawardene, the then member of the State Council moved a resolution for making Sinhalese the official language in the near future. C.W.W. Kannangaru, the then Education Minister, moved the amendment to include Tamil also which was accepted by 29 votes to 8. It is to be noted here that during the debate S.W.R.D. Bandaranaike, who became Prime Minister of Sri Lanka in 1956 and passed the 'Sinhala Only' Act also supported the move and stated, 'I do not see that there would be any harm at all in recognising the Tamil language as an official language.'[34] Later on the State Council at its meeting of 26 November 1946 accepted both Tamil and Sinhalese as official languages of the country, which raised high hopes that both the languages would be placed on a footing of equal prestige through legislation in no time. But subsequent developments caused much frustration and disappointment to the minority community, as their language was sought to be assigned an inferior status.

The last support the Tamil language had found from the United National Party and its leader S.W.R.D. Bandaranaike was in July 1951 when the latter had criticised the government for wily mighly attitude in the matter of taking a definite policy about official and national language and expressed the opinion in favour of two points – language and religion. At the sametime he pleaded for just treatment for Buddhism but emphasised that he never asked and did not ask then that Buddhism be made the state religion. It, however, changed its policy on the eve of general election of 1952 and emphasised special place for *Swabhasa* and Buddhism. In the first government of Sri Lanka both Sir John Kotelawala, the former Prime Minister, and D.S. Senanayake did not yield the mounting pressure exerted by Sinhalese groups for making Sinhala, the only official language of the country. Kotelawala was of the view that if the demand for Sinhala only was conceded today, sometime latter the demand for Buddhism would also be made and would have to be conceded and he was right in his assessment as Buddhism has already been provided a special treatment in the Constitution of the Republic of Sri Lanka. While the Senanayake argued that making the Sinhala the only official language was not in the interest of Sinhala population because this language was being spoken by a few millions in Ceylon only but the Tamil was spoken by a large number in India and other countries and thus the Sinhalese would be put to disadvantage vis-à-vis Tamils.

The Sinhala language issue became hot in the years from 1953 mainly due to misunderstandings created by the current interpretations given to the formula 'Parity of Status' for the Sinhalese and Tamil languages. The Sinhalese were of the opinion that parity of status implied a quantitative proposition which in its form would mean that all official records without exception would have to be maintained in both the languages throughout the length and breadth of the island. They maintained such a policy would lead to every Sinhalese child having to learn Tamil and because of larger population and better financial sources the Tamils would have a more advanced literature to offer than the Sinhalese. Also in the light of the Report submitted by the Unofficial Buddhist Committee of Inquiry in 1955, the decisive moment for the language problem appeared near ending. In 1956 both prominent political parties of the country – The United National Party and Sri Lanka Freedom Party had conceded, and the former had declared at its special conference in February 1956 that Sinhala would only be the official language of the nation. The Official Language Act No. 33 of 1956 made Sinhalese the official language of Sri Lanka. Enactment of the Act was followed by administrative orders, directing government departments to switch over to Sinhalese as the official language.

The step, on the one hand, proved to be an obstacle to racial integration and on the other, a hindrance to higher education for the Tamil - speaking children. It reduced the Tamils to a position of inferiority or semi-slavery. Bandaranaike, while tabling the Bill on 5th June 1956, in the House of Representatives, strongly defended the move and argued that without this legislation the Sinhala language will be reduced to a stage of inferiority and the language as well as the people will be pressed back almost to a point of elimination. But the language policy helped to bring about an intense feeling of togetherness among all the political parties of all complexions – the FP, the TC including those who resigned from the UNP as well as the UNP government before the dissolution of Parliament in 1956. The enactment of the Sinhala only Act by the Mahajana Eksath Peramuna (MEP) coalition government was done under the leadership of Bandaranaike. The emotions behind the passing of language policy led directly to a reaction from the Ceylon Tamils, who saw the legislation as a threat not only to their culture and their identity but also to their means of livelihood.[35] The immediate reaction to the threat of resurgent Sinhalese nationalism was to strengthen the hands of the Federal Party in Ceylon Tamil areas, and which sought a federal structure for Sri Lanka with local autonomy for the Tamil areas.

Further provisions regarding language policy of the Sri Lankan government were also incorporated in the constitutions of 1972 and 1978. The Constitution of Sri Lanka, 1972 in its chapter 2 article 7, laid down Sinhalese as the official language, as previously provided by the Official Language Act No. 33 of 1956. The Constitution further stipulated that all laws should be enacted or made in Sinhalese but would be translated into Tamil as per article 9 and that the language of courts, tribunals, and Conciliation Boards, established under the Constitution Board Act No. 10 of 1958, should be Sinhalese.

For the first time in the history of Sri Lanka, a number of concessions were given to allay the Tamil fears and anxieties. The Constitution, formally adopted by the Jayawardene Government on 7 September 1978, has recognised Tamil, along with Sinhalese, as a national language for legal, administrative, Parliamentary and educational purposes. A person has now the right to be educated through the medium of either language, and educational institutions providing for the one have to provide for the other. Competitive examinations also have to be held in both languages. The new Constitution has also abolished distinction between the citizens by descent and citizens by registration. The removal of the language barrier has happily paved the way for harmony and national unity whereby a new era of communal harmony and amity has ushered in Sri Lanka. An important pro-Tamil organisation, the Tamil United Liberation Front (TULF) welcomed the various concessions but regretted the absence of any reference to autonomy of Tamil majority areas in the North and the East and to guarantee against these regions being colonised by the Sinhalese so as to make eventually the Ceylon Tamil a minority.

Disappointments on Devolution of Power

After independence in 1948, the mass and the political leadership as well began pondering over the new pattern of political system which would be based on the federal style without using the term federation. In fact, the privileges enjoyed by minorities including the Tamils in the island took a U turn in Post-Independence era and internal scene changed particularly against the Tamils. The Presidential system which was adopted soon found to be unsuitable to the heterogeneous nature of Sri Lankan society, pushing the country into an ethnic mess. Prior to independence, the Tamil interests were looked after by the Tamil Congress who broke away from the Ceylon National Congress formed in 1919. In 1951 a split took place in the Tamil Congress itself and as a result the Federal Party (F.P.) came into existence under the leadership of S.J.V. Chelvanayakam who pleaded for a federal set-up in order to safeguard the rights of the minority Tamils. In the same year the Federal Party in its resolution also stated the formation of a separate state for the Tamil community in Sri Lanka.

Both the communities - the Sinhalese and the Tamils alongwith other groups awakened to safeguard their individual identity in Post-Independence era. In this context the Sinhala—Buddhist majoritarian became the forerunner. The two main groups-the Buddhist Committee of Enquiry and the Eksath Buddhist Peramuna began to enquire into the state of Buddhism in Sri Lanka. It resulted in the publication of a report in 1956 called 'Betrayal of Buddhism' which demanded several things for the protection of Buddhism in the country. It gave air to the language controversy and made the Sinhalese and the Tamils intensely hostile to each other. The enactment of the language policy the 'Sinhala only' by the coalition government under the leadership of S.W.R.D. Bandaranaike helped to bring about an intense feeling of togetherness among all the

Tamil political parties of all complexions—the Federal Party, the Tamil Congress including those who resigned from the UNP Party and the UNP government.[36] The Post-Independence political developments in the island only exacerbated communal disharmony that further strengthened the roots of alienation among the Tamil groups. In a sense, the unitary system of Sri Lanka has completely failed on account of the parochial and inhuman attitudes of the Sinhalese political society in satisfying the preserved aspirations of the multiethnic people and therefore, the demand of decentralisation of democratic processes has been raised from time to time.

The general sense of alienation among the Tamils and the government language policy passed in 1956 compelled the Federal Party to adopt a four-point demand at its annual convention held at Trincomalee in August 1956 with the threatening to take direct action by non-violent means if they were not met within a year. It included among other things (a) Enactment of a democratic constitution based on the federal principles and the establishment of one or more Tamil linguistic state or states, (b) Restoration of the Tamil language to its rightful place enjoying absolute parity of status with Sinhalese as an official language of the country, (c) Enactment of laws recognising the right to full citizenship on the basis of a simple residential test of all persons who have made this country their home, and (d) Immediate cessation of colonisation of traditional Tamil-speaking areas by the Sinhalese people. In the circumstances to accommodate the Tamil grievances and contain the communal killing, the then Prime Minister of Sri Lanka, S.W.R.D. Bandaranaike signed an agreement with Chelvanayakam in 1957 which is known as B-C Pact. It recognised the Tamil as the language of administration in the north and the east, and also provided some measure of autonomy for these regions.[37] This pact was supposed to permit reasonable use of Tamil in the Northern and Eastern Provinces and also for regional councils with powers in agriculture, education and selection of candidates for colonisation scheme.[38] But on account of the Sinhalese pressure and United National Party's opposition, the demand of the regional council for Tamils could not be contended by the government on the plea that any attempt towards federalism will be vicious for the unity and integrity of Sri Lanka. Likewise, the subsequent Dudley Senanayake-Chelvanayakam (D-C) Pact of 1965, though well-intentioned, and which dealt with, *inter alia*, regional autonomy also collapsed by 1968.

From the beginning, the Tamil parliamentarians along with others reaffirmed and reiterated their dedication in preserving the unity and integrity of the country, as they said "We are not asking for the division of Sri Lanka on the racial basis. We stand for division of the powers and thereby achieving unity in diversity." They described the federal system as the "Panchsheel", which means cooperation and co-existence. As part of its policy and to meet the Tamil demand of federalism, the Sri Lankan Freedom Party government headed by Mrs. Bandaranaike introduced a District Political Authority (DPA) system as a measure of the administrative decentralisation in 1973. The main duty of the district political authority was to control, direct and coordinate all matters pertaining to the district. However, the system failed on account of incapacity and the parochial approaches of the heads of DPA.[39] On the other hand, it created a psychological setback to the Tamils which led to the transformation of their demand from federal to the secession with the start of Tamil Eelam Movement.

Further realising the potentiality of the Tamil Eelam Movement, the United National Party government of J.R. Jayawardene formulated the new scheme for the devolution of powers in 1978 which was known as the District Development Council (DDC). It was consisted of the elected members of the parliamentary group and the executive committee headed by the district ministers who were under the control of and responsible to the President of Sri Lanka. As a result of its composition, the DDC had become an exercise in deception and had been puppets in the hands of President.[40] Consequently, the Tamils were obsessed with frustration and resentment. The new situation compelled the Tamil Federal Party change its name and manifesto, becoming the Tamil United Liberation Front (TULF) committed to independent Tamil state.[41]

The large-scale devastating communal riots of 1983 made the issue of devolution of power a burning topic in the country. Whereas July 1987 proposal of J.R. Jayawardene resulted in the signing of Indo-Sri Lanka Accord at the end of the month (29 July). The signed Accord had two aspects in which the first dealt with India's commitment to uphold Sri Lanka's sovereignty and territorial integrity on the condition that the latter agreed to grant a reasonable amount of autonomy to the Tamils to their satisfaction. The second aspect of the Accord dealt with Sri Lanka's commitment to disallow any extra-regional power to dabble in its affairs which had either a known or a potential intention to harm India's security interests in the region. In the Accord India expressed itself openly and unequivocally as being opposed to the Eelamist demand for a separate Tamil state in Sri Lanka, but at the same time brought pressure to bear on the Sri Lankan government to carry out its own pledges to effect a political solution of the ethnic crisis by implementing the principle of devolution of power from the centre to the provinces in Sri Lanka.[42] In general, the devolution of power from the centre to the provinces involved three basic issues; first, the extent of powers to be devolved; second, the relations between the centre and provinces; and third, the unit of devolution.

In one of its most controversial parts, the Accord had virtually acknowledged the Tamil 'homeland' demand by providing for a temporary merger of the northern and eastern provinces but at the same time recognised the justifiable reservations of the Muslims and Sinhalese communities in the eastern province by providing for breaking up the merger to allow the reversion of this province to its separate existence if a referendum so determined before the prescribed date.[43] As a follow up of the Accord, the Sri Lankan Parliament had passed the 13th Amendments to the constitution and the Provincial Council Act No. 42 to devolve power for the participation of the Tamil people into the democratic process. However, the Tamils considered all these provisions as biased and prejudicial as they had no real powers and almost all the powers rested with the Sinhalese. The said Amendment and the Provincial Council Act refused the constitutional recognition to the North-Eastern Province as areas of historical habitation of the Tamils. The devolution of power remained a controversial issue right up to the sign of the agreement in July 1987. The past conflicts on the overall problems of Sri Lankan Tamils aroused communal consciousness and antagonism. It took nearly fifty years (1920s-1970s) for the political mobilisation of the Tamil community—from communal ratios through balanced representation, responsive cooperation, federalism, to the demand of a separate state.

Role of Pro-Tamil Political Parties

The first political party of Sri Lanka was formed in pre-independence phase in 1919, namely, The Ceylon National Congress, on the pattern of Indian National Congress who fought for independence from colonial rule. The Ceylon National Congress was a broad-based party which included members from all ethnic groups. With the introduction of electoral politics along with territorial representation and universal adult franchise by the Donoughmore constitution in 1931, carefully adjusted the ratio of representation of the Sinhalese and the Tamils changed from

2:1 to 5:1. As a result for a long time the Tamils were effectively kept out of the power. On the issue of mode of representation, divisions within the ranks of the Congress party emerged. While Sinhalese leaders wanted to do away with communal representation and make territorial representation universal, minorities, including the Tamils, desired to retain it secure power for their communities. Gradually, the Tamils became communally conscious and fervent and divisions, being wide, the Tamils broke away and formed their own party, named, the Tamil Congress (TC) in 1944 under the charismatic leadership of G.G. Ponnambalam. In the year 1944 when the Soulbury Commission arrived to prepare the new constitution of Sri Lanka, the newly formed party (TC) demanded the balanced representation on the fifty-fifty scheme by which the minorities together would be assured of a number of seats equal to those obtainable by the majority. Though the fifty-fifty scheme was not granted, the Commission, however, provided for certain safeguards under which seats were distributed in the nine provinces.[44] The Constitution also prohibited the enactment of any law on matters affecting particular communities or religious groups.

Apart form this, there was also a gradual evolution of other moderate and liberal parties like the United National Party (UNP) and the Sri Lanka Freedom Party (SLFP). In September 1946, Don Stephen Senanayake broke away from the Ceylon National Congress and formed the UNP which advocated a liberal democratic order and became popular among the masses and there was a complete alignment of forces. It included conservative-minded political notables with the backing of a number of ethnocentric political groupings such as the Sinhala Mahasabha (SMS) and the Ceylon Muslim League and of sections of Ceylon and Indian Tamils.[45] Exactly five years later in 1951, an important political development was the split of the UNP. The Minister of Health and Local Government in the administration of D.S. Senanayake, S.W.R.D. Bandaranaike left the UNP with a group of supporters and founded the Sri Lanka Freedom Party. It emerged as a Party of moderate left, holding the centre between the UNP and the left. As the SLFP was more sympathetic to the cultural sensitivities of the Sinhalese, adopted a nationalist and anti-western posture.

After freedom from colonial rule in 1948, earlier in the general election held in 1947, the UNP was placed at the top of all political parties and formed the government under its leader D.S. Senanayake. The minority Tamils had come under the umbrella of the Tamil Congress who also joined the UNP government and served the interests of minorities well. One of the first acts of the first government of independent Sri Lanka was to enact the Citizenship Act of 1948, the Indian and Pakistani Residents (Citizenship) Act of 1949 and the Ceylon (Parliamentary Election) Amendment Act of 1949 which were aimed at disqualifying the Indian Tamils in the Up-Country Kandyan areas where numerical strength threatened to swamp the electorate.[46] The decisions taken by the UNP government of which the TC was a junior partner dissatisfied many of TC leaders and on the issue of deprivation of citizenship of the Indian Tamils, Ceylon Tamils, the party divided and ultimately one group split away forming a new political party called the Federal Party (FP) in 1949 under the leadership of S.J.V. Chelvanayakam.

The newly formed Federal Party represents Tamil nationalism and at the beginning they advocated federation with a future Dravidian sovereign state of south India. But later the opinion of the Party stabilised in favour of a Tamil homeland federated to a Sinhalese Ceylon. It pleaded federal set-up in order to safeguard the rights of the minority Tamils. Clearly, in contrast to the Tamil's Congress's moderate approach under Ponnambalam who continued to support the UNP government even after it initiated some discriminatory policies against the Indian Tamils. Perhaps it was one of the major causes of atmost poor performance of the party TC in the general election of 1952. It, however, continued to represent the views of substantial sections of middle class Jaffna Tamils who disapproved of the separatist politics of the Federal Party.

Thus, initially, following the independence years among the pro-Tamil parties were Tamil Congress and Federal Party. Especially, the Tamils of Sri Lanka have always supported their own parties at the ballot box and not one of the dominant blocs of parties in the country. As a result, the Sri Lanka Tamils, who are geographically concentrated in the north and east of the island, have almost exclusively returned candidates to Parliament from either the Federal Party or the Tamil Congress. This has resulted in the separation of the country into two different regions. Each of these regions has its own party system. The Tamil areas support the Federal Party (FP) later known as the Tamil United Liberation Front (TULF) or the Tamil Congress (TC), while the Sinhalese areas support the UNP or the SLFP bloc of parties.[47] The feeling of togetherness of the Tamils and the gradual growth of Tamil sub-nationalism and separatist sentiments must be seen in the context of the rising tide of Sinhalese nationalism after the end of colonial rule in the country.

By mid-1950s, the position of ruling UNP was undermined mainly due to bad economic condition in all sectors. The Sri Lanka Freedom

Party (SLFP), the break away faction of the UNP, improved its position rapidly by offering political change, social justice, economic independence from external control and other populist measures that attracted the masses. The Sinhala nationalism, which was in the offing after independence, led the warming of the issues relating to religion, culture and language. As demand the SLFP championed the cause of Buddhist Sinhalese and swept the polls defeating the UNP in the 1956 general elections. The SLFP, once in power, began to implement the Buddhist Sinhalese agenda and the first victim of the new government was language. In the year of its victory (1956) the government adopted the Official Language Act which declared Sinhala as the official language. It caused a reaction among the Tamils who perceived their language, culture, and economic position under attack. The Federal Party launched a Satyagraha that resulted in the famous B.C. Pact of 1957, but in 1958, Bandaranaike, under the pressure from militant Buddhists and the UNP opposition, abrogated the pact that he made with Chelvanayakam, the F.P. leader. Earlier in 1956 the F.P. led the opposition to the Sinhala Only Act with other leaders in staging a sit-down protest on the Galle Face Green, that caused a chain reaction of violence between the Sinhalese and the Tamils.

The Federal Party remained throughout active for Tamil cause and in August 1956 the Party had met in convention at Trincomalee where it presented a one-year ultimatum to Bandaranaike demanding (1) replacement of the present pernicious constitution by a rational and democratic constitution based on the federal principle; (2) parity of status for the Tamil language with the Sinhalese language; (3) repeal of the existing citizenship laws which discriminated against the Indian estate Tamil population; and (4) immediate cessation of colonising the traditional Tamil-speaking areas with Sinhalese people.[48] On being disappointed from the false promises of successive governments in early 1964, the Federal Party organised a Tamil only campaign in which it appealed to the Tamil-speaking public to transact all their business with the state in Tamil language.

With a view to get implemented the Tamil Language Act of 1958, the Federal Party also joined the Dudley Senanayake's National Government formed after 1965 general elections. But this time too due to SLFP pressure and the militant Sinhalese, it failed to get any further and the Federal Party resigned from the cabinet in 1968. The single Member of Parliament Murugeysen Tiruchelvam, who belonged to F.P. after his resignation as Minister of Local Government from the National

Government, pointed out in 1969 that though the Tamil Language (Special Provisions) Act of 1958 and 1966 were enacted to permit the use of Tamil language in the Northern and Eastern Provinces for the transaction of all government and public business and the maintenance of public records, whether such business is conducted in or by a department or institution of the Government, a public corporation or a statutory institution, the bills were not implemented and the education of the Tamils was affected. The Tamils were ignored for Government appointments, and for the import of South Indian films, the main entertainment of the Tamil people.[49]

In 1970 general elections the Sri Lanka Freedom Party fought the election in alliance with the left parties — the Communist Party (CP) and Lanka Sama Samaj Party (LSSP) — defeated the UNP and formed the government under the banner of United Front (UF). The UF had come to power with a mandate to provide the country a new constitution but it too like earlier, disappointed the federalists who wanted some more to be included as their constitutional right. On the issues crucial to the minority community — language and citizenship rights — the UF remained unrelenting.[50] With the UF coming into power, the Tamils feared that what little they had received from the UNP would become even less and an emotional speech was given in the House by M. Tiruchelvam, a F.P. member in which he said, "We the Tamils of this country have no other place to go to… . We are here forever as citizens of this country, as fellow citizens of the Sinhalese people.[51] He added further that the federalism we are asking is a federal form of government within the ambit of the Ceylon Constitution, under the control of the Central Government, with powers vested in the Central Government." While speaking he also prophesied, "As long as there is one Tamil man in Ceylon, we will not give up the cry of federalism.[52] Let us then, he urged, be a united country but with the rights of the people in the Northern and Eastern Provinces protected for ever."

The Sri Lankan Constitution of 1972 created a new unity and a new mood of militancy and the both taken together changed the whole scenario. Its immediate effect was the formation of the traditionally moderate Tamil Congress and also the non-political organisation representing the estate workers, the Ceylon Workers Congress (CWC) who consider themselves and are treated by the government as culturally and historically different from the Sri Lanka Tamils in the north and east. Although the Federal Party suffered some reverses in the general election of May 1970, it maintained its position as the leading Party of the Ceylon Tamils. It participated unwillingly in the proceedings of the Constituent Assembly but withdrew from it in June 1971 when its demands on federalism, language and citizenship were rejected. In May 1972 the Federal Party (FP) and Tamil Congress (TC) joined hands in a Tamil United Front (TUF) and they both rejected the republican constitution. At its national convention in May 1976, the TUF resolved to change its designation and became the Tamil United Liberation Front (TULF). With its new name the TULF had championed and piloted the cause of a separate state, the Tamil Eelam.

References

1. A. Jeyaratnam Wilson, *Politics in Sri Lanka, 1947-1979* (London : Macmillan Press, 1979), p. 2.
2. H.P. Chattopadhyaya, *Indians in Sri Lanka* (Calcutta : O.P.S. Publishers, 1979), p. 2.
3. S.R. Chakravarti, Swaroop Rani Dubey, P.C. Mathur and Virendra Narain (Authors), *Turmoil and Political Change in South Asia, Bangladesh, Sri Lanka, India and Pakistan* (Jaipur : Aalekh Publishers, 1978), p. 71.
4. Eric Meyer, 'Seeking the Róots of the Tragedy' in James Manor, *Sri Lanka in Change and Crisis* (Sydney : Croom Helm, 1984), pp. 154-55.
5. P.C. Roy Chaudhury, *Lands and Peoples of the World Sri Lanka* (New Delhi : Sterling Publishers, 1985), pp. 18-19.
6. A. Jeyaratnam Wilson, *Politics in Sri Lanka 1947-1979*, p. 3.
7. Iravatham Mahadevan, 'An Epigraphic Perspective on the Antiquity of Tamil', *The Hindu* (Madras), 24 June 2010.
8. Ibid.
9. *Census of Ceylon*, 1891, pp. 52-53.
10. H.P. Chattopadhyaya, *Indians in Sri Lanka 1947-1979*, pp. 11-19.
11. Ibid., pp. 30-31.
12. Leo E. Rose, 'Nepal, Burma and Ceylon' in Wayne Wilcox, Leo E. Rose and Gavin Boyd, (eds.), *Asia and the International System*, (Massachusetts : Winthrop Publishers, 1972), p. 231.
13. P.C. Roy Chaudhury, *Lands and Peoples of the World Sri Lanka*, p. 49.
14. Report of Agent T.L.R. Chandran, (1934), pp. 19-20.
15. S. Ranganathan's Annual Report for 1923 as quoted in H.P. Chattopadhyaya, *Indians in Sri Lanka, 1947-1979*, p. 125.
16. Ceylon Administration Report for 1931 – Report of the Controller of Labour, 1931, p. 20.
17. Gananath Obeyesekere, 'The Origins and Institutionalisation of Political Violence, in James Manor (ed.), p. 155.

18. V.N. Narayanan, 'Separating Tamils from the LTTE', *The Hindustan Times* (New Delhi), 9 August 1998.
19. A. Jeyaratnam Wilson, *Politics in Sri Lanka, 1947-1979*, pp. 7-9.
20. Gananath Obeyesekere, 'The Origins and Institutionalisation' of Political Violence, p. 157.
21. Kaufmann, Chaim, 'Possible and Impossible Solutions to Ethnic Wars', *International Security*, Vol. 20, No. 4, (1996), pp. 136-75.
22. P. Sahadevan, 'Negotiating Peace in Ethnic Wars', *International Studies*, Vol. 43, No. 3, (New Delhi : July-September 2006), p. 239.
23. Ibid., pp. 240-41.
24. S.W.R.D. Bandaranaike (ed.), *The Hand Book of the Ceylon National Congress 1919-1928* (Colombo: 1928), pp. 70-97.
25. Vinod F. Khobragade, 'Ethnic Politics in Sri Lanka – Political Solution to Tamil Cause and Military Solution to LTTE, *South Asia Politics*, Vol. 7, No. 11 (New Delhi : March 2009), p. 24.
26. Tom Farrell, 'For him no Sacrifice was too Great for the Objective of Eelam', *The Hindu*, 20 May, 2009.
27. S.R. Chakravarti, Swaroop Rani Dubey, P.C. Mathur and Virendra Narain, *Turmoil and Political Change in South Asia*, pp. 74-75.
28. Ibid., pp. 75-76.
29. D.L. Jayasuriya, 'Developments in University Education : The Growth of the University of Ceylon, (1942-1965), *University of Ceylon Review*, Vol. XXIII (April-October 1965), Nos. 1 and 2, pp. 83-153.
30. H.P. Chattopadhaya, *Indians in Sri Lanka*, 1947-1979, pp. 226-32.
31. Gananath Obeyesekere, 'The Origin and Institutionalisation of Political Violence', p. 158.
32. The Betrayal of Buddhism, *Report of the Unofficial Buddhist Committee of Inquiry* (Balangoda : 1955), p. 27.
33. James Manor (ed.), 'Introduction', pp. 8-9.
34. S. Muthiah, 'Legacy of a Dream', *The Hindu*, 24 January 2010.
35. Lucy M. Jacob, 'Regionalism in Sri Lanka', in Ramakant (ed.), *Regionalism in South Asia* (Jaipur : Aalekh Publishers, 1983), pp. 179-83.
36. Ranil Wicremesinghe, 'The Way to Resolve Sri Lanka's Political Crisis,' *The Hindu*, 6 April 2007.
37. Ibid.
38. Vinod F. Khobragade, 'Ethnic Politics in Sri Lanka – Political Solution to Tamil Cause and Military Solution to LTTE, pp. 27.
39. B. Muralidhar Reddy, The War is Over', *Frontline*, Vol. 26, No. 12, 6-19 June (Chennai : 2009), pp. 7-8.
40. Ibid., p. 8.

41. Wayne Wilcox, Leo E. Rose and Gavin Boyd (eds.), *Asia and the International System*, p. 229.
42. Vijaya Samaraweera, 'The Evolution of a Plural Society', in De Silva, K.M. (ed.), *Sri Lanka : A Survey* (London : 1977), pp. 88-89.
43. Lucy M. Jacob, 'Regionalism in Sri Lanka', pp. 176-77.
44. Ibid.
45. Calvin A. Woodward, 'The Growth of a Party System in Ceylon' (Providence : 1969), as quoted in A. Jeyaratnam Wilson, *Politics in Sri Lanka, 1947-1979*, p. 117.
46. Wriggins W. Howard, *Ceylon : Dilemmas of a New Nation* (New Jeresy : 1960), pp. 212-28.
47. Robert Oberst, 'Proportional Representation and Electoral System Change in Sri Lanka' in James Manor (ed.), pp. 118-19.
48. A. Jeyaratnam Wilson, 'The Tamil Federal Party in Ceylon Politics', *Journal of Commonwealth Political Studies*, Vol. IV, No. 2, pp. 117-37.
49. M. Muthiah, 'Legacy of a Dream', *The Hindu*, 24 January 2010.
50. Urmila Phadnis and Lucy M. Jacob, 'The New Constitution of Sri Lanka,' *India Quarterly* (October – December 1972), p. 297.
51. M. Muthiah, 'Legacy of a Dream', *The Hindu*, 24 January, 2010.
52. *Ibid.*

2

LTTE : FORMATION, STRUCTURE AND ACTIVITY

Dream of a Separate Tamil Eelam

Culturally, the island Sri Lanka is divided into two nations — Tamil and Sinhala. They have been rivals in the past; they are rivals in the present; and are likely to continue to be rivals in the future. It is a mosaic of self-aware communities distinguished from one another along ethnic, religious or linguistic basis. The political life of Sri Lanka has been closely bound up with these communal and other social differentiations. These traditional groupings formed the basis of politically most significant loyalties, interests and demands. The Sinhalese and Ceylon's Tamil communities could associate these loyalties with the past kingdoms and with specific territories. Because of the force of historical traditions, there emerged within Sri Lanka forms of identity among the majority Sinhalese and the minority Tamil communities of the country.[1] It has been recorded in the history that at the time of the Portuguese conquest there were three separate kingdoms in modern Sri Lanka – the Tamil Kingdom in the North, the lowland Sinhalese Kingdom in the south and the upland Kandyan Kingdom. Although the policies of the British were guided by the objective of creating a homogeneous society in the island, advancement of social mobilisation generated new aspirations and demands and widened concerned with educational opportunities, urban employment and government services heighting the potential for communal conflict.[2] Unlike India, where the government decided not to build the nation on the basis of religion, the nation building experiment in Sri Lanka was based on the language of the majority community, namely Sinhala and religion of the majority community, namely Buddhism that further paved the direction of nationalism on the basis of communal identity.

The Sinhalese and the Tamils are not separated by ethnic divide only but educationally, psychologically and geographically too. A recent study on the subject of national harmony revealed that there is no school in Ceylon where there is a positive, well-integrated and gradual programme for racial integration, working hand in hand with the community agencies, for the realisation of the aim of making the children better Ceylonese citizens. Under the psychological factor, the Sinhalese tend on occasion to group the indigenous Tamils with the Tamils of south India and view them in their entirety as the 'Dravidian peril'. Geographically Tamils, in general, reside in the northern and eastern parts of the island and the latter are conservative and community-conscious. Even when opportunities for employment and commerce took them to the Sinhalese areas, they developed there flourishing self-contained settlements of their own. These parting tendencies in both the communities developed and strengthened further due to the defective or biased progress in the constitutional history of the nation.

After independence in 1948s the economic issues gathered top priorities and was felt by the youths more intensely. At that time the industrial and agricultural expansion was not adequate to maintain the employment levels. The result was a body of frustrated educated young men and women who fell prey to communal appeals. The average middle class Sinhalese is in sharp competition with his Ceylon Tamil counterpart for white collar jobs and the commonly held image of the latter is that he is hardworking, clever, industrious and intensely communal. On the other hand, sections of the Ceylon Tamil intelligentsia look on the average educated Sinhalese as being lazy and foolish. The deterioration of Sinhalese-Tamil relations in the years after 1956 can be largely attributed to this fact. Earlier, the Sinhalese and the Tamils were self-conscious about their differences and were mutually suspicious, they were not hostile prior to the language issue. It was the political controversy surrounding the language dispute in the first decade of independence that generated the most severe regional feelings among the Ceylon Tamils. Consequently, the communal antagonism became sharper than they had been for generations.

When Sri Lanka achieved independence in 1948, the Soulbury Constitution of 1946 became the basic document of country's government. Soon thereafter, the island had adopted a Presidential system which was found unsuitable to the heterogeneous nature of Sri Lankan society, pushing the country into an ethnic mess. In fact, the unitary system in Sri Lanka has completely failed on account of the parochial and inhuman attitudes of the Sinhalese political society in satisfying the preserved aspirations of the multi-ethnic people and therefore, the demand of decentralisation of democratic processes has been raised continuously in order to accomplish socio-political equity. Basically, the decentralisation has been considered as one of the mechanisms to resolve the conflicts. The Tamils claimed that due to Sinhalese majority, the Tamil minority can not get access to political activities and participation in the governance and decision-making process of the country.[3] A strong section of the people believe even today that if Sri Lanka had been provided with the federal constitution at the time of independence, the Sinhalese and the Tamil leaders might have been able to bargain with each other from their political power bases at the centre and the regional prolonged ethnic conflict could been prevented.

On the issue of three citizenship acts passed by the UNP government of which Tamil Congress was a partner, differences arose in the rank and file of the party and a split took place in December 1949 under its leader S.J.V. Chelvanayakam. The new party was named as Federal Party and from the beginning it represents Tamil nationalism. Initially the Federal Party concentrated on three objectives : (1) an autonomous region for the indigenous Tamil-speaking peoples comprising the northern and eastern provinces linked to the rest of the island under a federal set-up; (2) parity of status for the Tamil language with the Sinhalese language; and (3) citizenship rights for all Indian Tamils who wish to make the island their permanent home.[4] Especially, after the language controversy of 1956, the Federal Party became the principal spokesman of the Ceylon Tamils, replacing its rival the Tamil Congress which had advocated responsive co-operation with UNP government. Years after independence, the government of the day initiated discriminatory policies harming the interests of the Tamils at large creating vacuum for conflicts and antagonism between the Sinhalese and the Tamils. The issues of discrimination responsible for bringing tussle and bickering were language, administration, education, employment, colonisation of land and power devolution.

The Federal Party formed in 1949 was totally devoted to the cause of a separate state for Tamil Eelam and, in fact laid the foundation of two-nation theory in Sri Lanka. It strongly pleaded in favour of a Tamil Eelam and stated in Party's resolution of 1951, 'The Tamil speaking people of Sri Lanka constitute a nation distinct from that of Sinhalese by every fundamental test of nationhood; firstly that of a separate historic past in this island at least as ancient and glorious as that of the Sinhalese; secondly by the fact of their being a linguistic entity, entirely different from that of the Sinhalese, with an unsurpassed classical heritage and a modern developed of language which makes Tamil fully adequate for all present day needs; and finally by reason of their territorial habitation of definite areas, which constitute over one-third of the island.[5] In fact, the political failure of democratic system and chief political parties in resolving Tamil grievances led to the demand of a separate Tamil state, the Tamil Eelam.

For the present situation of Sri Lanka, the political system adopted in 1948 and the succeeding governments that enjoyed power in a discriminatory manner were largely responsible. It is said that the history of relations between the Tamils and central government has been a succession of missed opportunities. Even before independence under the self-government allowed by the British since 1931, communalist attitudes dominated political life, culminating in the Tamil claim for parity of parliamentary representation between the Sinhalese majority and the minorities. Almost in the span of thirty years, the political life of the island nation was run by two major political parties- UNP and SLFP. In the first phase, each of these parties had a nine-year tenure – the UNP from 1947 to 1956 and the SLFP from 1956 to 1965. In the second phase, the UNP with its allies had a five-year-run, 1965-70, while the SLFP, with its partners completed its 1970-77 term. Despite their long and repeated innings, UNP and SLFP governments, which were clearly Sinhalese dominated, had toyed with the idea of concessions, and all promises came to nothing for the Tamil minorities of Sri Lanka.

Actually, the dysfunctional nature of the island's democracy remained unable to make a convincing argument that all the problems that might arise could be resolved within the framework of democratic institutions. As a result, in the politically active young people it has created a sense of nihilism which considers everything as permissive. In the political field it means a belief in violence for its own sake. In that kind of situation, the whole young generation would have no political aspirations except for protest for its own sake, reflects as to how deeply the dysfunctional nature of Sri Lankan democracy has affected the entire nation and particularly the young.[6] The abandonment of the rule of law and the authority of institutions which was already visible in 1958, became a much greater problem in the years that followed, with a similar political approach by subsequent governments and even radical experiments to undermine democracy and the rule of law.

The early writers, including the Tarzei Vittachi, a well-known author and journalist was of the view that the dysfunctional nature of Sri Lanka became visible in the early years of its rule. In his book, *Emergency 58:*

The Story of the Ceylon Race Riots, he pointed out that unfortunately the government made the mistake of throwing the baby away with the bath water. While repressive legislation and irksome, outmoded attitudes which had kept the masses in thrall had to be hurled away without delay, as it was vital for the peace and order of the country, especially in times of rapid social change to preserve and strengthen the rule of law and the authority of the officers who enforce the law.[7] This view was also supported by the Asian Human Rights Commission (AHRC), founded in 1984. It is Hong-Kong-based and defines itself as a regional non-governmental organisation (NGO), monitoring and lobbying human rights issues in Asia.

By 1970 all the major political parties in the country had expressly rejected democracy as a suitable form of government for the country. The government of Mrs. Sirimao Bandaranaike, which included a coalition of three major parties — the Sri Lanka Freedom Party, the Lanka Sama Samaja Party and the Communist Party — embarked on a new constitution spoken of as a home-grown constitution which was incongruously called a socialist constitution. In 1977 J.R. Jayawardene's United National Party was elected and in 1978 it abolished liberal democratic constitutionalism altogether in favour of creating a monster called the Executive President, who had more power than anyone under any government.[8] The mentality of this distrust of democracy will remain so long as democracy itself does not exist by way of functioning institutions within the country.

The decade 1970s was a decisive one in the political life of Sri Lanka. Sinhalese-Tamil relations deteriorated considerably during the period of United Front rule 1970-77. The Federal Party withdrew in June 1971 from the proceedings of the Constituent Assembly when the latter voted out its resolutions on language rights. In 1972, the majority of Tamil political groupings, including the powerful Indian Tamil CWC, formed the Tamil United Front (TUF) under the leadership of FP leader S.J.V. Chelvanayakam for the purpose of joint political action. In the same year Chelvanayakam on behalf of the TUF resigned his parliamentary seat to obtain a mandate for the establishment of a sovereign Eelam Tamil nation. In February 1975, a bye-election for the said seat was held at which Chelvanayakam obtained an overwhelming majority. The TUF, in its convention in May 1976, changed its name to the Tamil United Liberaton Front (TULF) resolving the restoration and reconstruction of free and sovereign, secular, socialist state of Tamil Eelam in order to safeguard the very existence of Tamil nation in this country. The Sinhalese paradigm of one country, one nation, one language and one people compelled the Tamil youths to rise against the Sinhalese chauvinism. With Tamil political leaders' failure in political bargaining and power politics, the Tamil youths raised arms against the government. The armed uprising gave birth to political violence as the only means. The armed struggle for the establishment of Tamil Eelam manifested in a variety of ways ranging from political protest to ethnic violence and terrorist insurgencies to guerilla warfare and ultimately the ethnic conflict became a central problem in Sri Lankan politics, which led to the emergence of political terrorism of Liberation Tigers of Tamil Eelam (LTTE).

Formation, Aims and Objects

The Liberation Tigers of Tamil Eelam (LTTE), which is also known as the Tamil National Army was founded on 5 May 1976 under the leadership of Velupillai Prabakaran. It was the failure of many years of peaceful demonstration by Tamil leaders in order to win their freedom from the successive Sinhala majority governments, who showed no concern for the Tamil grievances. It was the result of political and cultural rivalry between the Sinhalese and the Lankan Tamils and the ineptitude of the national leadership in reconciling their differences.[9] While some have interpreted this ethnic rivalry as a clash between two 'sub nationalism' that of the dominant Sinhalese Buddhist elite and of the minority Tamil elite of the northern peninsula,[10] more often it has been in political terms in which the Sinhalese have consistently sought to diminish the cultural and political salience of the Tamils in post-independence Sri Lanka.

The LTTE was avowed to achieve a separate state or Eelam through bloody and violent confrontation with the Sri Lankan state what had become unachievable by peaceful methods in over 28 years. The Political frustration had finally resulted in support for separatism, these same chauvinists were able to say that they had been right all along. So too the emergence of the Liberation Tigers of Tamils prepared to kill in furtherance of their aim to split up 'the island of the doctrine' merely served, for many Sinhalese people, to confirm their own misapprehension that Tamils are inherently violent people.[11] Historically, each of the political parties – the UNP and the SLFP, while in opposition, had played the role of a spoilsport. Ever since 1948 whenever the Government had taken an initiative to offer some accommodation to the Tamils, the then opposition had sought to politicise the issue by whipping up chauvinistic sentiments among the majority Sinhalese population.[12] During this period, Tamil militancy emerged in Tamil areas with plenty of Tamil militant organisations to fight for their rights against the oppressive rule of the Sinhalese.

In reaction to the policies of pro-Sinhala governments in Sri Lanka, earlier two dominant sections of Tamil parties – the Federal Party and the Tamil Congress united to form the Tamil United Liberation Front (TULF) in 1975 and it, in its Vaddukoddai resolution, adopted on 14 May 1976, called for the creation of a separate Tamil state of Eelam. Besides citing the existence of the historical Tamil Kingdom in the southern Jaffna districts as the legal basis for a claim to the Eelam state, nine additional reasons were given : the disfranchisement of Indian Tamils (1948 and 1949); Sinhalese colonisation of traditional Tamil lands; the Sinhala Only Act; the favoured position of Buddhism; inequality of opportunity; severance of ties with South India; permitting and unleashing communal violence against Tamils ; terrorism against the Tamil youths; and the 1972 Constitution.[13] The evolution of Tamil extremism around the mid seventies was of crucial importance and also developed due to the passing away of two important politicians of Jaffna, namely S.J.V. Chelvanayakam, the founder leader of Federal Party, and G.G. Ponnambalam, founder of the Tamil Congress. They both had been a great integrative and moderating force among the Tamils. Of the two, Chelvanayakam was the follower of Gandhian model of non-violence and also was called father of modern Tamil nationalism in Sri Lanka. He had been a tremendous charismatic force among the Tamils, cementing together the different and divergent sections and conflicting categories of thinking of members of highly individualistic community. He also held in check militant youth prone to violence in the community.

Terrorism in Sri Lanka began in 1970 with the formation of a militant student body called the Tamil Students Movement to protest government plans to limit access of Tamil students to universities. Very soon this movement went underground and turned to avert terrorist activities. Violence escalated in Jaffna from 1972 onwards, beginning with the publication of new constitution seen by the Tamil United Liberation Front (TULF) as anti-Tamil. The year 1972 witnessed the formation of two Tamil terrorist groups such as, the Tamil New Tigers (TNT) and Tamil Eelam Liberation Organisation (TELO), while other active Tamil guerilla groups included the Peoples Liberation Organisation of Tamil Eelam (PLOTE), the Tamil Eelam Liberation Army (TELA), the Eelam Peoples Revolutionary Liberation Front (EPRLF), and the Eelam Revolutionary

Organisation of Students (EROS). They all were averse to political bargaining and sought an armed solution to Tamil problem. For decades, the Tamils did not have an effective political leadership to articulate their just demands, with the mild-mannered leaders of TULF being seen as ineffective in countering Sinhala majority chauvinism.[14]

Vilupillai Prabakaran, the founder of LTTE, was born in Valvettiturai, a fishing town on the northern and eastern fringes of the island. The son of a minor civil servant father and a religious mother, he was said to have been a dutiful introverted child. Keeping all the developments of the time in view, he became a strong believer in violence and in 1972 formed the Tamil New Tigers (TNT) when most of the Tamil youths lost their patience in reform methods adopted by the Tamil parliamentarians. Soon Prabakaran became a wanted man known to the Jaffna police when he, in 1975 gunned down Alfred Duryappa, the mayor of Jaffna when he was on way to a Hindu temple. Months within the TNT was formed, it had morphed into the LTTE. Prabakaran drew up the charter and helped design the LTTE crest, a roaring tiger atop two crossed rifles and a halo of bullets set against a blood-red background. The Tiger had been the symbol of the Cholas, a Tamil dynasty which had dominated medieval south Asia.[15] Inspired by a young militant who had taken cyanide while in police custody, he compelled each LTTE member to wear a necklace with a cyanide capsule to be consumed in the event of capture. A lifelong devotee of Hollywood, he once cited Clint Eastwood as his role model. He watched action movies for inspiration, often using them as a training tool in Tiger camps.

For Prabakaran no sacrifice was too great for the objective of Eelam. In LTTE the Heroes Day (Maveerar Nal), the 27 November, which was also the birthday of Prabakaran, used to be celebrated every year with great pomp and show in the LTTE-controlled territory. On that very day, the lighting of the lamp by the supremo was to remember and commemorate the martyrs who have sacrificed their lives for the causes of Tamil Eelam. Sri Lanka watchers eagerly wait for this event, for the speech was an official prognosis of the immediate past and also contained indications for the future policy.[16] For example, in his Heroes Day speech following the withdrawal of the Indian Peace-keeping Force (IPKF), he made two important pronouncements : (1) Those who betray the cause of Tamil Eelam must be killed ; and (2) if ever Prabakaran betrays the cause of Tamil Eelam, you must kill him.[17] Throughout the years following the formation of LTTE, Prabakaran remained committed to the cause of Tamil Eelam and in one of the functions organised to mark the 7th anniversary of the 'Voice of Tigers' radio, somewhere in the Wanni, he said that the Tamils should be aware that the Sri Lankan government's aim was not just a military victory over the LTTE but the obliteration of the separateness of the Tamils of Sri Lanka.[18] There was a simultaneous propaganda war whose aim was to deny that the Tamils were a people with a totally distinctive identity, history, language, culture and above all a separate traditional homeland.

The Liberation Tigers of Tamil Eelam was a separatist organisation, which from the beginning, waged a violent secessionist campaign and sought to create an independent Tamil state in the north and east of Sri Lanka. For its avowed purpose, the LTTE had carried out civilian massacres, suicide bombings and various other high profile attacks, including the assassinations of several high ranking Sri Lankan and Indian politicians. They invented the suicide belt and pioneered the use of suicide bombing as a tactic. Unlike the old TNT, the LTTE was an elite, ruthlessly efficient, and highly professional fighting force, which as terrorism expert Rohan Gunaratna noted, he did by 'keeping numbers small, maintaining a high standard of training and enforcing discipline at all levels. The LTTE attracted many supporters among disenchanted Tamil youth. They carried out low-key attacks against various government targets, including policemen and local politicians. In practice, the militants' never-ending thirst for arms creates an illegal network of manufacturers, suppliers, financiers, transporters, and corrupt officials. Every point of this supply chain spawns more crimes-bribery, corruption, theft, illegal documentation, killing, extortion, subversion, and sabotage. The list seems endless.[19] The Asian trader's preference to keep secret accounts and to use the illegal hawala route for financial transactions aids the militants' arms trafficking. For about the last four decades Sri Lanka has faced the catastrophe of uncontrolled spread of illegal arms and the spiralling militancy. The LTTE was the most powerful Tamil group in Sri Lanka and used overt and illegal methods to raise funds, acquire weapons, and publicise its cause of establishing an independent Tamil state.

In Sri Lanka, soon after its formation, the LTTE emerged as perhaps the most lethal, well organised and disciplined terrorist force in the world. Initially, LTTE operated in cooperation with other Tamil militant group which shared their objectives and in April 1984, the LTTE formally joined a common militant front, the Eelam National Liberation Front (ENLF), a union between LTTE, the Tamil Eelam Liberation Organisation (TELO), the Eelam Revolutionary Organisation of Students (EROS), the People's

Liberation Organisation of Tamil Eelam (PLOTE) and the Eelam People's Revolutionary Liberation Front (EPRLF). Among them TELO usually held the Indian view of problems and pushed for India's view during peace talks with Sri Lanka and other groups. In contrast, the LTTE denounced the TELO view and claimed that India was only acting on its own interest. As a result in 1986, the LTTE broke from the ENLF. Soon thereafter, fighting broke out between the TELO and the LTTE and clashes occurred over the next few months. In fighting between the two, the entire TELO leadership and many of the TELO militants were killed by the LTTE. The LTTE attacked training camps of the EPRLF a few months later, forcing it to withdraw entirely from the Jaffna peninsula. The LTTE then demanded that all remaining Tamil insurgents join the LTTE. Notices were issued to that effect in Jaffna and in Madras. With the major groups including the TELO and EPRLF eliminated, the remaining Tamil insurgent groups, numbering about 20, were then absorbed into the LTTE, making Jaffna an LTTE-dominated city.

Normally in Sri Lanka the operation areas of LTTE can be divided into three regions : (1) In the northern threatre included Jaffna, Killinochhi and Mullaitivu districts and there the LTTE employed high and mid-intensity warfare. Since the mid-1990s, semi-conventional and unconventional insurgent and terrorist methods are also being used. With the loss of the peninsula in 1996, the LTTE had reverted to unconventional warfare, mostly sparrow tactics – hit and run methods. In the mainland, mostly in Wanni, the LTTE engaged the Sri Lankan troops semi-conventionally. This has become possible after the LTTE acquired artillery and heavy mortars. (2) In the eastern threatre falls Batticaloa, Trincomalee and Amparai districts where the LTTE stationed high, mid and low intensity warfare. Dependent on the LTTE force level, it will engage the troops semi-conventionally or unconventionally. However, insurgent and terrorist tactics predominate. (3) In the Southern threatre, LTTE's operations have been largely focussed on the Colombo, the capital. By targeting financial nerve centres and political leaders, this divisionary tactic of the LTTE has been highly effective. After steadily shifting the threatre of terror into the seat of the country's administration, LTTE's elimination of political and military leaders has adversely affected the morale of the security forces.

The freedom struggle of Tamil Eelam was not limited to the people of Tamil Eelam alone. Without the help of Tamil Diaspora spread around the world, it would become an uphill task for the Tamil people in Tamil Eelam to free themselves from the oppressive rule of the Sinhalese dominated Sri Lankan government. It is the responsibility of each Tamil world-wide to ensure that the birth rights of the Tamils in Tamil Eelam are won to enable them to live in freedom and dignity. Realising this, the Tamil Diaspora is actively involved in various forms of non-violent activities to expose the dark and ugly face of Sri Lankan state terrorism. Eelam Web show-cases some of these activities world-wide for the benefit of fair-minded people who care about the freedom of the Tamils of Tamil Eelam. The LTTE runs a wide network of publicity and propaganda activities with offices and cells located in at least 54 countries. The largest and most important centres are located in leading western states with large Tamil expatriate communities, most notably the UK, France, Germany, Switzerland, Canada and Australia. In addition to these states, the LTTE are also known to be represented in countries as far-flung as Cambodia, Burma, South Africa and Botswana. Its publicity networks covering Europe, Australia and North America, include also radio and TV satellites.

Organisational Structures

Military

The Liberation Tigers of Tamil Eelam (LTTE) aimed to create a separate homeland for the Tamils known as the Tamil Eelam (state) in the Northern and Eastern provinces of Sri Lanka. They control most of the northern and eastern areas and have conducted operations throughout the island. Its leadership is organised along a two-tier structure : a military wing and a subordinate political wing. Overseeing both is a central governing committee, headed by the LTTE chief, Velupillai Prabakaran. This body has the responsibility for directing and controlling several specific subdivisions, including an amphibious group, the Sea Tigers, an airborne group known as the Air Tigers, an elite fighting wing named after the Charles Anthony Regiment, a suicide commando unit called the Black Tigers, a highly secretive intelligence group and a political office headed by Thamilselvam and Anton Balasingham, widely known to be the political advisor and ideologue of the LTTE. The central governing committee also has an International Secretariat, which is in charge of the outfit's global network. Prabakaran heads the LTTE power structure, as chairman of its central governing committee and commander-in-chief of its army.

The LTTE cadres comprise men, women and children – both boys and girls. They are known for their high sense of discipline, dedication, strong determination, a high degree of motivation and innovation. All cadres are carefully indoctrinated on the authorised position : they are fighting against an unresponsive and discriminatory Sinhala majority for a separate state – Eelam; the cadres must banish all fear of death from their minds and be prepared to lay down their lives fighting the Government forces, or consume the cyanide pill fastened around their necks when capture is imminent. The LTTE places immense emphasis on the cult of martyrdom. All the LTTE fighters undergo a programme of rigorous training. A typical training schedule is spread over four months, during which they receive training in handling weapons, battle and field craft, communications, explosives and intelligence gathering, as well as an exhausting physical regimen and rigorous indoctrination.

The LTTE is organised into three main divisions : a military wing, a political wing and a fund raising wing. The military wing includes three specific subdivisions, which are directly controlled and directed by the central governing body. The subdivisions consisted of : (1) Sea Tigers – an amphibious warfare unit focusing on utilisation of naval firepower and logistics, mainly consisting of lightweight boats; (2) Air Tigers – an airborne group, consisting of several lightweight aircraft. It is known to be the world's first air force controlled by an organisation proscribed as terrorists; and (3) Black Tigers – a suicide commando unit, which has carried out between 100-200 missions. In the LTTE, recruits are instructed to be prepared to die for the cause, and are issued with a cyanide capsule to be swallowed in the case of capture.

The Sea Tigers is the naval force of the Liberation Tigers of Tamil Eelam and is lead by Colonel Soosai. It is believed to have about 2000 personnel and has become a potent threat to the Sri Lankan Navy at Sea. According to a 2006 publication of the Woodrow Wilson School of Politics and International Studies, the Sea Tigers has destroyed 35% to 50% of the Sri Lankan Navy's coastal craft. However, following its northern offensive, the Sri Lankan military reported recently that it captured Sea Tiger main base in Mullaitivu and several boat yards. While the Air Tigers was the air force of the Liberation Tigers of Tamil Eelam. The Air Tigers were believed to have operated five light aircrafts. The organisation was revealed in 2007 when it conducted its first air raid on the Sri Lankan Air Force base. It later conducted four air raids. With the Air Tigers, LTTE became the first non-state organisation to establish an air force.

The battalion Black Tigers is a suicide commando unit, which is known for carrying deadly attacks against the Sri Lankan Army and also the politicians who opposed their movement for a separate state for the minority Tamil. The creation of the Black Tigers is based on the LTTE's studies of Asymmetric warfare; thus using suicide cadres balance the government's greater resources. They are special operatives of the LTTE that commit suicide if needed to reach their destination. The LTTE are keeping the Black Tigers unit active, as witnessed by their commemoration ceremonies of Black Tigers Day on 5 July. Its cadres that volunteer for the Black Tiger unit get extensive training but are then believed to return to their previous unit, without revealing their assignment. The Black Tigers are believed to be the most effective unit of its kind in the world, as the rest of the LTTE is also secular, not driven by religious fanaticism. Apart from Black Tigers, there are also maritime Black Tigers and airborne Black Tigers. The maritime Black Tigers use small glass fibre boats loaded with explosives that ram Sri Lanka Navy vessels. Suicide attacks have also been conducted by divers, swimming into the Kankesantural naval base in the Jaffna peninsula and blowing up a large merchant vessel. The LTTE may have airborne Black Tigers; it is believed that the five microplanes at Iranamadu may belong to such a force, but no airborne attack has yet been attempted.

The Black Tigers are considered to be one of the most elite and lethal suicide bombers in the world. The first LTTE Black Tiger was Captain Miller who drove a small truck laden with explosives into a Sri Lankan Army camp in Nelliady, Jaffna peninsula, on 5 July 1987, killing himself and over 50 Sri Lankan soldiers. In January 1996, the LTTE carried out their deadliest suicide bomb attack, at the Central Bank, killing 90 and injuring 1400. In October 1997 they bombed the Sri Lankan World Trade Centre, and, in January 1998, detonated a truck bomb in Kandy, damaging the Temple of the Tooth, one of the holiest Buddhist shrines in the world. Notable Black Tiger operations are the suicide bombing of the late Indian Prime Minister Rajiv Gandhi by a female cadre, resulting in the death of herself, the Prime Minister, and 16 bystanders. The late Sri Lankan Prime Minister Ranasinghe Premadasa was also assassinated by an LTTE operative, killing 23 others unfortunate enough to be nearby. They also attempted to assassinate Chandrika Kumaratunga in 1999 during election campaigning; she survived the suicide blast with the loss of her right eye. More than 270 Black Tigers have died in various actions on land and sea, almost all in Sri Lanka. After their death, the cadre families are cared by the LTTE and the cadre's photo is listed in the Black Tigers Day commemoration.

The LTTE in general, have integrated a battle field insurgent strategy with a terrorist programme that targets not only key personnels in the countryside but also senior Sri Lankan political and military leaders in Colombo and other urban centres. The extensive training of their suicide units separates the Black Tigers from other suicide bombers around the world. The most recent Black Tiger operations were against the Sri Lanka army commander Lieutenant General Sarath Fonseka in April 2006 and Major General Parami Kulatunga in June 2006. While Fonseka survived, Kulatunga perished. Especially, the attack against Fonseka was typical of the Black Tigers detailed planning. They employed a woman, possibly pregnant, that penetrated the Army headquarters' security under the cover of visiting the hospital on the compound, checking her pregnancy. Manjula Devi, the female suicide bomber, lived with a Sinhalese family and she was fluent in Sinhalese.

Civil Administration

The LTTE had, since its control, established civil administration in the Tamil areas of northern and eastern region of Sri Lanka where the Sinhala government had no concern for the proper care of the public except when the tax collection was required. In the Tamil dominated areas the LTTE had for decades worked as a *de facto* government and discharged the responsibilities to see the effective functioning of civil administration with its own agencies, such as Tiger Courts, Tiger Police, Bank of Tamileelam and Voice of Tigers as radio and television. For the purpose of imparting justice properly, the LTTE had implemented a judicial system that included the courts to adjudicate in criminal and civil matters. The Tamil Eelam judicial system consisted of district courts, high courts, a supreme court and a court of appeal. The district courts handled civil and criminal cases. The two high courts handled criminal cases such as rape, murder, treason and arson. The supreme court had jurisdiction over the whole of Tamil Eelam. The courts were said to be effective and people who had a choice went to the Tamil Eelam courts rather than the Sri Lankan courts. The LTTE had also released law books that were updated. The court of law, with Tamil literates and scholars presiding over the hearings, had equal representation for all people and offer free hearings for the poor to ensure the upholding of justice.

The Liberation Tigers of Tamil Eelam had established a police force called Tiger Police which was well respected by the people for its tough stand on criminals and its zero tolerance policy regarding bribes within its members, worked in an effective manner in conjunction with the

Court of Law. Established in 1991, the Tiger Police was the other key factor in maintaining law and order. Prior to 2009 offensive, it had its headquarters at Kilinochchi. It was formed in all areas controlled by the LTTE. It claimed that its police force was the reason for the low crime rate, but critics of LTTE claim that police force was an integrated arm of the LTTE armed force and that the crime rate is low as a result of LTTE authoritarian rules. However, everyone agreed the police force and the judicial system was the reason for high degree of rule of law in the areas controlled by the LTTE.

The National Bank known as Bank of Tamileelam is another aspect of the civil administration of the LTTE's *de facto* government. Although it used the Sri Lankan rupee as its currency but offered higher interest rates than any bank of the island. Through this bank, various projects aiding the improvement of Tamil people in all walks of life such as farming, technology, small industries, are carried out. The bank with many branches throughout Tamil Eelam, also provides relief and loans to the civilians affected by the terror of the Sinhala government and its forces, to ensure that the people don't lose hope in their lives. In addition, the LTTE also ran its own radio and television stations. These entities were named the Voice of Tigers and National Tamil Eelam Television respectively. Both the radio and television channel were aired from the areas under LTTE control.

Social welfare and humanitarian assistance were also state functions of the LTTE administration. The LTTE established an education sector as well as health sector that offered services to the people under control. It created a human rights organisation, called Northeast Secretariat on Human Rights, that functioned to advocate the rights of the Tamils. Though not recognised by international government, it acted as a human rights commission. The commission communicated with the LTTE regarding complains of child recruiting which resulted in the release of the recruit. The Planning and Development Secretariat (PDS) was established in 2004 which acted as a needs assessment body responsible for studying the needs for people and formulating a plan for effective action in areas that needed humanitarian assistance. There were also many civil servants who worked in the LTTE-controlled areas who were directed by the LTTE but paid by the Sri Lankan government. A custom service was operated at the border by the Tamil Tigers.

The LTTE laid special emphasis on humanitarian assistance and in 2004 after the Asian Tsunami, it set up a special task force called the tsunami task force for human help to the people affected by tsunami. The Planning and Development Secretariat (PDS) was responsible for needs assessments for various humanitarian organisation to maximise effectiveness of resettlement reconstruction and rehabilitation. After the Tsunami, the PDS was responsible of coordinating and directing the NGOs involved in tsunami relief work. Further more, according to Tsunami Evaluation Coalition, the key NGOs that responded also claimed that the LTTE forces provided extremely efficient and focused leadership and support to the relief effort in the areas controlled by the Tigers. During the second round of negotiation between Tigers and the Government of Sri Lanka, an agreement was reached for a joint Post-Tsunami Operational Management Structure (P-TOMS). This mechanism would allow the government and LTTE to share funds for tsunami relief. However, this agreement was bitterly opposed by hardliners in the government and some moderates. As a result, the P-TOMS was challenged in the Sri Lankan Supreme Court, who put the said agreement on hold.

Recruitment of Women and Child Cadres

The overall ideology and principles of the LTTE, who also advocated equality for women from both male oppression and social oppression attracted many women into the LTTE ranks. For the first time, Women's Front of the Liberation Tigers (WFLT) was formed in 1983 followed by the creation of an all-female unit called the Freedom Birds in 1984. As a result LTTE became the first Tamil militant group to employ women as soldiers in the battlefield. Tamil women believe that their participation in the armed struggle will bring them advantage in a future peaceful society and allow them to take part in liberating their society. The Women cadres began their combat training in 1985 and in 1987, Prabakaran set up the first training camp exclusively for women in Jaffna for the second and successive batches. From the year 1987, a deliberate policy of recruiting women and children into LTTE cadres was initiated after the signing of the Indian Peace-keeping Force (IPKF) accord to offset a severe shortage of manpower, because of ever increasing casualties and the escalation of the conflict. By 1989, the women wing of LTTE secured its own leadership structure. This period reportedly witnessed the highest recruitment of women as it was also the time when women were the worst sufferers of the ethnic conflicts.

The women cadres of the LTTE undergo the same tough training as men, and like them, are classified into fighting, intelligence gathering, political and administrative units. Adele Ann, the Australian born wife of Anton Balasingham, the LTTE theoretician, in her book named *Women Fighters of Liberation Tigers*, published in 1989, described the decision by a Tamil women to join the organisation as a message to society that they are not satisfied with the social status quo; it means they are young women capable of defying authority; it means they are women with independent thoughts; young women prepared to lift up their heads. Later the LTTE chief Prabakaran, in an address to women cadres on International Women's Day on March 8, 1996, described the liberation of the Tamil woman as 'the fervent' child that was born out of the Tamil national liberation movement. Nearly one-third of the LTTE cadre comprise women, who have assigned duties on the battlefield, in the kitchen, and in medical camps as nurses. According to a report of *The Hindu*, 10 March 2002, nearly 4,000 women LTTE cadres have been killed since they began taking part in combat from 1985, joining the LTTE pantheon of over 17,000 heroes in the round about two decade-old conflict. Over 100 women killed belonged to the dreaded Black Tigers' suicide squad.[20] Women in the LTTE are allegedly forced to suppress their femininity and sexuality, which is regarded as a crime and an evil force that could sap their strength. Marriage is not allowed for women cadres up to the age of 25 and for men up to the age of 28. The proportion of female combatants was small until June 1990, but increased rapidly afterward. Apart from military roles, the female soldiers have also produced numerous publications and many of them are described as rich in culture and writing.

Recruitment of children as LTTE cadres began following the ethnic riots of July 1983. At this stage, LTTE chief Prabakaran selected Basheer Kaka, an LTTE leader from the harbour city of Trincomalee to establish a training base in the State of Pondicherry in India for recruits under 16. Initially, the child soldiers – affectionately referred to as 'Tiger Cubs, received non-military training, mostly primary education and physical exercise. By early 1984, the nucleus of the LTTE 'Baby Brigade' or 'Bakuts' was formed. Until 1986, the LTTE had sufficient adult units in operation and young recruits were put through the Tiger's standard grueling four-month training course as soon as they reached 16. The child fighters were originally a part of the Baby Brigade. After 1987, the LTTE integrated children with other units to offset heavy losses in combat. When the children were pitched into battle against Sri Lankan forces after 1990, the LTTE made training tougher.

Children have featured prominently in the LTTE's protracted guerilla and terrorist campaigns. According to an assessment done by the Sri Lankan Directorate of Military Intelligence, as much as 60 per cent of the LTTE's fighters were below 18 years of age. Another study in this regard was conducted by a UK-based Sri Lankan researcher Dushy Ranatunge which revealed that at least 60 per cent of the dead LTTE fighters were under 18 and were mostly girls and boys aged 10-16. He also revealed that almost all of the casualties were from Batticaloa, but after the escalation in the fighting following the LTTE assaults on the Kilinochchi. In the LTTE a typical unit of children was trained for four months in the jungle. Woken up at 5 A.M. in the morning, they assembled, fell in line, and their leader raised the LTTE flag. This was followed by the two hours of physical training, after which the recruits were engaged in weapon training, battle and field craft, and parade drill. During the rest of the afternoon, time was spent on both – reading the LTTE literature and further physical training. Lectures on communications, explosives and intelligence techniques continued into the evening. No contact was permitted between the camp and the children's homes during the training period. Sleep and food were regulated during training to build endurance. The trained child fighters were also prepared for battle by attacking unprotected or weakly defended border villages. Several hundred men, women and children have been killed by LTTE child combatants armed with automatic weapons guided by experienced fighters.

For the proper maintenance of LTTE's vast organisational structures, fund raising was an issue and it was done by the large Tamil Diasporas and as reported through drug running, particularly heroin from Southeast and Southwest Asia. The majority of financial support came from six main areas, all of which contain large Tamil Diasporas : Switzerland, Canada, Australia, the UK, the US, and the Scandinavian countries. The LTTE had established a wide network of offices and cells practically across the globe. They have secured a considerable degree of visibility in the United Kingdom – the headquarters of its 'International Secretariat' as well as in Canada, France, Germany, Holland, Switzerland, Italy, Sweden, Denmark, Norway, Australia and South Africa. These networks of offices and cells carry out propaganda, organise the procurement and movement of weapons and raise funds from the Tamil Diaspora. Thus the Western countries are the main territory for fund raising activities of the LTTE. The money raised from donations and enterprises are transferred into bank accounts of the Tigers and from there to the accounts of a weapon broker or the money is taken by KP operative themselves. LTTE's need for resources is mostly fulfilled by the Tamils who reside outside Sri Lanka. In 1995, when the LTTE lost Jaffna, its international operatives were ordered to increase by 50 % the amount raised from Tamils outside the island.

In the spheres of fund raising and weapon procurement, the LTTE is in a particularly advantageous position to traffic narcotics due to the highly efficient international network it had developed to smuggle munitions around the world. Many of these arms routes pass either directly through or very close to major drug producing and transit centres, including Burma, Thailand, Cambodia, Southern China, Afghanistan and Pakistan. Military and arms procurement played a vital part in the LTTE's battle against the government sources. The LTTE arms network is headed by Tharmalingam Shanmugham, alias Kumaran Pathmanathan and colloquially known as 'KP'. At the heart of the KP's operations is a highly secretive shipping network. The ships frequently visit Japan, Indonesia, Singapore, South Africa, Burma, Turkey, France, Italy and Ukraine, scouting for arms. In addition to setting up a number of lucrative businesses, the LTTE established a state-of-the-art boatyard that manufactured a dozen different boats, including a minisubmarine for debussing divers.

Although the LTTE was formed as a military group, it later transformed into a *de facto* government. It controlled sections of the regions through different wings such as Political Wing, Tiger Intelligence and International relations. The chief of Political wing was Anton Balasingtham, who also held a key past in major peace talks with Sri Lanka and the third party of Norway. After his death on December 14, 2006, B. Nadesan took over as political head and led the political wing of the LTTE. This political wing also played a critical role with regard to both peace process and local state building. However, LTTE's political wing did not participate in Sri Lankan parliamentary elections. The intelligence wing has helped the Liberation Tigers of Tamil Eelam with exclusive missions such as radars and more to prepare the military for an attack. Pottu Amman, the leader of the Intelligence Wing was believed to be shot by the Sri Lankan Army on May 19, 2009. While the international relations are believed to be the only LTTE wing to be standing after the Sri Lankan's Army final offensive, it is led by current leader Selvarasa Pathmanathan. From an unknown location, operating outside Sri Lanka, the International Relations wing is now going to lead the LTTE and Tamil Eelam into exile in regard to a provisional transnational government.

Initial Activities

Since its formation on 5 May 1976, the Liberation Tigers of Tamil Eelam has continued to pursue its objectives of a separate, independent Tamil Eelam through its policy of indiscriminate killing of all those the LTTE considered stood in its way, be they Sinhala or Tamil.[21] With the arrival of the LTTE on the centre-stage of Tamil politics, it was signalled by the murder of four policemen in Velvettithurai in April 1978. The incident triggered off a confrontation with the government that injected a new and most complex dimension to Sri Lanka's ethnic problem and eventually plunged the country into a virtual civil war. The then government of Sri Lanka headed by J. R. Jayawardene, without taking into consideration the effects, resorted to military suppression of the guerillas and failed to measure the challenge politically. As a result, the government first banned the LTTE and other similar groups in May 1978 and then imposed emergency in Jaffna in January 1979 that continued for a year. In addition, the National Assembly also adopted on 19 July 1979 the Anti-Terrorism Bill, but it did not curb terrorism and radicalised the extremists and boosted their popularity among the Tamils.

The incident of April 1978 took an alarming turn in the coming years. Perhaps in revenge, the Jatika Sevaka Sangamaya (JSS) had given it an unprecedented militancy. It had spread its tentacles into other areas of the country and the members of Parliament have created through the JSS and through other local groups in small market towns a complex, powerful network of organisations that can be put to political use. By the time a remarkable change has also occurred in the composition of political power brokers in the country even in village areas. Traditionally the vote and especially the village vote, was delivered or controlled by an educated village elite, coming generally from respectable families. This was true of all parties but especially, the UNP was the country's most important conservative party. At the close of the 1970s, this has changed or was fast changing; political power on the village level was in the hands of those who can control the unemployed and the discontented, primarily the youth. The new composition of Sri Lankan society gave birth to political violence in large numbers which had been documented by Lakshman Wickramasingha, the chairman of Civil Rights Movement

(CRM). On his records, there are several examples of these events which confirm the new mode of social structure. He has quoted a number of incidents which took place between 1978-81 in Sri Lanka.

On 15 June 1978 about 400 thugs, members of the JSS, threatened six section heads at the Thulhiriya Textile Mills and drove them of the premises. The six were forced to resign. The management was warned by the thugs not to allow the six people back. Likewise, on 3 January 1980, the Personnel Manager of the Peoples' Bank was abused and assaulted in his office by JSS officers, in the presence of several members of staff. In another incident on 4 July 1980, teachers at Maharagama Teachers Training College were picketing peacefully when Government transport bus No. 23 Sri 2549 came through the college gates carrying 27 people including a leader of the JSS. Thugs got out and began to assault the teacher trainees with rubber belts, stones, bicycle chains etc. Women were thrown to the ground and waste oil was poured over their clothes and into their eyes and ears. And lastly a series of violent acts occurred in jaffna in late May and early June 1981, of which the most serious was the burning of the public library by thugs from outside while the security forces did nothing to stop the arson. This was a profoundly symbolic act : the library contained priceless manuscripts pertaining to the identity of the Tamils of Jaffna. On the Buddhist side it was an unparalleled act of barbarism, since rarely in Sri Lanka's recorded history was there an example of book burning of this magnitude.[22] The pattern in these activities is clear : the gangs were organised, they came in government vehicles, they were sometimes accompanied by MPs and for the most part they belonged to the JSS, the trade union arm of the party in power. In several events, the government also dared to openly flout the Supreme Court decisions. By mid–1983 every Tamil was of the opinion that the violence against them was organised by the government, and especially by the JSS and the influential politicians who controlled this union.

Soon after the formation, LTTE had grown out to be a massive army with whole-hearted support of the Tamil people and some years later it maintained thousands of brave soldiers, with a naval wing that had become formidable in the subcontinent. And as the racist policies of the repressive Sinhala governments continued, it made the Tamil civilians to more and more hardships. In that kind of situation the LTTE had become the army that the Tamil people could look up to in order to put an end to all the troubles and win back the Tamil's homeland, Tamil

Eelam. The LTTE carried out their first major attack on July 23, 1983, when they ambushed a Sri Lanka Army troop transport outside Jaffna in which 13 Sri Lankan soldiers were killed. Still the Tamils were a dispossessed people, denied of even basic democratic rights and equal citizenship rights by an oppressive Sri Lankan state dominated by the Sinhala majority.[23] The incident of 23 July led to the Black July riots against the Tamil community of Sri Lanka.

Large scale anti-Tamil violence in the form of riots erupted in July-August 1983 in which at least several hundred people, almost all of whom were Tamils, were killed and many tens of thousands driven into hiding or to refugee camps and a vast number of Tamil homes and businesses were looted and burnt. In several areas, members and even units of the security forces led or abetted the rioting and much of the violence, particularly in greater Colombo seemed more carefully organised than on earlier occasions. A large number of killings were performed in particularly gruesome, sadistic fashion and corpses were often mutilated or burned. On successive days, 35 and then 17 Tamil prisoners in the Welikada jail were massacred by Sinhalese inmates and, according to some accounts, by prison staff as well. One of the most shameful aspects of the troubles of 1983 was the refusal of the minor staff of several hospitals to tend or care for wounded Tamils. In all the refusal cases the JSS may be culpable since the hospital system was almost totally controlled by it. Linked to the growing demand for separatism was a sense of shock and outrage not just at the scale of the violence but also at the manner in which Tamils had been killed in the riots.[24] The riots of 1983 were only the most recent of a series of incidents which have made Tamil Catholics and their priests more aware of their identity as Tamils. As a result, the Tamil Catholics have begun to take a renewed interest in Tamil culture.

Although without doubt there was a large element of organisation in the rioting, this does not mean that events can be explained solely in terms of manipulation by a few ringleaders. Apart from this the rioting of July 1983 showed three kinds of violence that occurred in that week. Firstly, there was the inchoate anger at the murder of 13 members of the security forces on the night of 23 July, but the localised appearance of the violence – the complete absence of violence in many towns and its gradual move outwards from Colombo, would suggest that this alone would not constitute a sufficient cause for what happened. The second and most common kind of violence was the calculated destruction of Tamil property by relatively small and well organised gangs; by and large the Tamil occupants of such property were given the opportunity to escape to the relative safety of the refugee camps. The third and most disturbing kind was the horrific murder of innocent Tamils. It is likely that some of these murders occurred in that first wave of blind rage. But the best documented massacres seem to have followed in a perverse but regular way from the relative calm of systematic and rational looting and burning. These massacres only begin to make sense, both to a troubled outsider and to Sinhalese people themselves.

The July 1983 anti-Tamil program meant-organised massacre led many Tamils to spontaneously support all Tamil militant groups that came up in its wake.[25] Before the incident the separatist sentiment is far from general in all the Tamil areas. Tamil who lived in areas with a Sinhalese majority were naturally the least receptive to separatism, knowing that they would be the first to be exposed to reprisals. Most of them, however, kept their links with their home areas which would allow them to return there if need be. But now they began to think in terms of SLFP who might, after all, be a better defender of their interests. The continuation of pro-Sinhala governments in the country resulted in large scale unemployment and frustration which became the principal stimulus to separatism. The young who remained in Jaffna were attracted by the separatist movement. Those, increasingly numerous, who found the means to emigrate towards the countries of the Persian Gulf, Europe and North America, naturally became the propagandists of separatism and its sources of money–a classical process.[26] In post–1983 period, the subsequent anger amongst the Tamil community resulted in numerous Tamil youths joining Tamil militant groups to fight the Sri Lankan government, in what is considered start of the insurgency in Sri Lanka.

Thus the incident of July 1983 was taken as the beginning of the ethnic conflict which followed attacks and counter attacks and support on both sides for violence. Since 1983, there had been on-and-off civil war, mostly between the government and the LTTE. As a result, hundreds of thousands of refugees were displaced internally or had fled to Tamil Nadu and around the world. From here onwards, the LTTE had begun its armed conflict with Sri Lankan government and relied on guerilla strategy that included the use of terrorist tactics. The Tiger had integrated a battlefield insurgent strategy with a terrorist programme that targeted not only key personnel in the countryside but also senior Sri Lankan political and military leaders in Colombo and other urban centres. After it, the LTTE had made its organisational structure wide and placed immense emphasis on the cult of martyrdom and a two-tier structure was formed. In addition there was also an International Secretariat, which was in charge of the outfit's global network. The full-scale ethnic war which erupted in 1983 sent thousands of young Tamils to Indian training camps. Many wealthy Tamils fled to the west and their contributions, not always voluntary, played a large part in funding the Tigers arsenal.[27] The LTTE maintained a fleet known as Sea Tigers and carried out air raids using Czechoslovak - built propeller – engined trainers. Since the late 1980s, the LTTE had conducted approximately two hundred suicide attacks. Targets have included transit hubs, Buddhist shrines, and office buildings. According to the Federal Bureau of Investigation (FBI), the LTTE invented the suicide belt and pioneered the use of women in suicide attacks. In later years the LTTE had strengthened itself significantly in Sri Lanka and abroad.

With a view to finding a political solution to the strife, J.R. Jayawardene, the then President of Sri Lanka, on 19 July 1987, proposed the creation of an autonomous unit comprising the Northern and Eastern provinces and other related provisions were also made in the scheme. The Jayawardene's proposal galvanised the peace process that soon culminated in the signing of an accord between India and Sri Lanka on 29 July 1987 which came to be known as Indo-Sri Lanka Accord. The signed accord had essentially two aspects. The first dealt with India's commitment to uphold Sri Lanka's sovereignty and territorial integrity on the condition that the latter agreed to grant a reasonable amount of autonomy to the Tamils to their satisfaction. The second aspect dealt with Sri Lanka's commitment to disallow any extra-regional power to dabble in its affairs which had either a known or a potential intention to harm India's security interests in the region. Following the signing of the accord, India sent a peace–keeping force to ensure that peace returned to the strife-torn Tamil areas. In operational terms this meant the disarming of the LTTE cadres. Between 1983-90 India tried out all possibilities – supporting the Tamil cause and militancy, helping the Sri Lanka Government and the Tamils to resolve their differences across the table, working with Sri Lanka to help evolve a consensus on devolution of Tamils and lastly, underwriting an acceptable minimum package for Tamils in Sri Lanka through the accord.[28] The new understanding opened a new chapter between the two countries with cooperation rather than confrontation. Before India intervened in 1987, more than 37 Tamil militant groups came into being. All these groups except the Liberation Tigers of Tamil Eelam surrendered arms after signing of the accord in 1987.

Unfortunately the much-publicised India-Sri Lanka Accord of July 1987 was not approved by the LTTE and its supremo Velupillai Prabakaran who had explained that the accord did not address any of the Tamil demands, namely, an end of the illegal Sinhala colonisation, recognition of the Tamils as a nation, the permanent merger of the northern and eastern provinces, and the withdrawal of Sri Lankan troops from the province and as such, refused to surrender without any credible guarantee that political power would be handed over to it. The refusal of the LTTE made the accord irrelevant in context of establishing ethnic peace in the country. Both processes – surrender of arms as well as cessation of hostilities were repudiated by the LTTE leadership on 7 October 1987 when they retaliated against the capture at sea by Sri Lankan forces of thirteen of their senior cadres. Earlier in August 1987 Prabakaran, while addressing more than 100,000 people in a rare public appearance in Jaffna, had vowed that only a separate state could offer a permanent solution.

Barring the LTTE, the India-Sri Lanka Accord was also disapproved by certain important elements in the Sri Lankan establishment. The most important among them was President Ranasinghe Premadasa, who was killed by a LTTE suicide cadre during a May Day rally in Colombo on 1 May 1993, and his then Security Minister Lalith Athulathmudali, who too, was assassinated later by a LTTE cadre.[29] The Janatha Vimukti Peramuna (JVP) was another militant Sinhalese leftist group who opposed the India-Sri Lanka Accord and rejected the proposals for federalism or power devolution. It escalated terrorist campaign in the south and stepped up its scheme of assassinations of politicians who support the accord. The JVP was very successful in recruiting bhikkus in its armed anti-accord insurrection. Its monks and bhikkus who joined army caused deep confusion among those who perceived Buddhism as a philosophy of peace and non-violence. To committed Sinhala Buddhist ideologues, however, violence can be justified to counter threat posed by the India-Sri Lanka Accord to the unity of land. Many Sri Lankan Buddhist who follow Lord Buddha's teachings that reject all sorts of division between human beings cannot sanction support or participation in violence. But even they were in deep anxiety about perceived threats to their religion which can be and have been manipulated politically.[30] Thus the Indian Peace-keeping Force which came to the island nation as part of the Accord had to face a rough weather in the trouble-plagued Sri Lanka.

The 1987 Accord ran into trouble within months after the Liberation Tigers of Tamil Eelam took up arms against the Indian Peace-keeping

Force. On 10 October in the same year the IPKF which had been invited to Sri Lanka by President Jayawardene, inaugurated their own military campaign against the Tigers which was still continuing without any immediate prospect either of a cessation of hostilities or a complete surrender of arms by all militant groups. In the meantime, the Sri Lanka's security forces were withdrawn to barracks and this development necessitated an Indian military presence in Sri Lanka, at first to oversee the token surrender of arms by militant groups, laterly to undertake a full-scale military offensive against the LTTE. Now the IPKF got bogged down in a guerilla war against the Tamil Tigers which made essential a progressive increase in its numbers as well as in the number and range of its weaponary.[31] The operation which started off as a conventional one in 1987, quickly changed into a full-fledged counterinsurgency campaign. However, even on this count, the IPKF proved itself.

After a year of IPKF's operation against the LTTE, in August 1988, the latter had confined to the Vanni jungles. Within a year of the IPKF completing operation Checkmate – I, normal life was restored in the northeast. The IPKF, despite some aberrations and limitations imposed by political dispensations, gave the people there a feeling of security and gained their trust. Although the IPKF failed to fully provide the equal rights for Tamils, it reduced the LTTE to a spent force. It was in this phase that Prabakaran lived in a massive fortified camp in the thick jungles of the northern Wanni region. By this time, despite the LTTE's cardinal rule of celibacy, Prabakaran had taken a wife, Mathivathani Erambu. Accordingly, the rules were amended for his cadres. Tigers were allowed to marry with Prabakaran's sanction. But the Tiger's code remained austere. Tobacco and alcohol were forbidden and the vial of cyanide remained. The year of accord (1987) also witnessed first LTTE suicide bombing in the northern town of Nelliady and formation of Black Tigers – a group of male and female suicide bombers whose explosives – laden belts had later been copied by Palestinian, Chechen and Iraqi groups. As reported in July 1988 by Krishna Chandra Pant, India's Minister of Defence, in the Lower House of Parliament that since 10 October 1987, 511 Indian soldiers had died and another 1526 had been wounded in battles with Sri Lanka's dominant Tamil guerilla group, the Liberation Tigers of Tamil Eelam. Since the time up to 31 May, India had spent 970 million rupees on the Sri Lankan operation.

The direct fight of LTTE cadres against the Indian Peace-keeping Force (IPKF) caused the death of 1255 Indian soldiers on Sri Lankan soil during their two years' stayal in the island nation. It was not so good for the health of LTTE because its strength as the most powerful of the Tamil guerilla groups in the island had depended to a large extent on the moral and material support that it derived from Tamilnadu state, at times both from the government and opposition ranks in the state, generally from the Tamil public and, on occasion, even from central government agencies such as Research and Analysis Wing (RAW), the intelligence arm of the Government of India. In post-Accord period when the LTTE went back on it and got involved in a war with the IPKF, relations between the LTTE and the Rajiv Government and between the LTTE and the All-India Anna Dravida Munnetra Kazhagam (AIADMK) government in Madras became sour.[32] The LTTE along with JVP had opposed the Presidential election held in December 1988 which saw much violence and rioting in Sri Lanka.

Later in February 1989, the Parliamentary elections were held in which the UNP won 125 out of 225 seats. Ranasinghe Premadasa, the new President of Sri Lanka, was also opposed to the Indo-Sri Lanka Accord of 1987 from the beginning and now began to press the Indian government for its withdrawal. In the meantime, Tamil politics in the northeast of Sri Lanka took a new turn, with other militant groups engaging themselves in a struggle for political power. The Premadasa government of Sri Lanka had been involved in political negotiations with the LTTE since September 1989, when a ceasefire between the two sides had earlier taken effect, gave the LTTE a temporary advantage in this struggle for power. The Indian government of the time headed by Rajiv Gandhi fixed December 31, 1989, for the withdrawal of IPKF from the island nation, it however, was extended up to 30th March 1990 when the new government took over in New Delhi under the Premiership of V.P. Singh in December 1989. The new government of India was of the view that the IPKF can not do for the Sri Lankan Sinhalas but Tamils alone can do for themselves and therefore, must live in peace and social stability.[33] A week ahead of the deadline (31 March), the last of the Indian Peace-keeping Force left Sri Lanka ending a historic two and a half year long chapter in relations between the two countries. Hardly ten hours after the IPKF left Sri Lanka, President Premadasa thanked India profoundly for drawing its troops completely and said, 'We were able to send home a mighty army not by war but by consultation.[34] India's step was welcomed by all including the United States of America.

Response and Reactions

Initially the Government of Sri Lanka refused to take the formation of LTTE in May 1976 as a serious matter and thought it to be like other militant organisations in the country because there were dozens of such groups dominated by Tamil youths who believed in direct use of violence to have their objective of Eelam state achieved. At the July 1977 elections in Sri Lanka J.R. Jayawardene's United National Party came out victorious and he became the Prime Minister of the island nation. Like predecessors the new UNP government also choose to overlook the TULF's separatist stand but admitting the previous mistakes, tried to pacify Tamil sentiments with a number of concessions that fell short of Tamil expectations. The use of Buddhist symbolism in official affairs was curtailed. On the issue of language, Article 14 F guaranteed 'the freedom to enjoy and promote his own culture and to use his own language'. Tamil now became a national language and the language of administration in the northern and eastern districts.[35]

In fact from 1948 until 1977, despite the fact that successive Sinhalese governments toyed with the idea of concessions, all promises came to nothing since the Opposition Party of the moment, either UNP or SLFP, constantly raised the communalist bidding, whilst the constant attitude of the Tamil leaders was to turn in themselves. It was the time when Sri Lanka's image in the international community was perceived as a success story of democracy in South Asia. Its achievements in conducting regular elections, education and health and literacy were admired even in the developed world.[36] The year in early 1978 witnessed the change over from Parliamentary system to the French type of Presidential government and adoption of a new constitution in August by the National State Assembly of Ceylon which came into force on 7 September by a declaration of the President of the Republic.

The new constitution adopted in 1978 was aimed to meet some urgent problems like the maintenance of national unity and territorial integrity and the Presidential system of government too gave due consideration to the question of minority rights. It laid emphasis on individual's rights in matters of freedom of speech and religion and formation of trade associations. It also abolished the distinction between citizens by residence and citizen by registration, benefiting the Indian Tamils who were so far treated as second-class citizens by earlier governments. Chapter IV of the 1978 Constitution recognised Tamil as an official and national language and provided for its use by right in the legislative, administrative, and judicial arenas as a medium of instruction.[37] The constitutional provisions were hailed by the Tamil leaders of Sri Lanka not as an ideal or a perfect one, but nevertheless, as a great improvement on all the constitutions that the country so far had as it had given the Tamils who had sweated and toiled to develop the Sri Lankan economy a rightful place and a new status.[38] In response, the Congress Working Committee, the main political party-cum-trade union representing the Indian Tamils even joined the Jayawardene government.

For most Tamils the new concessions appeared to be a classical case of too little too late, and for separatists, particularly the LTTE, it led nowhere in realising their 'Tamil Eelam' or 'Precious Land'. They soon were accompanied by attacks on government agencies that compelled to pass the Prevention of Terrorism Act which gave unbridled powers of search and arrest to the military and police. Earlier the political immobility of the moderate Tamil leadership allowed the rise of a number of militant factions who increasingly took to terrorist activities.[39] President Jayawardene subsequently began a series of negotiations on increased autonomy with the major Tamil political organisations on the island. But in contrast, the constitution that Jayawardene had adopted in 1978 had retained the unitary character of the state, out of the fear that decentralisation would ultimately lead to Tamil secession. The Westminster model has been replaced by a presidential system with concentration of power in the central government.

As promised in the new constitution in 1981, the government set up councils for regional devolution of power in the form of District Development Council. These councils, which were elected, but controlled by a district minister appointed by the central government, were intended to replace in time the traditional system of administration and make possible a gentle evolution towards a certain amount of autonomy. These councils failed within two years because of a variety of reasons. The Tamil leaders also asserted that the DDCs had done nothing in their two years of existence to free the district ministers from central tutelage. Another objection was raised that these bodies were established at district rather than at regional level, and therefore foster local particularism instead of contributing to the formation of an autonomous Tamil region. In the meantime, the Sinhalese extremists who were opposed to any plan of devolution of power to the Tamils became active in Sinhalese majority areas.

Serious rioting broke out in Sri Lanka in 1981, and in greater magnitude, in July 1983, unleashed an unprecedented wave of violence that engulfed the island and divided the Sri Lankan society. Violence, accompanying protests against Sinhalese discrimination, and demands from the Sri Lankan Tamil minority youth grew more pronounced after the riots of 1983 which convulsively wrecked Sri Lanka for over a week. The immediate cause ascribed for the outbreak of this large scale severe violence was the death of the members of the armed forces in northern Sri Lanka. Although there followed immediate reprisal in Jaffna, capital of north Sri Lanka, yet almost throughout the island violence within Sinhalese districts was directed against captive Tamil minority groups.[40] In post 1983 riots phase, the LTTE had enjoyed an unprecedented level of support and goodwill among the people of Tamil Nadu despite its record of killing Tamil militants of repute of TELO and hundreds of cadres of other groups including the PLOTE. Velupillai Prabakaran's mystique persisted and many Tamils ignored his seeming character aberrations.[41] Hence, Jayawardene's efforts to bring Tamils and Sinhalese together to negotiate a political settlement failed as the moderate TULF had already lost ground to the LTTE which were steadfast in establishing a separate state, the Tamil Eelam.

As a result of 1983 riots which killed a number of government soldiers, the Sixth Amendment to the Constitution was passed. It empowered the government to ban political parties that advocated secession and impose death penalty on those found guilty of advocating it. Consequently, all fourteen TULF members of Parliament had to resign, leaving the Lankan Tamils unrepresented in Parliament; thus control of political leadership passed into the hand of the militant faction, particularly the Liberation Tigers of Tamil Eelam. Since then violence on both sides increased alarmingly, as the Tamil militants have trained abroad with the Palestinian Liberation Organisation (PLO) and in South India. On the other the Sri Lankan military forces had trained in the past under the supervision of ex-members of Britain's Special Air Services and Israeli security specialists.[42] In the coming years the Government of Sri Lanka appeared facing serious internal crises from different fronts.

However, the response of the government and its prominent leaders on the racial riots of July 1983 disappointed many who hoped that government officials and politicians would act sincerely taking into account the seriousness of the situation. Although the President himself was not a racist, it was likely that his inaction was due to bad advice from groups within his own party. Even more incredible was that neither the President nor any member of the government appeared on national television or radio to exhort people to calm down, or to condemn the violence. Jayawardene himself made his speech five days later with practically no sympathy extended to those who suffered most – the

Tamils of Colombo.[43] Also the speech of other government leaders was designed to placate the Sinhalese community - not a word of compassion for the Tamils. Equally surprising was the fact that neither the President nor any minister of the government made an official visit to a single refugee camp to console the dispossessed. They simply viewed that the racial violence was not a product of urban mobs but as a mass movement of Sinhalese people in general, and hence perhaps, refused to extend compassion to those who actually suffered.

President J.R. Jayawardene in his speech on July 28 promised to introduce legislation to ban separatism or even the talk of it. He said further that because of the violence initiated by Tamil terrorists, the Sinhalese people themselves have reacted. While Premadasa, the then Prime Minister, was even more explicit, 'We have now taken a decision to include in the Constitution that even advocating a division of the country is illegal. No one would be able to even talk about it. Such a campaign will be made illegal. We would not only deprive those advocating any division of the country of their civic rights, we would even bring legislation to confiscate their properties. Those advocating any division of the country will not be able to talk about it even in a foreign land.[44] At the same time it was also true that the greatest destruction of property occurred in the areas represented by the Prime Minister himself (Colombo Central). According to the government scenario, those committing acts of violence were generally of the Sinhalese people. But the same view was not shared by the Tamils who suffered. Many Sinhalese and the foreign press who openly stated that the violence was condoned by the government or that it was the work of factions within the government. As a result of the riots the Tamil moderates have been virtually eliminated in this polarisation of forces, and more people, particularly the youths, who had seen or heard of the macabre nature of the riots were now likely to join the terrorist organisations.

In post 1983 riots phase, militancy became a known fact in Sri Lankan politics and society. President Jayawardene, since the day of his assumption of office, had been, in person, of the view that devolution of power was one of the best solutions the island nation can offer to the Tamils of Sri Lanka. On the other, the Tamils were demanding total independence because they were convinced that no Sinhalese government will grant the Tamils self-rule. For the purpose, they wanted the creation of a single Tamil homeland after merging the Tamil dominated areas of north and east. On the devolution issue, the Sinhalese including SLFP – the main opposition party was critical of Jayawardene's proposal and the former had also withdrawn from the All Party Conference (APC) which was convened to consider the superstructure that was being built to solve the ethnic conflict. Perhaps under pressure from the SLFP and Sinhala extremist groups, Jayawardene had to hastily retreat from the offered devolution package at the APC in 1983. The then government in Colombo had also refused to consider the merger fearing that it would be a stepping stone to secession. These developments made the Tamil militants harden their attitude regarding the separate Tamil Eelam and the TULF's moderate line was no longer acceptable to Tamil hardliners who earlier wanted either Eelam or nothing.[45] Failure of talks on devolution resulted in violence that continued mistrust between the two communities.

The unrest, lawlessness, and violence existed in the then Sri Lanka, compelled the Tamils to take shelter in India and hence the latter had faced a flood of refugees in the succeeding years. It was in the year 1981 that for the first time, the Indian government made representations to the Government of Sri Lanka regarding violence against Tamils during the ethnic riots of that year. The ethnic riots of 1981 in Sri Lanka were a relatively mild affair compared to the serious proportions of the anti-Tamil program of July 1983, which had been sparked off by an act of Tamil terrorist violence directed against the Sri Lankan army in the north. After the failure of devolution talks at Thimpu held in 1985, which was also represented by five extremist groups including the LTTE, several rumours spread regarding Sri Lankan authorities and militant activities. By the end of May 1987 to teach the militants a lesson, the Sri Lankan authorities stopped fuel and other supplies to the Tamil population of the north particularly in retaliation against militant attempts to flout central authority and collect taxes as well as of a military offensive mounted by Sri Lankan security in Jaffna peninsula. Faced with diplomatic as well as internal pressure from the political parties of Tamil Nadu, India decided to send relief supplies to Jaffna by boat but when Sri Lankan navy prevented, India air-dropped dry rations and vegetables. Sri Lanka severally criticised Indian action and even complained to the Secretary-General of the United Nations but, in response, lifted soon the six-month old fuel embargo on Jaffna peninsula. Keeping these developments in active consideration on 19 July 1987, President Jayawardene proposed the creation of an autonomous unit comprising the Northern and Eastern provinces.

The understanding between India and Sri Lanka on ethnic issue ultimately resulted in the signing of an agreement called Indo-Sri Lanka Accord at the end of July 1987. Though the conflict was between the Tamil and the Sinhalese people, India and Sri Lanka signed the peace accord instead of India influencing both parties to sign a peace accord among themselves. The peace accord assigned a certain degree of regional autonomy in the Tamil areas with Eelam People's Revolutionary Liberation Front (EPRLF) controlling the regional council and called for the Tamil militant groups to lay down arms. As a follow up of the accord India sent a peace-keeping force, named the Indian Peace-keeping Force (IPKF) to Sri Lanka to enforce the disarmament and to watch over the regional council. Although the Tamil militant groups did not have a role in the agreement, most Tamil groups accepted it and laid down arms except the Liberation Tigers of Tamil Eelam (LTTE). It subsequently refused to hand over their weapons to the IPKF. Thus the LTTE was found engaged in military conflict with the Indian Army and launched its first attack on an Indian army ration truck on October 8, killing five Indian para-commandos.

In the circumstances, the Government of India and the IPKF in Sri Lanka faced a difficult choice. India can order an all-out assault on the Tigers; or it can concede the validity of LTTE's objections to the present scheme of devolution, and put pressure on President Jayawardene to introduce safeguards. At last Indian government decided that the IPKF should disarm the LTTE by force, and the former had launched a number of assaults on the LTTE including a month-long campaign dubbed *Operation Pawan* to win control of the Jaffna from the LTTE. The ruthlessness of this campaign, and the Indian army's subsequent anti-LTTE operations made it extremely unpopular among many Tamils in Sri Lanka. The then Government of Sri Lanka, having some understanding with the LTTE on devolution of power, demanded that the IPKF be backed and as a result of the consultations with the Government of India the IPKF was withdrawn in March 1990. Withdrawal of the Indian Peace-keeping Forces from Sri Lanka opened a new chapter in the ethnic history of island nation.

References

1. Lucy M. Jacob, 'Regionalism in Sri Lanka' in Ramakant (ed.) *Regionalism in South Asia* (Jaipur : Aalekh Publishers, 1983), p. 175.
2. Vijaya Samaraweera, 'The Evolution of a Plural Society', in K.M. De Silva (ed.), *Sri Lanka : A Survey* (London : 1963), pp. 88-89.

3. Vinod F. Khobragade, 'Re-Thinking Power Devolution in Sri Lanka' *South Asia Politics*, Vol. 6, No. 1 (New Delhi : May 2007) pp. 23-24.
4. A. Jeyaratnam Wilson, *Politics in Sri Lanka 1947-79*, (London : Macmillan Press, 1979), pp. 41-42.
5. Vinod F. Khobragade, 'Ethnic Politics in Sri Lanka – Political Solution to Tamil Cause and Military Solution to LTTE, *South Asia Politics*, Vol. 7, No. 11 (New Delhi : March 2009), pp. 24-25.
6. B. Muralidhar Reddy, "Democracy Deficit and Two Movements", *Frontline*, Vol. 26, No. 12 (Chennai : June 6-19, 2009), pp. 22-23.
7. Ibid.
8. Ibid.
9. *Inter-Racial Equity and Nationality in Sri Lanka* (Colombo : Marga Institute, 1985), p. 13.
10. A. Jeyaratnam Wilson, "Race, Religion, Language and Caste in the Subnatonalism of Sri Lanka", in Michael Roberts (ed.), *Collective Identities, Nationalism and Protest in Modern Sri Lanka* (Colombo : Marga Institute, 1979), pp. 462-73.
11. Jonathan Spencer, "Popular Perceptions of the Violence : A Provincial View", in James Manor (ed.), *Sri Lanka in Change and Crisis* (London : Croom Helm, 1984), p. 192.
12. *The Hindustan Times* (editorial), 5 September 1998.
13. For the Vaddukoddai Resolution, see *Race Relations in Sri Lanka* (Colombo : Centre for Society and Religion, 1978), pp. 79-83.
14. Malini Parthasarathy, "The Mirage of Eelam", *The Hindu*, 24 April 2009.
15. Tom Farrell, "For him no Sacrifice was too Great for the Objective of Eelam", Ibid., 20 May 2009.
16. V. Suryanarayan, 'Explaining Prabhakaran's Persistence Defiance', Ibid., 21 December 2007.
17. Ibid.
18. *The Hindustan Times*, 20 February 1998.
19. R. Hariharan, "Militancy and Small Arms Proliferation", *The Hindu*, 20 April 2007.
20. Ibid., 10 March 2002.
21. Jorge Heine, "Misapplying Responsibility to Protect in Sri Lanka", Ibid., 27 June 2009.
22. Gananath Obeyesekere, "The Origins and Institutionalisation of Political Violence", in James Manor (ed.), pp. 163-66.
23. Malini Parthasarathy, "The Mirage of Eelam", *The Hindu*, 24 April 2009.
24. R.L. Stirrat, "The Riots and the Roman Catholic Church in Historical perspective", James Manor (ed.), p. 210.

25. R. Hariharan, 'Sri Lanka : Need to Restore Trust', *The Hindu*, 18 May 2010.
26. Eric Meyer, "Seeking the Roots of the Tragedy", in James Manor (ed.), pp. 145-48.
27. As quoted in *The Hindu*, 20 May 2009.
28. R. Hariharan, "The Discarded Accord and the Unwanted War", Ibid., 7 August 2007.
29. *The Hindustan Times*, 2 November 1997.
30. Vinod F. Khobragade, "Ethnic Politics in Sri Lanka – Political Solution to Tamil Cause and Military Solution to LTTE", p. 26.
31. Shelton U. Kodikara, "The Indo-Sri Lanka Agreement of July 1987 : Retrospect", in *South Asian Strategic Issues – Sri Lankan Perspectives* (New Delhi : Sage Publications, 1990), pp. 168-70.
32. Shelton U. Kodikara, "Internal Politics and Foreign Policy : Prospects for Indo – Lanka Relations in the Nineties", in *External Compulsions of South Asian Politics* (New Delhi : Sage Publications, 1993), p. 233.
33. Rajkumar Singh, *Relations of NDA and UPA with Neighbours* (New Delhi : Gyan Publishing House, 2010), pp. 320-21.
34. *The Hindustan Times*, 26 March 1990.
35. Shaukat Hassan, "Problems of Internal Stability in South Asia", in Shelton U. Kodikara (ed.), *External Compulsions of South Asian Politics,* pp. 270-71.
36. *The Times of India* (editorial), 2 June 2009.
37. *The Hindu* (editorial), 28 January 2008.
38. *Asian Recorder*, 1-7 October 1978 (New Delhi : 1978), pp. 14533-34.
39. Bruce Matthews, "The Situation in Jaffna", *The Round Table*, No. 290, April 1984, pp. 34-37.
40. Bertram E.S.J. Bastiampillai, "Ethnic Conflicts in South Asia and Inter-state Relations Especially in Relation to Sri Lanka", in Shelton U. Kodikara (ed.), *South Asian Strategic Issues : Sri Lankan Perspectives* (New Delhi : Sage Publications, 1990), pp. 89-90.
41. R. Hariharan, "The Moment of Truth for the LTTE," *The Hindu*, 5 February 2009.
42. Shaukat Hassan, "Problems of Internal Stability in South Asia", pp. 270-71.
43. Gananath Obeyesekere, "The Origins and Institutionalisation of Political Violence", pp. 167-69.
44. Ibid.
45. Bertram E.S.J. Bastiampillai, "Ethnic Conflicts in South Asia and Inter-state Relations Especially in Relation to Sri Lanka, p. 92.

[illegible] [illegible]
28. [illegible] ... Times, [illegible]
[illegible]
29. *The Hindustan Times*, 2 November [illegible]
30. [illegible], Political Solution to [illegible] Military Solution [illegible]
31. [illegible] 11 July 1987 [illegible]
32. [illegible]
33. [illegible]
[illegible]
[illegible]
38. [illegible]
39. [illegible]
40. [illegible] Publications, 1990, pp. [illegible]
41. [illegible]
42. [illegible] "Problems of Internal Stability [illegible]", pp. 280-[illegible]
43. [illegible] "The Origins and Internationalisation of [illegible]"
44. Ibid.
45. [illegible]

3

LTTE'S EELAM STRUGGLE AND POWER SHARING

Post – IPKF Violence and Politics of North-East Merger

In 1987, the Indian Peace-keeping Force was sent to Sri Lanka on the specific request of President Jayawardene, as peace-keepers of a tenuous agreement for a cessation of hostilities. Some arms were turned in, but trust was never high on either side and fighting between the IPKF and the LTTE cadres continued unabated for over two years – both sides experiencing heavy losses. The last member of the IPKF, which was estimated to have had a strength of well over 50,000 at its peak, left the country in March 1990 after a due consultations between the two governments. However, as time went on, the Indian forces began to meet with stiff opposition from all sides. First the Indian intervention itself was unpopular among the Sinhalese majority for giving India a major influence and it became a source of nationalist anger and resentment as the IPKF was drawn fully into the conflict. The IPKF experience had many political consequences for Sri Lanka. One of these was the conviction in the decision-making circles in the government and in the minds of most Sri Lankans, that questions concerning the Tamils of Sri Lanka – whether these relate to their security or to devolution of power must be sorted out by Sri Lankans themselves. Ultimately, the Sri Lankan government, fearing a large scale rebellion began to grow, at the presence of IPKF, allegedly entered into a secret deal with the LTTE, which culminated in a ceasefire. According to some reports, the government even armed the rebels with a view to such back the Indian force. Thus a shaky peace initially held between the government and the LTTE, and peace talks progressed towards providing devolution for Tamils in the north and east of the country.

After consultations with the Sri Lankan leaders and on their request, India withdrew IPKF in March 1990 as latter's policy on Sri Lanka rested on three pillars – commitment to the unity and territorial integrity of Sri

Lanka, an equal commitment to the rights and the well-being of Tamil community as ethnic harmony in this country depends on this factor and lastly the progress and stability of Sri Lanka with all its people. 'It is in our interest to see Sri Lanka as a strong and stable society .... since the lack of stability has a tendency to spill over and affect us and involve us in a way would rather not be involved.'[1] Ranasinghe Premadasa, the President of Sri Lanka also thanked the Indian Prime Minister for withdrawing its troops from the country without attaching any condition and expressed gratitude to the government and people of India for respecting Sri Lanka's sovereignty.[2] Initially the IPKF was deployed to tame the LTTE and its forced departure in the aftermath of a pact between the Sri Lankan Government, LTTE and the JVP proved an eyewash for all concerned. Even today, it is not an easy task to deal with terrorism as a political force, and the failure of Sri Lankan governments to evolve a coherent policy in this regard is not a matter for surprise. All democratic governments have had great difficulty in evolving such a policy even when, as in Italy in the 1960s, and 1970s, and to a much greater extent in Sri Lanka in the period 1987-89, terrorist groups held the country to ransom, and reduced political life and public activity to a pitiful parady of its once vibrant past.[3] To be successful in counter insurgency, a political strategy with a matching military strategy would have to go hand in hand. This requires strong leadership commitment to a vision. These were missing in Sri Lanka and political success became the major consideration. President Premadasa used the ploy of sending back Indian troops to win the Presidential poll. In India, the political opposition played the same game.[4] The change of leadership midstream in both countries made it difficult for the IPKF to meaningfully operate in the absence of a clear political agenda.

But in the entire game plan the Liberation Tigers of Tamil Eelam was clearly a gainer who took full advantage of President Premadasa's antipathy to the Indian dispensation that made supply of arms to the LTTE even as it was fighting the war. With the departure of the Indian army having lost 1255 soldiers Velupillai Prabakaran, the leader of LTTE unleashed his vengeance against all perceived enemies, internal and external. Earlier a number of small arms proliferated to the civilian population as a result of the deployment of IPKF in 1987. A large number of army deserters with small arms have also been a source of criminal acts in the island following the withdrawal of Indian forces. Even on withdrawal, most experts agreed that it was ill-timed exit. It happened before the administration could consolidate itself in the northeast, whereby it ensured the resurgence of the LTTE. Very soon in June 1990 a tricky situation arose with the resumption of violence in the Tamil dominated regions of Sri Lanka and Ceylon sought moral support from India.[5] On the sudden and complete pull out of the IPKF from Sri Lanka, one analyst rightly predicted that things might take an ugly turn and suggested, 'Premadasa should guard himself against excessive euphoria on having succeeded in sending off the IPKF. For him the troubles are just starting. Particularly, since the LTTE has given away nothing, not even the arms it has collected. It has filled the military vacuum that the IPKF has left and will soon fill the political vacuum left by the collapse of the EPRLF government and the demoralised Tamil groups. It is possible that it will abide by this time for the Eelam and in the meantime accept the limited political autonomy that has been granted to it 'Tamil Province'.[6]

Exactly as anticipated, the LTTE gaining complete control of the north and east, continued to systematically eliminate opposing Tamil groups. Varatharaja Perumal, the former chief minister of the North-East Provincial Council, who received the support of IPKF during his brief tenure in office, was compelled to take refuge abroad on the departure of the IPKF, and those of his party cadres of the Eelam People's Revolutionary Liberation Front (EPRLF) who remained in the island became the subject of attack by the rival LTTE. The Council has been in abeyance since Varatharaja Perumal and his colleagues unilaterally declared the independence of Eelam on the eve of the departure of the IPKF, making themselves *persona non grata* to the government of Sri Lanka, and forcing themselves into exile.[7] Thereafter, Tamil politics in the northeast of Sri Lanka took a new turn, with other Tamil militant groups engaging themselves in a struggle for political power. Although for the time being, the LTTE's dominance in military spheres was tacitly accepted by the government and the latter had been engaged for the last one year with the LTTE leadership to bring it into the mainstream of democratic politics in the island, yet the LTTE had refused to give up arms even after the IPKF departure and feared that a premature surrender of their arms might have exposed them to the wrath and revenge of rival militant groups. LTTE's position with arms and military might have made them the most powerful of the Tamil militant groups and consequently provide an edge in the politics of northeast region.

But very soon the goodwill that the Sri Lankan government and the LTTE had earned evaporated and a new phase of violence emerged which ultimately led to the resumption of fighting between them in the first week of June 1990. The Sri Lankan security forces became alert in early June when the LTTE cadres started constructing bunkers and fortifying sentry points in the north and east and began a form of tax-gathering and resorted to hijacking vehicles and storing foodstuffs. On 7 June 1990, one soldier of the Sri Lanka Gajaba Regiment died and nine were injured following an attack by the LTTE in Thandikulam, near Vavuniya in the northern province.[8] Again on 11 June, 300 heavy armed Tigers walked into the Batticaloa police station, seized the weapons and asked 280 policemen to clear out. Soon they surrounded nearly all police stations in the Tamil and Muslim areas of Batticaloa and Amparai districts and forced the police to surrender. The Tigers took about 600 policemen as captives and 200 of them were reported killed. In another incident the Tigers killed 11 soldiers who were returning to their camp after buying provisions. They also began to attack army camps in the Batticaloa district.[9] All these events virtually ended the dialogue which had gone on between the government and the LTTE. The then government of the island nation was of the view that the present time was a transitional phase in the politics and would end soon with the creation of the provincial police force and the installation of a new provincial government in the Tamil-speaking areas.

The LTTE and the Sri Lankan government despite the eruption of violence continued their talks on political issues. The substance of the talks between them was not made public, but it was easy to surmise that the continuance of the existing merger of the Northern and Eastern Provinces would have been a high priority as Dr. Anton Balasingham, spokesman of the party observed, 'Once the provincial council elections are held and once we have proved to the world that we are the authentic representatives of our people, we will open up negotiations with Sri Lanka with regard to an appropriate political model.[10] The LTTE had also made it known to the Sri Lankan authorities that the dissolution of the North East Provincial Council, the holding of fresh elections to this council, and the repeal of the Sixth Amendment to the Sri Lanka constitution, were the essential preconditions for it to enter the political mainstream and work towards the solution of the ethnic question in the island. The Sixth Amendment of the constitution declared the advocacy of separatism at reasonable offence, and which required all members of parliament, provincial council, Supreme Court and High Court judges, and high officials to take an allegiance to the constitution. This amendment was justified on the ground that there should not be any constitutional constraints to our liberty to articulate our practical views and that it would help to build confidence and trust among the Tamil people and contribute towards ethnic reconciliation and communal harmony. All the Tamil groups including the EPRLF, EROS, and the TULF had supported the repeal of the sixth constitutional amendment.

The Government of Sri Lanka responded favourably to the political demands of LTTE and early in July 1990, it amended the Provincial Council Act to permit the dissolution of the North East Provincial Council, and to provide for fresh elections to take place in the region. The repeal of the Sixth Amendment, too, took on a new perspective and government seemed to consider the repeal, but it was constrained by virtue of the fact that it did not command the required two-thirds majority in Parliament. However, once again, the good look environment was vitiated by the LTTE attacks on government security forces in the middle of the talks. In the meantime the Sri Lankan authorities also expressed the view that in the present situation the repeal of Sixth Amendment would be interpreted as a tacit endorsement of the separate state by the government, and that oath of allegiance to the constitution are common features of democratic politics the world over.[11] In Sri Lanka's case the oath of allegiance is to the unity of the state, and that it cannot now be retracted without serious injury to the government's public image.

At thc juncture it was not clear whether the LTTE wanted war with Sri Lankan security forces or a share in the political power. LTTE's decisions and behaviours had surprised many who commended the role of the Government of Premadasa. *The London Times* wrote that most diplomats in Colombo felt that the present government of Sri Lanka was making generous concessions to try and reach a peaceful solution and to end Sri Lanka's seven-year civil war.[12] The paper also quoted a western diplomat as having said that the tigers could have got everything they wanted at the negotiating table. On the other hand, was the view of Dr. Anton Balasingham, head of the political wing of the LTTE, who justified the change of front by the organisation and alleged that President Premadasa was trying to catch them in a peace-trap and weaken them, in consequence of which our moral as a guerilla organisation will be seriously affected. He also charged for the unprovoked gunfire by the Sri Lankan police on the Tiger members. The clashes escalated into a full-fledged war when the Sri Lankan army confined in the barracks came out and engaged in armed confrontation with the Tigers.

In this unstable situation, Philip Comtesse, head of the International Committee of the Red Cross in Sri Lanka, as a gesture of goodwill, declared the unilateral ceasefire by the LTTE on 31 December 1990. It was done to promote peace and harmony and create conditions of normalcy in the North and East and also intended to be a prelude to peace talks as the Sri Lankan government responded positively and reciprocated the ceasefire.[13] It, however, was followed by a statement of Krishna Kumar (Kittu), an LTTE spokesman in London, who laid down three conditions for the successful fruition of such talks : namely, recognition of a Tamil homeland in the North and East, self-determination for Tamils in this region, and recognition of a Tamil National Army, either as a separate unit or as part of the Island's security forces. The London statement with new conditions had raised doubts in Sri Lankan government circles as to whether the LTTE had really given up its separatist goals. Doubts were also raised regarding laying down of arms by the LTTE—a condition considered to be an essential prerequisite for such talks not only by Sri Lankan government but also by most of the Tamil militant groups and political parties. Ultimately the LTTE's stand on the matter, that 'laying down of arms is not in our history' is but an end to any hopes that the ceasefire would lead to any political negotiations at all. Despite this the Sri Lankan government responded to the LTTE call by giving a seven-day trial period effective from 3 January 1991. In the period of ceasefire, claims and counterclaims were made regarding its violation by both the parties. After the expiry of seven-day trial period, the government called off its ceasefire and resumed hostilities against the LTTE.[14] It was reported that behind the unilateral declaration of LTTE's ceasefire was its declining position in the Indian state of Tamil Nadu, from where it always gained moral and material support and the change of guard which took place in India in December 1989.

Although violence and talks for provincial autonomy between the LTTE and the Sri Lankan security forces continued simultaneously, with the rise in terrorist violence and insecurity, the government resorted to some drastic measures. It implemented some draconian laws which compromised the principle of justice and democratic rights. Presidential powers were increased in an effort to restore stability. But the LTTE, on its part, continued the fighting and was marked by two key assassinations carried out by the organisation. First, in May 1991 the former Prime Minister Rajiv Gandhi and 16 others were killed by a female suicide bomber at an Indian election rally. Further the situation in Sri Lanka had gone beyond control when President Ranasinghe Premadasa was assassinated on 1 May 1993 by a LTTE cadre. After the withdrawal of IPKF, the LTTE took significant parts of the north and established many government-like functions in the areas under its control. Between 1990 and 1995 the Tigers ran the northern Jaffna peninsula as a mini state with Prabakaran as its absolute ruler. The fighting briefly halted in 1994 following the election of Chandrika Kumaratunga as President of Sri Lanka and the onset of peace talks, but fighting resumed after LTTE sunk two Sri Lankan Navy boats in April 1995.

Even in this adverse situation, the Government of Sri Lanka earlier in August 1991 set up a Parliamentary Select Committee (PSC) to recommend ways and means of achieving peace and political stability in the country. Headed by a SLFP MP Mangala Moonesinghe, the PSC called for written representations. From the beginning, the PSC got bogged down with one single issue whether or not to agree with one merged North-Eastern province. While the Tamil parties including the Ceylon Workers Congress went on repeating their demand for the merger of the north and east, the Sinhala parties including the SLFP and UNP members within the PSC kept opposing it. In the circumstances the purpose of PSC's formation was bound to fail because neither the Sinhalese nor the Tamils were willing to budge from their uncompromising positions about the North-East merger and all hopes were rested on the Chandrika Plan, put forward by Chandrika Kumaratunga who won presidential election held in 1994. She came out with a detailed devolution package within the framework of a proposed new federal constitution. Soon after assuming office, the President announced a package aimed at assuaging minority Tamil sentiments and giving a degree of self rule to Tamils who have long demanded a separate home-land.

The proposed scheme of federal constitution was to give the federating units much more power than any time in the past. It also talked about the permanent merger of the Northern and Eastern provinces in which the Tamils would have their say. But on the issue the People's Alliance (PA) government was under pressure from the UNP in particular and the Sinhala-Buddhist forces in general. Although Lakshman Kadirgamar, the Foreign Minister of Sri Lanka had said that, we have reached agreements on a large number of issues but a handful eludes us. He went on to spell out the problem areas as the nature of the Sri Lankan state, the merger of north and east, police power in new provinces and control of land in the provinces.[15] These are the core issues basic to the solution of the ethnic problem and hence, clearly under pressure, the People's Alliance government retracted from its original stand on federalism and went in favour of more safeguards for the central authority. It was seen that the power of the centre was not diminished and the integrity and security of the nation was not compromised. In fact, any attempt by the Tamil minority in Sri Lanka to seek its legitimate rights encounters stiff opposition from the majority Sinhala community. It is also generally realised that the concept of 'federalism', indeed the very word itself, which comes somewhat naturally in India, excites tremendous passions in Sri Lanka. To a small country it conjures visions of secession. Therefore, the lofty notion or concept of unity in diversity which, again one tends to take for granted in India, has fewer takers among the majority Sinhala community. This obduracy has resulted in an approach which has been highly counterproductive for Sri Lanka and the Sinhalese, in particular.[16] The proposal of federalism was vehemently opposed by the UNP and it even warned that any change in the constitution will be dangerous.

However, despite the continued stalemate with regard to Kumaratunga's devolution proposals, the Tamil minority in Sri Lanka remained hopeful for peace, security and honourable settlement of its problems because the President herself was genuinely committed to devolution and the Tamils put the blame on the UNP and Sinhala chauvinists both within and outside the ruling party. 'She is the first Chief Executive of Sri Lanka to have said openly that injustice has been done to the Tamils in the past 50 years, and that devolution is the only answer to the problem.[17] Indeed, the President had made this devolution package in 1995 after talks with the LTTE over the last two and half years of deliberations. Although the Tamils were particularly unhappy with the current proposal to hold referenda in the East on the question of the merger of the North and East to form a single Tamil province, yet the Tamil community of the country is in no doubt that the package is by far the best on offer from the majority Sinhala polity in the island's turbulent history since independence in 1948.[18] Unfortunately, Kumaratunga's efforts at negotiating with the Liberation Tigers of Tamil Eelam broke down in April 1995, when the latter had dramatically ended the ceasefire by sinking two naval gunboats anchored in the Trincomalee naval base. Since then the government had followed a two-track diplomacy : containing the LTTE militarily and finding a political solution to the ethnic problem.

Devastating Attacks and Talks Side by Side

The Sri Lankan government of Chandrika Kumaratunga was genuinely interested in resolving the ethnic issue through devolution of power and merger of North-Eastern regions of the country with a referendum to be conducted in eastern part on the matter. Barring some reservations of the UNP, the main opposition party, there was a general consensus in the country that devolution of power to the provinces was a must for a solution of the long-pending ethnic issue.[19] The offered devolution framework of Kumaratunga's administration was a step forward the 13th Amendment resulting from the Indo-Sri Lanka Accord (1987). The new proposal enshrined the concept of a 'union of regions' that had strong federal connotations. But even this, failed in satisfying all the groups of the Tamil community in Sri Lanka. The Indian origin Tamils in the country feel that they are being sidelined and ignored by the People's Alliance (PA) Government whose devolution proposals have no meaning for the community. S. Thondaman, Chief of the Ceylon Workers Congress (CWC), in a letter to the secretary of the ruling Peoples Alliance had bitterly complained that neither the Government nor the devolution proposal have addressed the basic and pressing problems of the community.[20] He also charged the government in his letter dated 25 July that particularly in Colombo they are harassed by the police for being Tamils.

However, the devolution package was a no way forward for the emotive issue of a separate homeland for Sri Lankan Tamils for which the Liberation Tigers of Tamil Eëlam have waged a bloody armed insurrection for the last 14 years. Despite the fact that all the Tamil militant groups have now laid down arms and joined the democratic mainstream, the LTTE is still fighting. After failed peace talks with the new government in 1994, the Sri Lankan authorities pursued a 'War for Peace' line. In a series of military operations that followed, the Sri Lankan Army re-captured the Jaffna peninsula, the heart land of Tamil in the country. In the situation, the LTTE signalled its rejection of these promising circumstances by abruptly terminating a ceasefire offered by the Kumaratunga government as a prelude to peace negotiations. With this the island was plunged into fresh war with the Tigers following a declaration by Kumaratunga's administration that peace would have to be achieved 'through war'. Further offensives followed by both sides over the next three years. In late 1995, Sri Lankan forces launched a massive campaign to retake the rebel-held north. The LTTE were expelled from Jaffna but 60,000 government troops found themselves hemmed in over the next few years as the Tigers captured large areas of the Vanni and the eastern province. The south was also hit by a spate of savage Black Tigers strikes.

The ongoing fighting between the LTTE and the Sri Lankan security forces was intensified in the first week of October 1997 in which more than 150 LTTE fighters were killed and over 200 injured in a major confrontation with advancing Sri Lankan troops on the Mankulam-Mullaitivu road in the north-east region of Puliankulam. In the war 34 soldiers of Sri Lankan forces were also killed and 60 injured in the fierce battle. The rebels used mortars and heavy arms and attacked Army defences around Kanagarayankulam and also slightly damaged an MI-24 helicopter gunship of the Sri Lankan forces. In reply as reported by a top Sri Lankan Army general in-charge of the operations against LTTE in the north, the LTTE suffered heavy casualties and the latest Army offensive had blunted the LTTE's military capability to a great extent. "We are destroying the LTTE's military machine. We have dealt a severe blow to the LTTE. Now is the hour for the whole country to join us and help annihilate the LTTE. That will bring a political solution, closer to fruition."[21] Both the Army and the LTTE were locked in Sri Lanka's worst ever battle to regain control of the 65 - kilometres highway, which is the main supply route connecting northern Vavuniya with Jaffna peninsula. The Government had so far secured about 20 kilometres of the road in the five month long offensive. The heavy resistance put up by the LTTE had slowed down the advance of the troops. Over 700 troops had been killed and 4000 injured so far.[22] In addition to these heavy fightings, there were also other minor confrontations which took place in Madam in Jaffna district in which one soldier was killed. In another incident the LTTE attacked the Arantalawa police station in the southern district of Amparai, killing six and injuring 15 policemen. The police station was completely damaged and weapons were taken away by the rebels. According to Army sources, 10 rebels were believed to have been killed in the attack.

By the time the LTTE had also moved to damage the country's economy. Earlier in January 1996, the organisation had carried out a blast which destroyed the Central Bank building. Another successful attack was made in October 1997 which was meticulously planned and executed. This explosion wrecked the prestigious World Trade Centre along with two luxury hotel buildings in Colombo's commercial hub. As a result, at least 26 people were reported killed, while over a hundred others sustained injuries. The Tamil Tiger guerillas virtually rammed with an explosive-laden truck into the hostel parking.[23] In general, it was felt that irrespective of the breakthroughs it had been claiming in its military operations against the LTTE, the Sri Lankan Government would need to tone up its security apparatus. The blast probably was also intended to send a massage to the Sri Lankan Government that despite the setbacks it had suffered in the north and the loss of international support, the LTTE still retained its capability to strike at will.[24] Therefore, a negotiated settlement of the ethnic question remains the only way to end the ongoing civil strife.

Sri Lanka's continuing ethnic war had also affected country's economy in other ways and its engagement in countering terrorism led to the expenditure in relation to national security, increasing from about 1.5 percent of Gross Domestic Product (GDP) in the early 1980s to nearly 6 percent in the late 1990s. Studies conducted by the Central Bank of Sri Lanka and the Institute of Policy Studies have estimated the cost of terrorism to be around 1 to 1.5 per cent denial of economic growth each year.[25] Although the deficit declined from around 20 per cent in the mid-1980s to less than 10 per cent in the 1990s and to around 7 per cent in recent times. It remains high in terms of fundamental macroeconomic norms. Moreover, overall national savings showed a modest growth from 12 per cent of GDP in 1980 to 16 per cent in 2004.

At the height of ethnic strife and economic decline, several contextual studies were made including one at New Delhi. Top Indian experts felt that there was no possibility for peace in Sri Lanka without bringing the LTTE to the negotiating table. Defence analyst Major General Ashok K. Mehta, who was general officer in command (GOC) South and commanded the Indian peace-keeping operation in Sri Lanka and former Foreign Secretary J.N. Dixit felt that the ground situation in the island nation was no different from what it had been when the IPKF left Sri Lanka after a two and-a-half year attempt to eliminate the LTTE. General Mehta, participating in a panel discussion on the current situation and Sri Lanka's emerging international equation at the India International Centre (IIC), at New Delhi, in November 1997, said 'there was some sort of illusion in the minds of the Sinhalese people and the clergy about a military victory over the LTTE. At best, the LTTE can be marginalised but can not be eliminated. While there was a lack of a national consensus on the part of the Sinhalese, the LTTE was a highly motivated force numbering about 15000.[26] He also added that though the Sri Lankan Army had physical control of Jaffna town in the north-eastern parts of the island, they had cleared only about 25 kilometres of the 75 kilometres main supply land route. Holding on to Jaffna town using the air corridor would be an expensive proposition. Even if the land route was cleared, the manning of the 75 kilometre long route would be a difficult task and the Army would be a target for LTTE attacks.

J.N. Dixit, former Foreign Secretary and Indian High Commissioner during the IPKF operation in Sri Lanka, in his presidential remarks said that the situation was not the same today. During the IPKF days the LTTE had been confined to small bushes but were now confined to large forests. The panel discussion was also participated by C.R. Jayasinghe, Sri Lankan deputy High Commissioner, who said that his government had the backing of the people for the devolution of power.[27] He also maintained that the Sri Lankan government had promised to resolve the genuine grievances of the Tamils. The military option had been resorted by his government only after exhausting all other efforts. But Dr. V. Suryanarayan, another participant, who was visiting Professor for Diplomacy, School of International Studies at Jawaharlal Nehru University, New Delhi, narrated the facts of this militant organisation and said that the LTTE, with its cult of martyrdom and cyanide culture had annihilated its dissenters or, whoever obeyed the New Delhi - Colombo dictates. It was a Pol Potist organisation never tolerating dissent and had drawn support from various parts of the globe. They wanted to be recognised as a nationality and be the sole representative of the Tamil. They wanted devolution of power only for the north-east region and not for the entire country. They wanted two Parliaments, two Prime Ministers and were not willing to consider any federal set-up.[27]

Meanwhile, at the end of October 1997 General Anuruddha Ratwatte, Sri Lanka's Acting Defence Minister had claimed that 90 per cent of the battle to marginalise the LTTE had been won.[28] He maintained while addressing the Foreign Corresponds Association at Colombo that the Sri Lankan armed forces were poised to launch a final assault to successfully conclude Operation Jayasikurui whose aim was to capture the Vavuniya Kilinochchi Main Supply Route (MSR) and bottle up the LTTE in the Wanni, reducing them to a jungle guerilla outfit incapable of disrupting normal life in the populated areas of the Tamil north and east.

The partial success of Sri Lankan security forces encouraged the Government of Sri Lanka to move in the direction of peace efforts with new energy. It took an important step towards healing old ethnic wounds by reopening an important library in northern Jaffna. Mangala Samaraweera, the Media Minister of Sri Lanka, inaugurated the library in January 1998 and said on the occasion that it was a significant step in correcting the historic injustices committed against Tamils and would re-establish harmony between the majority Sinhalese and the minority Tamil Communities. This library will become, I hope, a bridge between the people of the north and the people of the south in our island home. The books in this library will become, I hope, the building blocks of peace.[29] The library, considered a rare storehouse of Tamil literature and old manuscripts, was allegedly set ablaze by police in June 1981 and became a rallying point for Tamil youths to join rebels fighting for a separate homeland in Sri Lanka's north and east. Side by side, a significant peace movement also developed in the 1990s, with peace camps, conferences and meditations, and many kinds of training, research, and outreach to bridge the two sides at all levels. In later years, born out of a need to institutionalise the peace process, the Secretariat for Coordinating the Peace Process (SCOPP) was established on 6 February 2002 with the approval of the Cabinet of Ministers. The Secretariat was headed by Bernard Goonetilleke (2002-2004), Jayantha Dhanapala (2004-2005) and Dr. Palitha Kohona (2006-2007). The Sri Lankan government, with some success, pressed other governments around the world to outlaw the LTTE, interfering with fund-raising activities.

Violent activities and opposition to Sri Lankan peace proposal continued by the LTTE and on 25 January 1998 the organisation targeted Buddhist sites, most notably the historic Dalada Maligawa or 'Temple of the Tooth', the holiest Buddhist shrine in the country located in the town of Kandy. Thirteen worshipers, including several children were killed by the bombing. As a result, the government had augmented security at a number of religious sites island-wide including the most revered Temple of Tooth. The year 1998 also witnessed a cheerless golden jubilee of Sri Lanka's independence as its celebrations were boycotted not only by the LTTE but by all Tamil parties including the TULF and they had a point. They argued that the Tamils have lost grievously since Independence when the country was declared a Sinhala-Buddhist one. Their peaceful struggles for equality were met by batons and bullets and when they took to armed struggle, bombs and shells began to rain on them. Political packages never got off the ground.[30] They also criticised the present devolution package put forward by the Chandrika Government which was caught in uncertainties, with the opposition UNP rejecting it outright.

Once again, the Sri Lankan security forces and the LTTE were poised for a major battle in Mankulam, the cost of which was going to be high in terms of human lives. On the side of Sri Lankan forces, the morale was palpably high as the Major General Srilal Weerasuriya had said, "The LTTE was not as fighting fit as before. They are facing a recruitment problem and commitment is not as high as before. More and more are surrendering now."[31] With a view to open a land route to northern Jaffna peninsula from the southern region and after losing two naval ships, the Sri Lankan forces had launched on 24 February 1998 the final thrust of Operation Jayasikurui (Victory Assured) against Tamil rebels. Earlier in the successful attack of LTTE's Sea Tigers, some 50 soldiers and sailors were killed. In the operation Sri Lanka deployed some 30,000 soldiers and they were supported by the air force and navy. As per plan, the troops broke out of the forward defence line at the northern town of Mankulam, part of which was wrested from the LTTE and began advancing under artillery and air cover towards the town centre which was under rebel control. Troops had in the last ten-month operation captured about 50 kilometres of the Vavuniya-Kilinochchi road and have to cover about 24 kilometres to link up with the troops at the northern peninsula. The battle for the strategic highway, which would give the military access by road to the north, had till February 1998 claimed over 1,000 soldiers' lives and left at least 2,000 rebels dead.[32] In course of the operation, the government forces received a major setback in September 1998 when the LTTE guerillas attacked the Sri Lankan army camps at Kilinochchi and killed at least 600 troops. The Tamil Tigers appeared to have regained control of Kilinochchi to the extent of putting paid to the Sri Lankan government's hopes of securing the land route to Jaffna in the foreseeable future.[33] On the other hand, all this exposed the tenuous nature of the Sri Lankan government's capacity to control the north. In the process, the Tigers had demonstrated their ability to spring back into action with great ferocity even at a time when their morale and prowess was suspected to have been considerably diminished through two years of fighting.

Unfortunately, still there were several roadblocks to evolving a national consensus on finding a solution to the ethnic issue. The two main political formations in the country were unable to see eye to eye with each other. The habit of Sinhala chauvinists to raise war-cries every time, the question of conceding to some of the demands of the minority Tamils was raised, had further worsened the chances of a peaceful solution.[34] It was the position when a survey conducted by Colombo University had found that most Sri Lankans think that war alone will not solve the ethnic problem and that there is no guarantee that once the LTTE is defeated, there will be peace. The survey conducted by Professor S.T. Hettige, Head of the Department of Sociology of the Colombo University revealed that 77.4 per cent of the respondents said "no" when asked if military action alone would solve the ethnic problem, just 20.7 per cent said that war was the only way. To the question on how to solve the problem only 9.3 per cent said "by defeating the LTTE". Only 6.9 per cent said that peace would be ensured by defeating the LTTE, 77.8 per cent favoured a non-military way of bringing lasting peace. Most wanted some kind of a political solution by accommodation. When asked to specify what they wanted done in this respect, 22.2 per cent said the minority Tamils should be given equality with the majority, another 18.6 per cent suggested communal amity as a must for a lasting solution.[35] Thus the study clearly indicated that the bulk of the Sinhalese at the grassroot level did not believe in a purely military solution and it gave a lie to the theory touted by a section of media that the Sinhalese favoured war.

Gradually, although for the time being, an environment of talks and peace appeared possible. In his Heroes' Day speech on 27 November 1998, LTTE supremo Velupillai Prabakaran had offered to talk with third party mediation if the Government met two conditions. First, the armed forces must vacate aggression which meant that it must go back to the pre-1995 position when the LTTE controlled Jaffna and the Wanni and, second, normalcy should be restored in the war zone. But the Government rejected the conditions saying that the LTTE must talk about a political solution eschewing the demand for Eelam, and that too within a pre-determined time frame. Further details were declared by Srilal Weerasooriya, the Army Commander Lieutenant General of Sri Lanka, who said that talks or no talks, the Army will not withdraw from the area which it has liberated from the LTTE. In an exclusive interview to the state-owned paper *Daily News*, Weerasooriya stressed that we are against withdrawing because past experience has shown the LTTE renegading. In the past on three or four occasions this has resulted in several deaths. "Let us talk from where we are."[36] He also made it clear that he was not a warmonger. As a soldier, I am 100 per cent for peace. If there is a definite chance for peace, we are all for it. But it has to be peace with meaning. I think there needs to be a political solution. Earlier, the Premadasa and Chandrika Governments had agreed to a ceasefire prior to talks and each time, the LTTE had used the ceasefire and the meandering talks to build itself up and move into new areas stealthily. Also, every time it had broken the true unilaterally catching the armed forces completely off guard, the General added.[37] Earlier in August 1998 Sri Lankan President Chandrika Kumaratunga ruled out a ceasefire during any talks with the LTTE. She said that her government was ready for talks, but only under certain conditions. One of them was that there would be no suspension of the military operations against the LTTE during the talks, till such time it became clear that the talks were definitely leading to a solution.

The offensive attacks of Sri Lankan security forces against the LTTE continued unabated and at the beginning of the year 1999 in February according to the Defence Ministry 15 LTTE rebels were killed and six others injured in two different clashes between Sri Lankan troops and the guerillas in the northern Wanni region near Vannivilankulam and troops also recovered a number of arms from.[38] In the next month in the ongoing battle 33 Sri Lankan troops including an officer were also killed and 158 wounded in the north of Elephant Pass as per a government communiqué. The Ministry of Defence (MoD) release said that the LTTE had infiltrated Vathirayan under mortar fire cover, and that troops were engaged in clearing the affected areas. A tank used by the LTTE was destroyed and a large number of LTTE cadres were dead in the battles.[39] But the Tamil sources claimed that the LTTE was jockeying for a better military position before sitting down for any talks with Sri Lankan government with Norwegian facilitation.

Before the talks with Norwegian facilitation, a major attack was undertaken by the LTTE Sea Tiger squads in April 2000 who landed in Nagarkovil in north Vadamarachi and were moving south to link up with a group that had established a beachhead east of Elephant Pass. Simultaneously, the LTTE had shelled Palai and Yakkachi in Thenmarachi, north of Elephant Pass, from Pooneryn, across the Jaffna lagoon. Its amphibian cadres had breached sections of the A-9 highway there. In addition, a 1000 strong special Tiger unit under Karuna was awaiting deployment. The fighting had already taken the lives of seven Sri Lankan officers and 114 other ranks, besides 60 LTTE fighters. According to analyst Dayan Jayatilleka, 'it is wrong to work on the premise that Prabakaran is after Jaffna or that he is jockeying for an advantageous position to be better able to bargain in the forthcoming talks. Jaffna has never been crucial to him having vacated it twice before. Nor have talks been important for him, as he has quit them many times before. His aim now is to break the backbone of, or even decapitate the Sri Lankan army by destroying a base like Elephant Pass with 17,000 men in it. He is trying to do a 'Dien Bien Phu.'[40] In response to the erupted heavy fighting, President Kumaratunga held a crisis meeting with the top brass because the LTTE had taken parts of the road linking Jaffna with Elephant Pass (EP) through Thenmarachi, and also parts of the road linking Point Pedro with Mullaitivu through Vadamarachi. The President had ordered top defence brass to stay put in Jaffna to personally conduct the operations to blunt the LTTE's ferocious onslaught against Jaffna and Elephant Pass.

However, despite the heavy fighting given by the LTTE against the Sri Lankan security forces, it was reported that the continuing war in recent years had gnawed into the LTTE's pool of trained and experience technicians. The LTTE had short of men, though it had enough armaments. This was acknowledged by those who claimed proximity to the organisation. In the meantime, an inter-religious group headed by Professor Kamburugamauwe Vajira, the former Vice-chancellor of the Sinhala and Pali University, visited Mannar and Vavuniya in February 1999 whose aim was to build bridges with the people of those areas who were frustrated by the situation and to find out their grievances at first hand.[41] He said further : 'It was also our intention to allay the perception of the Tamil community that the Buddhist clergy were against a negotiated solution to the problem. In course of the visit, the group also met LTTE leader Tamilchelvam and Karikalan beside others at Mallawi. The LTTE leaders expressed their willingness to seek a solution to the problem through negotiations and said they were perturbed by certain elements in the south who were keen to continue the war. Earlier too the Tamil Tigers had indicated their preference for negotiations on the 'principles enunciated at the Thimpu talks.' This, hopefully, should allow some space to the other Sri Lankan Tamil parties whose opinion and role are essential for arriving at a durable and democratic solution.

The change of mood in favour of solution in the year 1998 and 1999 also witnessed on the part of treasury as well as opposition sides of the Sri Lankan politics. In September 1998, leader of the opposition in Sri Lankan Parliament and Chief of the UNP, Ranil Wickremesinghe expressed his desire to talk to the LTTE to end the war. He suggested that any talk with the LTTE should be preceded by an all-party conference to work out a genuinely unified stand on a political settlement. His call for a dialogue with Tamil Tigers had raised the hope that nation's two political parties could, for once, be geared to evolve a consensus on the ethnic conflict. The proposal of UNP was equally significant because it had suggested that the exercise be preceded by building a consensus among the southern political parties and an unconditional ceasefire. It had underlined the need for a mediatory role by a third country 'not affected by the LTTE' in getting the dialogue underway. Apart from the opposition, Chandrika Kumaratunga, the President of Sri Lanka, on 4 February 1999, speaking on the occasion of country's 51st Independence Day said, 'It is time for all of us to find a just and satisfactory solution taking into serious consideration the great loss of life and property caused by unpatriotic elements. Without naming LTTE, she added further that let us dedicate ourselves to achieve peace, prosperity and unity, preserving the rich diversity of all, thus ensuring economic and social stability. The present dispensation of Sri Lanka seemed more willing 'to solve the ethnic issue in the larger interest of the country.' Fortunately, despite the LTTE's periodic attempts to sabotage the peace process and its ruthless elimination of several high profile Tamil and Sinhala leader who were sincerely committed to the peace process, there was still a determination to bridge the ethnic gap on the part of leaders.

In the general election held in October 2000, no party got a clear mandate to form the government. In the year 2001 an LTTE assault destroyed half of the air force's planes and the incident dampened the economy and government hopes for a military solution of the problem as well. It, however, was regained in December 2001 when as a result of the mid-term election, the UNP led by Ranil Wickremesinghe formed the government with the support of SLMP, its pre-poll alliance partner. In 2001, the LTTE had also dropped its demand for a separate state. Instead, it stated that a form of regional autonomy would meet its demand on political and economic issues for the Tamil community of Sri Lanka. With the idea of initiating peace talks with the LTTE, the government announced a month's ceasefire which was reciprocated by the LTTE the very next day. At the end of the period, the new government again extended the ceasefire by another one month. The peace process had been mediated by Norway, a country that had often found the favour with both the government and the insurgents, ultimately the confidence building measure worked and on 22 February 2002 a long term ceasefire agreement was signed between the Sri Lankan government and the LTTE. Soon in March 2002, both sides signed an official Ceasefire Agreement (CFA). As part of the agreement, Norway and the other Nordic countries agreed to jointly monitor the ceasefire through the Sri Lanka Monitoring Mission (SLMM).

As a result of the Ceasefire Agreement signed in 2002, both the Government of Sri Lanka and the LTTE maintained peace to a greater extent. But some accuse the LTTE of using the ceasefire to build up its forces. The LTTE also continued to be accused of abducting school children and killing political rivals. The LTTE used the opportunity of prolonged peace to build warfare strategies including air force. It procured advanced arms to fight against government reviving civil war in a more powerful way and even started air attacks.[42] As regards the number of forces, varying reports were given by the government. According to an estimate, the LTTE's deployment increased from 9,390, before the ceasefire agreement was signed, to 16,240 towards the end of 2002. On January 22, 2003, the Sri Lankan President's office indicated that the LTTE had increased its fighting forces during the ceasefire period by 10,000 cadres, most of whom were children. Citing intelligence sources, Presidential spokesperson Harim Peiris said that the LTTE strength had increased from around 6,000 cadre before the February 2002 ceasefire agreement to 16,000 and charged that kidnapping for forcible recruitment was a major recruiting mode of the outfit. Further, on January 8, 2004, Sri Lankan President Chandrika Kumaratunga alleged that the outfit increased its military strength during the truce period by recruiting over 11,000 guerillas. The LTTE had increased its cadres by three times from around seven thousand to over 18,000. Quite a few of them were small children and the forcible recruitment was going on.

In the year 2005, the Presidential election was held in Sri Lanka which was boycotted by the LTTE. It however, claimed that the people under its control were free to vote. The new government of Sri Lanka came into power in November 2005 with Mahinda Rajapaksa as the President of the island Republic. It demanded in the same year to abrogate the ceasefire agreement, stating that the only possible solution to the ethnic conflict was military solution, and that the only way to achieve this was by eliminating the Liberation Tigers of Tamil Eelam.

Receding of LTTE's Image and Dream of Eelam

Other countries alike in the history of independent Sri Lanka, there are two shades – the moderate and the extreme which have dominated the politics and society of the island nation. As a predecessor to the LTTE in the 1960s, Marxist groups sprang up to fight the cause of economic freedom for the oppressed people that led to the beginning of armed resistance and civil war in 1970s. In the decades following the freedom of the country, the Tamils supported a more federal system through Federal Party. On 14 May 1972, the various Tamil political parties came together to form Tamil United Front (TUF) threatening to take non-violent direct action against government in order to win the right of Tamil nation on the basis of right to self-determination, if the government failed to take their aspirations into account.[43] But the Tamil youths believed in revolutionary methods to accomplish their objectives. Consequently, the Tamil youths adopted violent means becoming the powerful political force to compel TUF to reconsider its long cherished objective of federal system to form Tamil Eelam. As a result, the TUF was renamed as the Tamil United Liberation Front (TULF) in 1975, resolving the restoration and reconstitution of free and sovereign, secular, socialist state of Tamil Eelam in order to safeguard the very existence of Tamil nation in this country.

With Tamil political leaders failing in political bargaining and power politics, the Tamil youths raised arms against the government. The concept of a separate nation, Tamil Eelam, was proposed by the Tamil United Liberation Front (TULF) in 1976. As the TULF was a coalition of Tamil parties, it went to campaign in the 1977 elections for an independent state of Tamils in Sri Lanka. They won and went to Parliament to represent the northern and eastern provinces. The Government of Sri Lanka banned the TULF from Parliament for advocating an independent state for the Tamils. Thereafter, talk and nonviolent actions continued on the part of TULF, but the youth started to form militant groups, some funded by bank robberies, while military presence in the north also grew simultaneously.

The Tamil youths sought the means of armed struggle for the establishment of Tamil Eelam and Velupillai Prabakaran was one of them who founded the Liberation Tigers of Tamil Eelam on 5 May 1976. The arms uprising gave birth to political violence as the only means and as a result Tamil militancy emerged in Tamil areas with plenty of Tamil militancy organisations to fight for their rights against the oppressive rule of the Sinhalese. On the other hand, divergence exists in trying to date the ethnic conflict between the Sinhalese majority community and the Tamil minority community and the anti-state violence from groups of young Tamil militants, called separatist terrorist by the Sri Lankan state. Initially, violence was directed against Sri Lankan Tamil police officers, later, force began to be manifested against all security officers, Sinhalese or Tamil either from the police or armed forces.[44] At first there was a plethora of different resistance groups. The Liberation Tigers of Tamil Eelam's position attempting to learn from Palestine, was that there should be only one. Over the time the LTTE, often bloodily, merged with or eliminated almost all the other groups. However, when

Prabakaran formed the LTTE in the early 1980s, it was a democratic group and decisions were taken collectively by a central committee. Since then it had grown out to be a massive army with the wholehearted support of the Tamil people and contained thousands of brave soldiers. In later years, it became the army that the Tamil people could look up to in order to put an end to all the troubles and win back the Tamil's homeland, Tamil Eelam.

In the history of Liberation Tigers of Tamil Eelam, the riots of July 1983 proved a turning point as it encouraged the Tamil groups of Sri Lanka to use overt and illegal methods to raise funds, acquire weapons, and publicise its cause of establishing an independent Tamil state. In this incident large scale violence accompanied protests against Sinhalese discrimination, while demands from the Sri Lankan Tamil minority youth grew more pronounced after 1983.[45] The LTTE began its armed conflict with the Sri Lankan Government and had relied on a guerilla strategy that included the use of terrorist tactics. In post-riots periods there had been on-and-off civil war, mostly between the government and the LTTE. The aggressive postures and activities on the part of the LTTE and by late 1984, it became obvious that the Tamil United Liberation Front (TULF) apparently had forfeited their right to represent the Tamil because they had evacuated from the north and east of Sri Lanka to Tamil Nadu abdicating their functions and responsibilities as Tamil People's representatives.[46] All initiatives were now, seized by Tamil guerilla terrorists, to the Sri Lankan government and, as always, the former had considered the latter as colonial power with whom the time for peace had passed earlier.

By then the organisational discipline of the LTTE had also undergone a significant change. In 1984, Prabakaran shocked his colleagues when he introduced the oath of personal loyalty to him. In an operation reminiscent of the Nazi tradition, a strong conformist culture with internal spy networks had already been built. The material needs of the cadre were well looked after. There were patrons in India. Well known at that time in India was the 'Green boat'. Those whom Prabakaran assessed as of independent thinking, were sent in it to India ostensibly for deployment. In reality they never reached their destination. The green boats were generally used – often carrying innocent citizens who would sink to death as the boat hits a rock or gets shelled and the blame laid on Sri Lankan authorities.[47] Thus Prabakaran, with an overwhelming desire to emerge as the *Thanipperum Thalaivar* (the sole leader) of Tamils systematically eliminated not only the rival militant groups and their leaders but also charismatic Tamil political leaders such as Amirthalingam who could eloquently put across the Tamil case to the international community.[48] For a longer period; the LTTE enjoyed an unprecedented level of support and goodwill despite its record of killing Tamil militant leaders of repute such as Sri Sabharatnam of the Tamil Eelam Liberation Organisation (TELO) and hundreds of cadres of other groups including the People's Liberation Organisation of Tamil Eelam (PLOTE), the Prabakaran mystique persisted and many Tamils ignored his seeming character aberrations.[49] Not surprisingly, the Prabakaran's bloody journey to the top, left the Tamils without a strong political leadership or party. His history was one of achievements through killings, assassinations and violence.

In later years, the Federal Bureau of Investigation (FBI) of the United States of America had described the Liberation Tigers of Tamil Eelam as a 'dreaded terrorist organisation, amongst the mostly dangerous and deadly extremist outfits in the world' that claimed to be the sole representative of Sri Lankan Tamils and pursued the secessionist goal of Tamil Eelam in an uncompromising way. For all its success in building over time, low-intensity fighting capabilities that are the envy of extremist and terrorist organisations the world over.[50] Thus, by all accounts, the foundation was laid for a unique fighting force made up mostly of children and women– persons who were hazy about the aims and methods of the organisation, motivated to kill and to be killed without thinking. In the decade of 1980s, a Tamil journal in Canada carried photo feature who proudly proclaimed, 'Today Tamil children who should carry books are seen with AK-47 rifles hanging on their soldiers. These fighters stand guard surrounding Sinhalese army camps and borders of Tamil Eelam.'[51] It seemed to the Sri Lankan Tamil community that it was not until the rise of Tamil militancy that Colombo felt the need to sit up and listen to the angry voices of the alienated Tamils.

In post-1983 periods, the initiatives and efforts of Indira Gandhi, the then Indian Prime Minister, and Gopalaswamy Parthasarathy, her envoy, to bring about a solution ended unsuccessfully but their endeavours made an attempt to satisfy both the Sri Lankan government and the moderate Tamil United Liberation Front (TULF). In the scheme the TULF was to abandon their claim for Eelam, and independent Tamil separate state, and instead were to accept provincial councils that could provide a degree of autonomy to the north and east of Sri Lanka where Tamils lived in a majority. The hopeful structure collapsed because J.R. Jayawardene's All Party Conference was boycotted by Bandaranaike's

Sri Lanka Freedom Party (SLFP). As a result the militant Tamils in turn hardened their demand for a separate state; and the TULF's moderate line was no longer acceptable to Tamil hardliners who wanted only Tamil Eelam and nothing else. Continuing violence, anarchy and oppressive measures in the coming years, paved the way for signing the Indo-Sri Lanka Accord of July 1987.

The Indo-Sri Lanka Accord was signed on 29 July 1987 by J.R. Jayawardene, the President of Sri Lanka and Rajiv Gandhi, the Indian Prime Minister. It contained several provisions to satisfy the contending parties and both the dignitaries agreed on generalities while the responsibility and task of bringing the TULF and Tamil militant separatists to agree to conditions of the peace accord entailing their obligations and responsibilities were left to be tackled by the Indian Government.[52] India got obliged to assist Sri Lanka militarily if armed separatists disregarded the terms of the peace accord, such as the ceasefire or the surrender of weapons within a stipulated time. Also, India became committed to expel Tamil separatists living in Tamil Nadu. Further more, the northern and eastern provinces were to be welded into a single linguistic unit, an agreement to be tested for political acceptability by the eastern province through a referendum after an interval of an year or so. For a long time the merger of the northern and eastern provinces into one unit had been mooted by Tamil agitators, inspite of Sinhalese and some Muslim opposition in earlier discussions on grounds of linguistic commonality and also for buttressing security to the Tamils who argued that a united north and east would enhance their strength and safety. Sinhalese and Muslims together, outnumbered the Tamils in a part of the eastern province and hence, they feared dominance by the northern Tamils in one unit scheme. Following the peace accord an Indian Peace-keeping Force (IPKF) was dispatched to the island nation and with this other provisions of the agreement also became operative.

Pursuing the provisions, all other militant groups except the Liberation Tigers of Tamil Eelam (LTTE) had accepted the accord and surrendered arms and other war materials. The LTTE had counted several causes for its rejection of the accord but political issues remained on the top of LTTE's agenda. It vehemently opposed the candidate of EPRLF, another militant group, and instead named three candidates for the position which were rejected by India. Subsequently, the LTTE found itself engaged in military conflict with the Indian Army and the former had launched first attack on the IPKF in October 1987. The Government of India then decided that the Indian force should disarm the LTTE by force while the latter had declared their intent to continue the armed struggle for an independent Tamil Eelam. Initially, for three months the Indian troops had kept the Tamil guerillas under pressure and Indian intelligence officials have held talks with Sadasivan Krishnakumar, the Tigers' representatives in Madras. The aim of the Madras talks had been to find a formula that will induce the guerillas to surrender their arms and allow elections to be held in northern and eastern Sri Lanka. The eruption of fierce fighting between the LTTE and the IPKF resulted in a devastating blow to the former and took the life of about 1,200 members of the latter. It took Prabakaran two decades to rebuild the LTTE after the mauling he received at the hands of the Indian Peace-keeping Forces from 1987 to 1990. The IPKF found itself engaged in a bloody police action against the LTTE throughout its stayal in Sri Lanka and after due consultations it was withdrawn at the end of March 1990. In succession an LTTE squad had assassinated Rajiv Gandhi, the former Prime Minister and signatory of the peace accord, on 21 May 1991. As a result India became the first country to ban the LTTE as a terrorist organisation whose supreme, Prabakaran, continued to be wanted as Accused No. 1 in the Rajiv assassination case.

The LTTE's engagement at war with the Indian forces for more than two years in Sri Lanka and its assassination of Rajiv Gandhi in May 1991 gave the organisation a shattering blow to its strength and image as well. India trained the LTTE in the 1980s and created the Frankenstein monster. It must atone for this grievous mistake by actions to disband and wind up the LTTE. Despite enjoying India's hospitality for years and after welcoming the peace accord it teamed up with the Sinhala hard-liner, President R. Premadasa. It betrayed India by killing more than a thousand Indian army personnel of the IPKF sent to the island to enforce the Agreement. Thus, the LTTE needs to be dealt with as part of the problem – not part of the solution.[53] Gone are the days when the Tamil people of Sri Lanka, particularly who belonged to Jaffna region, felt that only the struggle of the type and magnitude waged by Prabakaran can assure us a life of dignity. We see no vested interest in the LTTE's struggle except our deliverance.[54] The anti-India activities of the LTTE made India its principal enemy and ensured that the gains of a decade unravelled in no time.

But as earlier India genuinely wished that a ceasefire following the LTTE's offer and Sri Lanka's positive response would have held and stabilised. We still hope that all efforts would be exerted in this direction and lead to meaningful and sustained negotiations with the participation of all concerned parties. We believe that only a negotiated political settlement within the framework of the unity and territorial integrity of Sri Lanka, which takes into account legitimate Tamil demands, can lead to a durable and lasting solution.[55] And, on the opposite, was the thinking and strategy of LTTE who had concentrated, in later years, all its political energies on ensuring its own fascist control of northern Sri Lanka. As a consequence, it had been unable to provide sensitive and alert leadership which would necessarily include the capability to engage with the wider situation and respond in a timely manner to the opportunities to advance the Tamil cause as and when they arose.[56] The first such occasion was provided in 1985 in the form of Thimpu Declaration which was attended by five Tamil militant groups including the LTTE. The said Declaration caught the international imagination as it asserted that Tamils were a nation with the right to self-determination and a homeland. On the other hand, it also increased the pressure on the Sri Lankan state to respond to the demand for power sharing with the Tamil minority.

For most of us except the LTTE, the Indo-Sri Lanka Accord of July 1987 was a path-breaking achievement which marked a paradigm shift in Sri Lanka and promised a genuine transition to a federal type of power sharing structure. Internationally too the accord was welcomed and India as well as Sri Lanka were praised to solve the ethnic conflict. Almost all nations disapproved the idea of solving the issues militarily. But according to Prabakaran the accord was to prevent involvement of outside forces in Sri Lanka, and tackling the Tamil problem was only a byproduct.[57] Thus the LTTE's short-sighted and adventurist positions had cost the Tamil ethnic cause dearly even as valuable time had been lost in the failure to consolidate the gains achieved through political negotiations. When later a vengeful Prabakaran carried out the assassination of Rajiv Gandhi, popular support in Tamil Nadu for the LTTE dried up and the Eelam Tamil cause was pushed to the backseat even in political rhetoric.

The Indo-Sri Lanka Accord of July 1987, barring other controversies, was the best solution of the ethnic issue ever devised by the two Governments. It was not only suitable for the national sovereignty and integrity of both countries but for the regional interests too as it debarred external powers to interfere in the regional affairs or any dispute between the nations. But for its failure, responsibility mainly went to the LTTE who refused to surrender arms and continued its avowed for the Tamil Eelam. Very recently Douglas Devananda, Sri Lanka's Social Welfare Minister in the Mahinda Rajapaksa government and leader of the Eelam

People's Democratic Party (EPDP), in November 2008, in course of interview given to *The Hindu*, blamed the LTTE that the demand for ceasefire is made only when the organisation is militarily weakened. The LTTE has cynically used ceasefire and talks to strengthen itself militarily – to rest, rearm and recommence fighting. He emphatically said that till Prabakaran is alive he would not allow anyone to solve this problem. His real problem is that he can not survive in a democratic environment. He needs a piece of dreamland called Eelam that he can rule as a dictator.[58] Devananda also added further that after the Indo-Sri Lanka agreement every leader in office has attempted to solve this issue but the LTTE had walked out of talks every single time on some excuse or the other.[59] He expressed the government's wish to put an end to the politics of militancy and move towards a negotiated political settlement.

In this way in post Indo-Sri Lanka accord period and particularly after the assassination of Rajiv Gandhi in May 1991, the who had proactively intervened in Sri Lanka to help the Tamils, the LTTE started dissipating its goodwill in India. Going a step further it also colluded with its 'sworn Sinhala enemy' President Ranasinghe Premadasa, to get the Indian forces off its back and sending them out of Sri Lanka. However, the LTTE did not use its newfound bonhomie with the President for the benefit of the Tamils. Instead, it killed Premadasa after carrying out a blood bath of thousands of cadres of the Eelam peoples Revolutionary Liberation Front. Their only sin was that unlike the LTTE they had accepted the Indo-Sri Lanka accord.[60] The LTTE relentlessly pursued the members of the EPRLF leadership who had taken refuge in India and killed many of them in Chennai. No amount of political or parochial rhetoric is going to repair the damage done to the LTTE's image. Although for several years, some political parties and fringe groups in Tamil Nadu had been involved in ineffective chauvinistic propaganda and activities to enable the LTTE to stage a political comeback in India. They got no political purchase for the simple reason that the overwhelming majority of the people of Tamil Nadu, something like 95 per cent, did not want a reprise of the secessionist campaigns and violent activities of the Tamil Tigers in one of India's most peaceful States.[61] The other mainstream parties of the country that have no love lost for the LTTE found themselves taking a strident stand on the Sri Lankan Tamil question. Appropriately, the *Home Ministry 2005 Annual Report to Parliament* also confirmed that the LTTE had been targeting pro-Indian Sri Lanka politicians and assassinating them.

But above all, the LTTE interfered in the internal affairs of India by financing some Indian political elements, in providing training to certain Indian extremist organisations, and by extending insurgency infrastructure to bandits such as Veerapan. It also laundered the black money of some Indian politicians through its illegal Eelam Bank in the Jaffna area. India can not allow such erosion of law and order within its own borders. In reality the LTTE must be understood to be part of an international terror network. It was involved in smuggling narcotics into India, circulating fake currency notes to buy medicines and diesel, and engaging in passport fabrication and hawala operations.[62] Prabakaran's faith in a military solution, rather than a political one, prevented him from taking the easy way out. He continued to procure modern weapons and arms even as he spoke of peace. He did everything to scuttle the peace process and took advantage of the weaknesses of Sri Lanka's polity to bring it to an end.

There is no doubt in the fact that since its inception, the LTTE had showed no faith in constitutional methods or in solving any issue with political negotiation. Likewise, it had no faith in devolution; any devolution of power within one Sri Lanka; it stood committed to Tamil Eelam through armed struggle and had shot down even constitutional proposals that mooted some kind of federal solution.[63] Also, within a decade of its formation, the LTTE's goodwill for other Tamil militant groups and political parties, the TULF in particular, who represented a moderate view in Sri Lankan politics, evaporated as signs of their proclivity for extreme violence emerged in their savage internecine fighting. One by one, TELO, PLOTE and EPRLF were devoured by the LTTE, which was determined to establish its hegemony as the sole representative of the Tamil people. Even as other groups, led by the TULF were using India's good offices to press Colombo for a framework that would devolve powers to the Tamils and allow for a merger of the northern and eastern provinces that could constitute a Tamil homeland, the LTTE was disdainful of these parleys.[64] In 1990, Suresh Premachandran, the new General Secretary of the EPRLF and Jaffna District MP, was of the view that the LTTE deceived all those who genuinely attempted to negotiate with them to settle the North's issues amicably and expressed the belief that the only way out for the government was to arrive at a solution with other Tamil groups, declaring that the EPRLF would extend its support to the government for such a solution.[65] The LTTE-EPRLF feud was likely to be one of the permanent features of Tamil politics in the island.

In an effort to make political solution possible, the Government of Sri Lanka had started dialogue with other Tamil militant groups and Sri

Lankan political parties, including Tamil political parties with a view to isolate the LTTE permanently from the political process. All other Tamil militant groups and political parties had renounced a separate Eelam in their search for a constitutional solution of the Tamil problem. But with the passage of time the moderate Tamil United Liberation Front (TULF) agreed to the LTTE's being the Tamil's sole representative in any talks with the Sri Lankan Government. The TULF's President M. Sivasithamparam made it in an interview but added, 'Nobody can deny that the TULF has made a major contribution to the Tamils' struggle and that it has been responsible for bringing the Tamils' struggle to the current decisive stage.[66] In March 1998 when TULF's nominee Sarojini Yogeswaram was sworn in as the Mayor of the northern town of Jaffna, it declared that the Tamil Tigers should be recognised as the legitimate representatives of the island nation's largest minority and that it was also ready to step down in favour of the Liberation Tigers of Tamil Eelam if the government and the main opposition party recognise the Tigers as the sole representative of the Tamil people and resume negotiations with them.[67] It appeared that TULF's announcement was not made due to the fear of LTTE. But in the context of continued killing of TULF leaders by the LTTE, V. Anandasangaree, the Vice-president of the organisation, had appealed to the LTTE to stop the killing, recognise the TULF as a *satvik* or moral force struggling for the Sri Lankan Tamil cause, and allow it to function. Extending a hand of friendship, he also said that the TULF had never acted against the LTTE hence it should not consider the TULF its enemy, and recognise it as a peaceful movement.[68] It all tarnished LTTE's image in and outside the island nation. The LTTE was also weakened following mutiny in its ranks in 1995 and 1998 that affected negatively its recruitment momentum.

At the close of the decade 1990s, despite the fact that the LTTE had no fund crunch and coming in at a steady flow alright, after the manner in which the organisation had eliminated all rival groups and established a regimen of terror, the biggest problem for the LTTE had been fresh recruitment. Unlike earlier, according to the independent University Teachers for Human Rights (Jaffna), was poor. 'Those who join are scattered individuals rather than groups of persons. In the early nineties, the LTTE would easily recruit children of the ages 9 and 10 and girls of 14 and 15 for training in the use of weapons but now parents are resisting.[69] At one of the recruitment camps that the LTTE had organised to recruit the cadres, its senior spokesman was reported to have said, 'We have got plenty of money, weapons and ammunition, but, we suffer casualties in battle. Unless you join us in large numbers we cannot resist the enemy with the same intensity.[70] Especially after the takeover of Jaffna by the army and its claim that all but 41 square kilometres of area in the northern province is under army control – the biggest problem for the LTTE had been fresh recruitment. Perhaps keeping the scarcity in view, the high command of the LTTE planned to declare a 'state of war' in the areas under its command in Wanni. From the economic points of view, the most crippling economic blow for the Tigers was the loss of Jaffna, where the LTTE had a well-oiled administrative system going with collection of taxes and other funds easy and smooth.

As then, the LTTE was suffering from a crisis of credibility. According to the United Teachers for Human Rights (UTHR), most of the recent recruits to the LTTE were persons stopped on the street, brainstormed, given promises of glory and pledges to look after the family. Even the Tamils were tired of its policy of 'response-no-response' – agreeing for talks to gain time and striking when talks were about to begin. What all that meant was that the LTTE was in the process of natural disintegration within itself and also within its base population. Here the prediction of Rajni Thiranganama, who was dedicated to the LTTE in the eighties and spent about half a dozen years with the LTTE to realise the true nature of the organisation and its leader, and who favoured peaceful path of struggle and for the reason, she was executed in 1989 by the order of Prabakaran, wrote in her report on the Tamils' struggle entitled 'Broken Palmyra'; 'The Tigers' history, their theoretical vacuum, lack of political creativity, intolerance and fanatical dedication will be the ultimate cause of their own break-up. The legendary Tigers will go to their demise with their legends smeared with the blood and tears of victims of their misdoings. A new Tiger will not emerge from their ashes.'[71] Thus the Tamils are caught between the 'devil and the deep sea'.

In total from the year 1998 the general population of Tamils in Sri Lanka began to be alienated from the LTTE and its dream 'Tamil Eelam'. It seemed that the Tamils needed liberation from both sides. They have to politically defeat LTTE if they want to regain the space to live in peace with dignity. Given the present scenario, with an internationally isolated LTTE ploughing a lonely furrow, the Tamils feel that Eelam is not attainable. The passion for Eelam is clearly dimming, though given the deep-seated suspicions plaguing Sinhalese-Tamil relations, Eelam is still seen as the 'ideal' or 'permanent solution'. Even a pro-LTTE journalist admitted that there is no great support for it even in the Tiger heart. People would settle for a unified Sri Lanka provided the North and East are merged and designated 'the Tamil Homeland.' Land is the main issue.[72] And a major reason for the Tamils disillusionment with the Eelam was the poor shape of the LTTE. It had not been able to retake Jaffna lost in 1995. Its weakness was evident in the areas under its control in Batticaloa district. Receding of the dream of Eelam was also felt in the Heroes Day message of the year (27 November 1997) in which the LTTE itself had climbed down from the high horse of Eelam. Prabakaran on that day had scaled down his goal from Tamil Eelam to Tamil Homeland, which is the moderates' demand.[73] As there was a government-sponsored devolution package in Parliament and as an alternative the opposition United National Party had proposed asymmetrical devolution or devolution restricted to the Tamils.

Politics of Power Devolution in Sri Lanka

The Tamils in Sri Lanka are an integral part of the population mostly concentrated in Jaffna area which is close to the mainland of India and also called the traditional home of Tamils-Ceylonese and Indian.[74] The Sri Lankan Tamils, who constitute the majority of the Tamils are concentrated in the northern and eastern provinces while the Indian Tamils are mostly concentrated in the plantation areas situated in the central highlands. The Ceylon Tamils are also called the indigenous Tamils and are the descendants of those Tamils who reached Sri Lanka in the wake of Chola invasions beginning with the rule of the Chola Prince. The Ceylon Tamils ultimately settled in Northern and Eastern provinces which constitute the dry zone of Sri Lanka.[75] The Indian Tamils had been brought from the Indian mainland by the British to work on the coffee, tea and rubber plantations in the island. In the northern and eastern arid regions where the scope for agricultural development was limited, people looked towards other means of employment. Here a large number of Tamils, mostly from the cultivator caste of Vellala benefited from English education provided by schools and colleges set up by the American missionaries. They found excess to jobs in the colonial administration and in the various upper-bracket professions. A sizable number of Tamils from more modest background also moved out and settled in Colombo to avail of the opportunities provided by boom in trade and commerce.

Before the independence of Sri Lanka, the first ethnocentric political party, named Tamil Congress, was formed in 1944 to work on the basis of responsive co-operation with the Sinhalese. It was followed by the formation of Federal Party in December 1949 who was more responsive to the Tamil demands and aspirations as well. The Tamil Congress was Jaffna-centred, while the Federal Party sought to unite under its leadership the Tamil-speaking peoples of the north and east, the Tamil-speaking Muslims, and the Indian Tamil plantation workers. The Federal Party activists represent Tamil nationalism but in the beginning advocated federation with a future Dravidian sovereign state of south India. Thereafter opinion stabilised in favour of a 'Tamil homeland federated to a Sinhalese Ceylon. In early seventies (1972) the F.P and T.C. joined hand in a Tamil United Front (TUF) and in 1976 resolved to change its designation and became the Tamil United Liberation Front (TULF).[76] By the time several militant groups were also formed who were dominated by Tamil youths having no faith in peaceful means and were determined to achieve their goal of separate state – Tamil Eelam through waging war against the Sri Lankan authorities. As a result of ethnic divide and strife, riots on larger scale erupted in July 1983 which paved the way for Indian intervention and signing of the Indo-Sri Lanka Accord between India and Sri Lanka with the provision to merge the northern and eastern provinces of the island nation.

The peace accord signed in July 1987 in one of its most controversial parts, virtually acknowledged the Tamil homeland demand by providing for a temporary merger of the northern and eastern provinces but at the same time recognised the justifiable reservations of the Muslims and Sinhalese communities in the eastern province by providing for breaking up the merger to allow the reversion of this province to its separate existence as a referendum so determined before the prescribed date. In Sri Lanka's case devolution of power from the centre to the provinces involved three basic issues : first the extent of the powers to be devolved; second, the relations between the centre and provinces; and third, the unit of devolution. The unit of devolution remained a problem issue right up to the time of the signing of the July agreement.[77] However, under the agreement there was no permanent merger. It was a temporary merger to be followed by a plebiscite – a referendum among the people of the Eastern province so that they could decide whether they could merge it or not.

In fact, the provision of referendum had brought to the fore the ethnic tensions in the Eastern province, because in this peculiar province roughly there are one-third Tamils, one-third Muslims and one-third Sinhalese. Given the ethnic composition, it was very clear that Muslims and Sinhalese of the Eastern province would not vote for a merger. And so keeping the composition of the region in view for the time being temporary merger was provided to be followed by a referendum. The developments succeeded in the passing of the 13th Amendment to the constitution of Sri Lanka in September 1987 which envisaged province as the unit of power and devolution of powers between the centre and the provinces as a solution to the ethnic crisis.[78] A notification on the temporary merger of the two provinces were issued on 7 September 1988, by President J.R. Jayawardene. But for a variety of reasons successive governments have not been able to implement various provisions of the 13th Amendment. After the withdrawal of IPKF in March 1990, the issue of power devolution became an active issue in the island's politics.

In post-withdrawal phase, the future of Provincial Councils figured prominently in the political discourse in Sri Lanka, as a general device for political devolution of power, and as a specific instrument for granting regional autonomy to the Tamils of the North and the East. It is also to note here that majority of Tamil opinion, as represented both by the political parties and the militant groups, would never be reconciled to the demerger of the Northern and Eastern Provinces, and since these parties and groups have clearly renounced the idea of the separate state and shown their willingness to enter the political mainstream within the framework of the unity of Sri Lanka, the government and all Sinhala political parties must, in the interests of peace and national harmony, endeavour to meet the aspirations of these parties and groups.[79] Politically, the Sri Lankan government commenced preparations for working out a model through which power could devolve on the recoganised provincial councils.

In August 1991, the then Government of Sri Lanka had set up a Parliamentary Select Committee (PSC) to recommend ways and means of achieving peace and political stability in the country under the headship of Mangala Moonesinghe, a SLFP Member of Parliament, who called for written representations from all parties concerned. The PSC from the beginning faced the delicate issue of merger of the North-Eastern provinces in which the Tamil parties including the Tamil Workers Congress (CWC) went on repeating their demand for the merger of the north east, while the Sinhala parties with the SLFP and UNP members within the PSC kept opposing the Tamil's proposal. In course of the deliberations with the parties, it became obvious that the Sri Lanka Muslim Congress (SLMC) had emerged as an interested party and it wanted to have its share of the cake too, which meant that it was supporting the North-Eastern merger without sufficient safeguards for the interests of Muslims in provinces.

Ultimately, during deliberations and in the Interim Report that the PSC had issued on 16 December 1992, entitled 'Matters Agreed Upon By A Majority of the Members, ignored the views of Tamil parties and gave weightage to the anti-Tamil parties on North-East issue. It noted that the agreement were (i) on the establishment of two separate units of administration for the Northern and Eastern Provinces, (ii) to adopt a scheme of devolution on lines similar to those obtaining in the Indian Constitution, and (iii) to devolve more subjects that are in list III or to dispense with the list. On the day the agreements were issued, were rejected by the Tamil parties. The failure of the PSC was evident because neither the Sinhalese nor the Tamils were willing to budge from their uncompromising positions about the North-East merger. It, however, was mainly the failure of politics and the style of politics that did not allow for the resolution of conflict.

With a view to provide peace and stability to the island nation, the Chandrika Plan came out with a detailed devolution package within the framework of a proposed new federal constitution when Chandrika Kumaratunga became the President of Sri Lanka. It proposed to give the federating units much more power in comparison to previous years. It also talked about the permanent merger of the Northern and Eastern provinces in which the Tamils would have their say. But according to a constitutional provision, a minimum of two-thirds majority was required to pass an amendment to the constitution of such nature. The then People's Alliance had only a simple majority in the Parliament and it was not possible to pass the amendment without the support of United National Party (UNP). The politics and deadlocks on the issue of North East began in Sri Lanka clearly thereafter. This sorry state of affair continued despite the fact that both the UNP and the PA had promised not to use the ethnic issue for political gains under the Fox Plan, an agreement which was brokered by Britain's Liam Fox on 25 February 1997. According to it, the two leading Sri Lankan political parties should chalk out a joint strategy prior to holding talks with the LTTE.[80] However, the said pact was criticised by the National Movement Against Terrorism (NMAT). The NMAT was of the view that a bi-partisan strategy on the ethnic issue was needed as a whole and opposed any talks only with the LTTE.[81]

In fact, Chandrika Kumaratunga came to power with a promise to find a political solution to the island's ethnic issue but when her efforts to negotiate with the LTTE failed and the latter had ended the ceasefire agreement, she again turned to devolution package in order to have a peaceful and stable Sri Lanka. However, over the issue the United National Party – the main opposition party of the island was staunchly opposed to changing Sri Lanka's unitary constitution. Sections within the UNP were also bitterly opposed to merging the northern and eastern provinces to form a contiguous homeland for the Tamils. The homeland theory cannot be encouraged as said by Stanley Kalpage, who represented the hardliners was totally opposed to federal set-up.[82] Even the devolution package was opposed by a member of the Peoples Alliance who publicly criticised the merger of the northern and eastern provinces.

Among the critics of the devolution plan were the UNP leader Ranil Wickremesinghe and former foreign minister A.C.S. Hameed who realised that only way of solving the ethnic issue was through a political package and their party is willing to give the Tamils their due. But several other analysts held the view that the UNP did not want to let Kumaratunga take the credit of actually working out a fair deal for all sections in the country.[83] According to the view of Chandrika Kumaratunga who was prepared to bring to fruition her radical proposals for devolution and had told the coalition partners in a meeting that she had got a mandate for bringing about peace to the country. In case of not passing from the Parliament, the next move of Peoples Alliance would be to hold a non-binding referendum.[84] There is already a provision for a non-binding referendum in the 1978 constitution but the UNP was also opposed to making the non-binding referendum a substitute for Parliament.

Ultimately, at the end of September 1997, the Sri Lankan Cabinet decided to hold a referendum in the districts of eastern province on the question of the merger of the northern and eastern provinces to form a single North-East Tamil province.[85] It followed in the next month the approving of the devolution package by the ruling coalition despite a devastating bomb blast by the LTTE, a day before the approval. However, the Tamil parties hoped that the government would not be deterred by the blast and would go ahead with the devolution package, stop the war and begin negotiations with the LTTE.[86] The Tamils, in general, feel that a package, however good, cannot be implemented without the LTTE's express consent. The recent blast was an indication of LTTE's view that peace could not be brought about by marginalising it, ignoring it, banning it or suppressing it. In Sri Lanka many considered the devolution package a good strategy as the LTTE or anybody else would not be able to complain that the government had nothing concrete to offer. But in this context, President Kumaratunga had made it clear that there was no possibility of holding talks with the LTTE before it abjured war and terrorism, and agreed to discuss her government's devolution package.[87] She added further that the majority of Tamils living in the North East, the area of conflict, were for peace and the devolution package.

The Government of Sri Lanka appeared determined to implement its devolution package despite criticisms of the scheme from various quarters. Mangala Samaraweera, the powerful Media Minister of the country, said to the Capital's radio correspondent that if need be, the government would hold a referendum even outside the framework of the present constitution. Any constitution would have to reflect the will of the people.[88] He was of the view that all the ethnic groups in Sri Lanka, the minority Tamils and majority Sinhalas, desperately wanted devolution, ethnic harmony and peace. He also held lack of devolution responsible for the secessionism in Sri Lanka. 'It was under the unitary constitution that Prabakaran got transformed from being a leader of a lunatic fring to being an internationally known liberation fighter. Quoting the examples of India, Belgium and Canada, the minister refuted the charge that the devolution would lead to secession.[89] Political observers of the island believed that President Kumaratunga would go ahead with the devolution proposals for two reasons, (i) the common Sinhala and Tamil are for devolution and the peace it would bring (ii) there is international pressure, basically from the West. David Tathane, the British High Commissioner, had publicly said that the government should come out with a credible offer if the LTTE were to be induced to come for peace talks. In the absence of such an offer, the Sinhalas and the Tamils would be condemned to live separately or Eelam would be inevitable.[90] Among other charges, the government had rebuffed the Sinhala Commission's report as the 'biggest conspiracy' against the Sinhala people which would only benefit the rebel Tamil leader Prabakaran and the international arms dealers who wanted the war to continue.

With the coming of a BJP - led government in India, the pro-Tamil groups of Sri Lanka felt relief and perhaps hoped New Delhi to intervene in the matter. Meanwhile, in the last week of April 1998 Nagendra Nath Jha, the former Indian Ambassador and Convenor of BJP's Foreign Affairs Committee, had said that South Block is working on a 'concrete, palatable and immediately implementable proposal to resolve the Sri

Lankan ethnic conflict. He also added that India should take a 'friendly interest' in what was happening in Sri Lanka.[91] His statement annoyed Sinhalese while cheered Tamils and had triggered speculation about India's intentions. Although earlier several countries including the US had offered mediation between Colombo and the LTTE to bring an end to the bleeding war, the statement of former Indian Ambassador was taken seriously, if not by the government whose Minister of Constitutional Affairs Professor G.L. Peiris adopted a soft line and said that a friendly interest did not mean interference or involvement, but by the media, especially the pro-Sinhala. However, Douglas Devananda of the EPDP urged N.N. Jha to press New Delhi to revive the moribund Indo-Sri Lanka accord and see that 13th amendment was implemented in letter and spirit.[92] Objecting the remarks which created a storm of sorts in the country, a foreign ministry official while talking informally to newsmen said that Sri Lanka would certainly object to India or for that matter any other country working out a package for the solution of the ethnic question, as this was essentially an internal matter to be solved by Sri Lankan themselves.[93] On the whole Jha's views on merger was refuted by the Sri Lankan government saying that it was against a full merger.

Further, in response to Peoples Alliance devolution package, the United National Party (UNP) also submitted a constitutional proposal to Professor G.L. Peiris, the chairman of the Parliamentary Select Committee (PSC) in March 1998. The UNP's proposals were related to four subjects : fostering a Sri Lankan identity; devolution of power to the provinces; local government; and the legislative powers of the Parliament. It based its proposals on the devolution of power on the existing 13th amendment, with a Central list, Provincial list and an indeterminate Concurrent list. Whereas, the proposal was in favour of the unitary nature and provinces were given less powers. In the context of devolution of powers, the constitutional proposal of the UNP brought disappointments for the TULF, the moderate Tamil Party, and M. Sivasithamparam, the President of the Party, had complained that the Central list had everything, leaving only minor subjects to the provinces. The devolution of subjects under this list would be based on the needs of a province and the PSC is charged with the task of working out a mechanism to enable such devolution.[94] The TULF leader had also objected to the provision for dismissing a provincial government on the ground that it did not implement a law passed by the Parliament.

Apart from the constitutional proposals, leader of the opposition in the Sri Lankan Parliament and chief of the United National Party, Ranil

Wickremesinghe had said at the end of August 1998 that he wanted to talk to the LTTE to end the war immediately. In an exclusive interview the leader gave to *Sanjeevi*, a Jaffna Tamil Weekly, he noted that any talks with the LTTE should be preceded by an all-party conference to work out a genuinely unified stand on a political settlement. On the issue of talks both the UNP and the Tamils were agreed that the government and the UNP must make a united stand.[95] But in contrast was the view of Sri Lankan government who wanted to finish the war first and then talk to the LTTE. To some extent, the government had also sidelined the LTTE politically by propping up the other Tamil groups. The UNP's suggestion for immediate talks with the LTTE was also welcomed by *The Hindustan Times*, the daily newspaper in its editorial on 5 September 1998.[96] It wrote that the call for a dialogue with the Tamil Tigers had raised the hopes that the island nation's two main political parties can, for once, be geared to evolve a national consensus on the ethnic conflict.

After a long gap in November 2005, Mahinda Rajapaksa took over as the President of Sri Lanka and he began to look over the whole issue of ethnicity and the LTTE with new vision and context. First of his initiatives was formation of All Party Representative Committee (APRC) in 2006 to find political consensus on power sharing between the conflicting communities. The report of the APRC stated that the final political package would require a constitutional amendment, that some of its provisions will also need to be approved in a referendum, and that all this will take time once a favourable climate is established.[97] As a historical step both the UNP and SLFP signed a Memorandum of Understanding (MoU) in October 2006 to cooperate in all the spheres of national interest but the parochial and narrow interest of both parties killed it.[98] In a landmark development on devolution of power, the Sinhala nationalist Janatha Vimukthi Peramuna (JVP) moved the Supreme Court of Sri Lanka on 21 July 2006 and challenged the temporary merger of the country's north and east as a single administrative unit.[99] The JVP's petition was admitted in the Supreme Court.

The temporary merger of the two provinces in 1988 was a consequence of the 1987 Indo-Sri Lanka Accord. The merger was to have been preceded by de-weaponisation and followed by a referendum within a year on whether the arrangement should continue. Counsel for the JVP have argued before the Supreme Court that the gazette notification on the temporary merger of the two provinces issued on 7 September 1988, by President J.R. Jayawardene, was invalid as the merger was neither preceded by a surrender of weapons nor followed by a referendum as envisaged by the Parliament.[100] The JVP had roped in the President's counsel, H.L. de Silva, to argue its case. De Silva, who is also the head of the newly constituted 15- member multi-ethnic experts' panel, has strong views on the subject of sharing of powers among various communities.

These developments on the merger of north and east had sparked concerns among the moderate, albeit marginalised Tamil parties and all those yearning for de-escalation of tension. Although the JVP had always been opposed to the merger, yet it never deemed necessary to knock on the doors of the apex court, since the two units became one in 1988. In a far-reaching judgement, the Sri Lankan Supreme Court on 16 October 2006, ruled that the 1987 order by the President of the island merging the two provinces was not in keeping with the country's constitution and that they should, therefore, be separate provinces.[101] In this regard there were assurances from the highest level that the Government would not interfere with the apex court verdict and nothing would be done to complicate the matters. Now, the challenge before non-extremist Tamil political parties is to show the courage and wisdom to go for genuine devolution of power.

References

1. *The Hindu* (Madras), 5 June 1990.
2. *The Indian Express*, 27 March 1990.
3. Dayan Jayatilleka, 'A Sri Lankan Analysis – Dixit's Testament : A Critical Review', *Mainstream*, Annual, (1977), p. 109.
4. R. Hariharan, 'The Discarded Accord and the Unwanted War' *The Hindu*, 7 August 2007.
5. *The Statesman*, 22 June 1990.
6. N.S. Jagunnathan, 'The End of a Misadventure' The *Indian Express*, 2 April 1990.
7. *The Sunday Times*, 29 April 1990.
8. Shelton U. Kodikara, 'Internal Politics and Foreign Policy : Prospects for Indo-Sri Lanka Relations in the Nineties', in *External Compulsions of South Asia Politics* (New Delhi : Sage Publications, 1993), pp. 226-28.
9. *Daily News*, 5 July 1990.
10. *The Island*, 9 May 1990.
11. Shelton U. Kodikara, 'War and Peace : Options for the LTTE', *The Sunday Observer*, 1 July 1990.
12. As quoted in Ibid., 8 July 1990.
13. Ibid., 31 December 1990.

14. Shelton U. Kodikara, 'Internal Politics and Foreign Policy : Prospects for Indo-Sri Lanka Relations in the Nineties', pp. 232-35.
15. Seema Guha, 'The Lankan Tug-of War', *The Times of India*, 28 July 1997.
16. N.N. Jha, 'India –Sri Lanka Relations', *India Quarterly*, Vol. L, Nos. 1&2, January-June, 1994 (New Delhi : Indian Council of World Affairs, 1994).
17. *The Hindustan Times*, 13 November 1997.
18. Ibid.
19. Rajkumar Singh, Relations of NDA & UPA with Neighbours (New Delhi : Gyan Publishing House, 2010), p. 334.
20. Malini Parthasarathy, 'The Mirage of Eelam', *The Hindu*, 24 April 2009.
21. *The Hindustan Times*, 21 August 1997.
22. Ibid.
23. Ibid., editorial, 17 October 1997.
24. Ibid.
25. P.B. Jayasundera, 'Moving to Create More Fiscal Space', *The Hindu*, 5 July 2008.
26. *The Hindustan Times*, 2 November 1997.
27. Ibid.
28. Ibid., 1 November 1997.
29. Ibid., 16 January 1998.
30. Ibid., 4 February 1998.
31. Ibid., 20 February 1998.
32. Ibid., 26 February 1998.
33. Ibid., editorial, 2 October 1998.
34. Ibid.
35. As quoted in Rajkumar Singh, *Relations of NDA & UPA with Neighbours*, p. 348.
36. *The Hindustan Times*, January 1999.
37. Ibid.
38. Ibid., 16 February 1999.
39. Ibid., 30 March 2000.
40. Ibid., 4 April 2000.
41. Ibid., 16 February 1999.
42. Vinod F. Khobragade, 'Ethnic Politics in Sri Lanka – Political Solution to Tamil Cause and Military Solution to LTTE', *South Asia Politics*, Vol. 7, No. 11, March 2009 (New Delhi, 2009), p. 26.

43. Ibid., p. 25.
44. Bertram E.S.J. Bastiampillai, 'Ethnic Conflicts in South Asia and Inter-state Relations Especially in Relation to Sri Lanka', in Shelton U. Kodikara, *South Asian Strategic Issues – Sri Lankan Perspectives* (New Delhi : Sage Publications, 1990), p. 89.
45. James Manor (ed.), *Sri Lanka in Change and Crisis* (Sydney : Social Scientists Association of Sri Lanka, 1984) as quoted in Ibid., p. 92.
46. *The Weekend*, 12 July 1987.
47. V.N. Narayanan, 'Separating Tamils from the LTTE', *The Hindustan Times*, 9 August 1998.
48. R. Hariharan, 'Sri Lanka : Need to Restore Trust', *The Hindu*, 18 May 2010.
49. R. Hariharan, 'The Moment of Truth for the LTTE', in Ibid., 5 February 2009.
50. Ibid., editorial, 18 October 2008.
51. V.N. Narayanan, 'Separating Tamils from the LTTE'.
52. *Sunday Observer*, 26 July 1987.
53. Subramanian Swamy, 'Sri Lanka Crisis and India's Options'. *The Hindu*, 29 November 2006.
54. V.N. Narayanan, 'Between the Devil and Deep Blue Sea', *The Hindustan Times*, 8 August 1998.
55. *Foreign Affairs Record*, vol. xxxvii, No. 1 January 1991 (New Delhi : Ministry of External Affairs, 1991), pp. 7-8.
56. Malini Parthasarathy, 'The Mirage of Eelam', *The Hindu*, 24 April 2009.
57. *Sun*, 6 August 1987, as quoted in Shelton U. Kodikara (ed.), *South Asian Strategic Issues – Sri Lankan Perspectives*, p. 110.
58. B. Muralidhar Reddy, 'Fight Against LTTE and Move Towards Political Solution Should Go Hand in Hand', *The Hindu*, 26 November 2008.
59. Ibid.
60. R. Hariharan, 'The Moment of Truth for the LTTE', in Ibid., 5 February 2009.
61. Ibid., editorial, 18 October 2008.
62. Subramanian Swamy, 'Sri Lanka Crisis and India's Options', in Ibid., 29 November 2006.
63. Ibid., editorial, 31 March 2008.
64. Malini Parthasarathy, 'The Mirage of Eelam', in Ibid., 24 April 2009.
65. Shelton U. Kodikara, 'War and Peace Options for the LTTE', *The Sunday Observer*, 8 July 1990.
66. *The Hindustan Times*, 5 October 1997.

67. Ibid., 13 March 1998.
68. P.K. Balachanddran, 'TULF Seeks LTTE's Permission to Function', in Ibid., 6 January 1999.
69. V.N. Narayanan, 'Between the Devil and Deep Blue Sea', in Ibid., 8 August 1998.
70. Ibid.
71. V.N. Narayanan, 'Separating Tamils from the LTTE', in Ibid., 9 August 1998.
72. P.K. Balachanddran, 'Eelam : a Receding Dream' in Ibid., 19 January 1998.
73. Ibid.
74. P.C. Roy Chaudhury, *Lands and Peoples of the World – Sri Lanka*, (New Delhi : Sterling Publishers, 1985), pp. 48-49.
75. H.P. Chattopadhyaya, *Indians in Sri Lanka* (Calcutta : OPS Publishers, 1979), p. 100.
76. A. Jeyaratnam Wilson, *Politics in Sri Lanka, 1947-1979* (London : The Macmillan Press, 1979), pp. 150-54.
77. Shelton. U. Kodikara, 'The Indo – Sri Lanka Agreement of July 1987 : Retrospect' in *South Asian Strategic Issues – Sri Lankan Perspectives*, p. 166.
78. B. Muralidhar Reddy, 'Full Implement of 13th Amendment Recommended', *The Hindu*, 24 January 2008.
79. Shelton U. Kodikara, 'Internal Politics and Foreign Policy : Prospects for Indo – Lanka Relations in the Nineties', in *External Compulsions of South Asian Politics*, pp. 239-40.
80. *The Hindustan Times*, 7 March 1999.
81. Ibid.
82. Seema Guha, 'The Sri Lankan Tug-of War', *The Times of India*, 28 July 1997.
83. Ibid.
84. *The Hindustan Times*, 27 August 1997.
85. Ibid., 30 September 1997.
86. Ibid., 17 October 1997.
87. Ibid., 18 October 1997.
88. Ibid., 18 November 1997.
89. Ibid.
90. Ibid., 26 September 1997.
91. Ibid., 27 April 1998.
92. Ibid.

93. Ibid., 8 May 1998.
94. Ibid., 8 March 1998.
95. Ibid., 2 September 1998.
96. Ibid., editorial, 5 September 1998.
97. *The Hindu*, editorial, 28 January 2008.
98. Vinod F. Khobragade, 'Ethnic Politics in Sri Lanka – Political Solution to Tamil Cause and Military Solution to LTTE', p. 26.
99. B. Muralidhar Reddy, 'The JVP Makes Its Move', *The Hindu*, 25 July 2006.
100. Ibid.
101. B. Muralidhar Reddy, 'Sri Lanka : Uncertainty asDe-merger Nears', in Ibid., 29 November 2006.

4

PEACE INITIATIVES AND CEASEFIRE AGREEMENT

Antecedents of Peace Initiatives: 1957 & 1965

Conflicts between any two people, cultures and countries are not unnatural or unusual. In fact, in today's context of competitive policies for limited natural resources and the tendency to maintain upper hand in control of such resources and relationships, conflicts are inbuilt. Hence, conflict resolution approach is a sustained way of endeavouring for enduring peace. But peace is not a constant phenomenon. It is a situation at a point of time and between a set of countries, often neighbours.[1] Peace building is a process over time and requires to be nurtured and sustaining, rather more deliberately. Trust or mistrust between countries or groups engaged or tend to engage, in conflict determines the state of global peace. If suspicion, friction and tension and the resulting conflict situation could be avoided, peace is more likely to be prevailed.[2] Further, such situation can be sustained only when certain deliberate initiatives and efforts are made by various stake holders. Failure to conflict resolution is a potential challenge to internal stability and occurs more in the underdeveloped regions of the world than elsewhere.

In Sri Lanka's case, the ethnic divide between the Tamils and the Sinhalese has widened after the independence of the country in 1948 and after decades of violent confrontations. In that also early years the political dominance of the Sinhala community in Ceylon was not seriously challenged, as the minority had usually avoided direct confrontations in favour of accommodations with the Sinhali political leaders who preserved their established privileged positions in economy and government service.[3] In the absence of an effective and genuine federal, democratic arrangement, no working solution to the crisis will ever be possible as has been amply demonstrated in island nation's case. The main problem with plural societies is the divergent way in which common political principles are approached, interpreted and acted upon. This often leads to contrary and contradictory perceptions about political processes and to inevitable clashes of interests.

The ethnicity related war in South Asian region is a common phenomenon particularly in Bangladesh, India, Pakistan and recently in more violence in Sri Lanka. It is a large scale violent incident entailing an organised and prolonged military engagement and confrontation between regular government forces and highly mobilised insurgent or militant groups. There is continuity in fighting : military attacks/ operations are extended over a considerable part of the country's territory. Importantly, the warring parties and their grievances and goals are solely defined in ethnic terms. Whereas the government represents the dominant majority ethnic group, civilians belonging to the minority ethnic community invariably constitute the insurgent or militant forces.[4] In the situation winning the war is the fundamental objective of the combatants and compromise is hard to negotiate so long as the asymmetry of power between the ethnic parties is not altered. In general, ethnicity has gained prominence in today's politics for two additional reasons. First the growth of sectarian political parties throughout the region has amplified and redirected ethnic issues to the political limelight. These parties have risen or have been resurrected by parochial interests, because of government's inadequacy or inability to remove ethnic grievances. These parties differ from national parties in that they have a narrow political base; represent the interests of only particular ethnic groups or segments thereof; and are dedicated to achieving political ends through violence. Second, the ethnic factor in South Asian Politics is sustained also by the international role of the regional countries.[5] For instance, the Pakhtoonistan movement in the NWFP has been inspired and sustained by successive Afghan governments and the Sri Lanka's Tamil secessionist movement received full support from the neighbouring Indian state Tamil Nadu.

In general, the separate cultural identities of the regions, far from losing social significance and becoming blurred have in fact reasserted their cultural and regional identities by politically mobilising themselves in order to confront the state system which has failed to recognise or protect their interests. The Sri Lankan Tamils have rejected the continued validity of national symbols and values and have redirected their allegiance to ethnic symbols and values in order to fight for greater influence within their societies.[6] The present position of Sri Lanka have been interpreted by some as a clash between two subnationalism, that of the dominant Sinhalese Buddhist elite and of the minority Tamil elite of the northern peninsula.[7] But more often it has been seen in political terms in which the Sinhalese have consistently sought to diminish the cultural and political silence of the Tamils in post-Independent Sri Lanka. Despite the fact that there was an apparent communal harmony during the British period in Ceylon, the seeds of the cleavage between the Sinhalese and the Tamils were laid in the colonial Sri Lanka. The first wave of discontent was felt by the minorities during the independence movement when the practice of communal representation, prevalent during the colonial administration, was abandoned and fearing the dominance of Sinhalese in the new system, the Tamils began to agitate for equal sharing of legislative and executive powers.[8] The volume of grievance formation increased in the post-Independence era of the island country.

Unlike India from the early years of administration, the Government of Sri Lanka, following the majoritarian principle decided to build the nation on the basis of religion (Buddhism) and language namely Sinhala. The decision at large, of Bandaranaike's government pertaining to language, education and settlement schemes affected the Tamil community both politically and economically. Apart from the official language policy and passing of the 'Sinhala Only' Act in 1956, the other important factor that intensified the Tamil fears of marginalisation and suppression was the 'land colonisation' of traditional homeland of the Tamils by Sinhalese population. As a result, the Bandaranaike's centrally sponsored settlement schemes were viewed with suspicion as efforts to alter the demographic composition of the eastern province, the traditional homeland of the Tamil population.

Although the first ethnocentric political party, the Tamil Congress was formed in 1944, due to divergence of approach on several issues, a split took place in the party after five years and in 1949, the Federal Party (FP) emerged that sought to unite the Tamil speaking peoples of the north and east. The party, despite the fact that it poorly performed in 1952 general election, gradually improved its position and from 1956 onward, the party had become a potential force and voice of the Tamils as well in Sri Lanka's ethnic politics. Ethno-politics and increasing Tamil militancy forced the government to respond and to initiate very conducive measures so that the political violence and terrorism would be eliminated from Sri Lankan politics.[9] The government of pro-Sinhala and anti-Tamil policies caused a chain reaction of violence between the two communities in sensitive areas throughout the island. In line the Federal Party held its annual convention in August 1956 at Trincomalee and had made the four demands and threatened to take direct-action by non-violent means if they were not met within a year. The demands included (i) replacement of the present pernicious constitution by a rational and democratic constitution based on the federal principle; (ii) parity of status for the Tamil language with the Sinhalese language; (iii) repeal of the existing citizenship laws which discriminated against the Indian estate Tamil population; and (iv) immediate cessation of colonising the traditional Tamil-speaking areas with Sinhalese people.[10]

In the background of the above demands made by the Federal party and the tension built up in the months that followed, the party was invited for negotiation by the Prime Minister and the agreement reached was a compromise settlement. The first initiative was taken on 27th July 1957, and known as the Bandaranaike-Chelvanayakam (B-C) Pact to solve the problems of language, power devolution, colonisation, education, etc. This pact had given Tamils a degree of regional autonomy including control of the land in their areas. Under the agreement the federal demand was accommodated with a scheme for the establishment of regional Councils for the various administrative districts or provinces in the island, including a single regional council for the northern province and two or more for the eastern. These councils would have powers delegated to them by Parliament in respect of a number of subjects. The language demand was made by the offer that Tamil would be recognised as the language of a national minority and that it would, without infringement of the official language, be made a language of administration in the northern and eastern provinces.[11] Likewise, on the question of colonisation, Bandaranaike conceded that his government would not utilise the instrument of colonisation to convert the majority Tamil-speaking population in the two provinces into a minority. The citizenship issue, it was agreed, would be resolved with Ceylon Workers' Congress (CWC) and Democratic Workers' Congress (DWC).

The agreement, however, was from the Federal party's point of view not a final solution but an adjustment. The pact was supposed to permit reasonable use of Tamil in the Northern and Eastern provinces and also for regional councils with powers in agriculture, education and selection of candidates for colonisation scheme.[12] But on account of the Sinhalese pressure and United National party's opposition, the demand of the regional council for Tamils could not be contended by the government on the plea that any attempt towards federalism will be vicious for the unity and integrity of Sri Lanka.[13] In 1958 succumbing to the pressure from militant Buddhists and the UNP Opposition, Bandaranaike abrogated the pact that he had with Chelvanayakam. Retreat from the pact resulted in the swing of Tamil opinion more firmly behind the Federalists. The Tamil demonstrations led to counter-riots and ultimately to the island-wide holocaust in 1958 and the declaration of emergency. In a desperate attempt for compromise, the Tamil Language Act was passed in 1958 which provided for the 'reasonable use' of Tamil in education, public service entrance examinations and administration in the Northern and Eastern provinces. It was passed in the absence of the Federal Party leaders who were in detention.

On issues related to ethnicity, Sri Lanka began to boil often and in early 1964, the Federal Party organised a 'Tamil only' campaign in which it appealed to the Tamil-speaking public to transact all their business with the state in Tamil language. The campaign had caused some problems for the administration. In mid-1964 the party also announced plans for a direct action, but before this could be organised, Bandaranaike's coalition government suffered parliamentary defeat and after the general election of March 1965, the UNP leader Dudley-Senanayake, was abliged to fall back on the Federal Party to form his national government. Thus the second initiative was made in 1965 by signing the Dudley Senanayake-Chelvanayakam Pact to provide language status, to establish district councils and to confer citizenship on the people of Indian origin. The two leaders met on 24th March 1965 and discussed in detail matters relating to some problems over which the Tamil-speaking people were concerned and Senanayake agreed that action would be taken by him to ensure a stable government. The provisions of this agreement were implemented, except for that dealing with district councils. The Prime Minister had a Bill prepared for this purpose but had to drop it in July 1968 when faced with a revolt of his backbenchers. Consequently, Tiruchelvam, a Federal Party MP and Minister in Senanayake's cabinet resigned from the ministry and the signed pact too collapsed with this. Thus, though well intentioned it was, it could not contribute much to harmonise the relations between the two communities.

The Thimpu Talks of 1985

In the background of earlier developments on the issue of devolution of power, the Thimpu talks of July 1985 was held between the representatives of the Sri Lankan government and those of six Tamil groups which included the moderate TULF and five extremist groups, namely, LTTE, TELD, EPRLF, EROS and PLOTE. The issue of power devolution was put in every enquiry commission, talks, and meetings like Presidential Commission to study and enquire on power devolution in 1979, Annexure C Proposal initiated by India and All Party Conference of Sri Lanka in 1983, Thimpu Talks initiated by India in 1985, 19 December Proposal from Indian government in 1986, Devolution Package of Sri Lankan government in 1995 etc, but all in vain.[14] Despite plenty of measures and efforts, even not a single effort, or any scheme from many, could bridge the difference between ethnically segregated people of the Sinhalese and the Tamil Communities whereas the Sinhalese government failed to compromise to devolve powers to the Tamils. However, the year of talk (1985) was a dramatic moment that caught even the international imagination and at least increased the pressure on Sri Lankan authorities in this regard.[15] India played a positive role in its preparations.

In the ethnic history of Sri Lanka, its riots of July 1983 was a watershed which cast a dark shadow on Indo-Sri Lanka relations and compelled the latter to help seek the island nation in solving the problem. On the one hand, it encouraged the Tamil population of Sri Lanka to support all the Tamil militant groups and instigated New Delhi to express grave concern about the holocaust on the other. After the riots, Narasimha Rao visited Sri Lanka and returned to India being acquainted with the prevailing situation and discussions with the Sri Lankan government. Although earlier to this after the riots of August 1977, Morarji Desai, the then Prime Minister of India, had sent his emissary S.A. Chidambaram to study the situation. Yet under Indira Gandhi, as the relations and understanding between the two countries had waned, the dispatch of a cabinet minister, although no surprise, was unwelcome.[16] This time one reason must be admitted was that the Jayawardene government was unable to face down India's relentless pressure because the former suffered from a crisis of legitimacy following the referendum of December 1982. Therefore, it was unable to mobilise the broad nationalist masses around it in a manner that is usually quite possible for regimes under external siege.[17] Indian and Eelamist guerilla pressure on the UNP government, willy-nilly prised upon some democratic space in the changed context.

After Narasimha Rao, on the initiative and efforts of Indira Gandhi, the then Prime Minister of India, Gopalaswamy Parthasarathy was sent to Sri Lanka as her envoy to bring about a solution of the ethnic issue in the country. During July 1983 anti-Tamil riots, the Tamil Nadu government of AIADMK came under severe pressure from Tamil people and the opposition party DMK to take up the Sri Lankan Tamils issue with the central government of India. To express solidarity with the Sri

Lankan Tamils, the parties of Tamil Nadu had been agitating and campaigned. Therefore, M.G. Ramchandran, the then Chief Minister of Tamil Nadu, had asked the Indian Prime Minister to take up the issue at the appropriate level highlighting that the arson, rioting and ruthless killing of Tamils were highly disturbing.[18] They also urged the Indian government to take proper step to save the innocent Tamils in Sri Lanka from the cruel attacks. The increasing pressure of Tamil Nadu made Indian government concerned about its domestic security perspectives, to national interest and unity and integrity of India.

The sustained efforts of Indian negotiator Parthasarathy had resulted in a short conceptual paper called 'Annexure C', jointly drawn up by India and Sri Lanka. It provided a broad framework within which details of the political solution were to be worked out. Their endeavours attempted to satisfy both the Sri Lankan government and the moderate TULF. There was a provision for the TULF to abandon their claim of independent state and instead they would get provincial council that could provide them a degree of autonomy. The concept paper along with others were to be considered in the All Party Conference (APC) and as a follow up J.R. Jayawardene, the President of Sri Lanka convened the first meeting of APC in January, 1984. But the APC, however, lost its all party character after the withdrawal of the major opposition party of Sri Lanka, the SLFP and the Mahajana Eksath Peramuna (MEP) from the conference. As a result, the President invited the religious organisations to participate in the deliberations. The last meeting of the APC was held in December 1984 and the proposals put forward by the Sri Lankan President fell far short of the proposals prepared by Indian envoy G. Parthasarathy. The President's proposal envisaged for coordination of the already existing District Development Councils and it did not mention about the delegation of powers to these bodies. The scheme was also opposed by the SLFP, Buddhist religious organisations and other prominent member of the ruling United National Party (UNP). Ultimately the APC's deliberations had ended in failure with varying interpretations by the Sri Lankan government and the TULF leadership.

However, the valuable outcome of the whole exercise was the acceptance by the leaders of India and Sri Lanka that there was no alternative to a political solution; military onslaught to quell Tamil militancy needed to be abandoned. It was also recognised that no final solution to the ethnic conflict could emerge without the agreement of the TULF and other militant groups. And for the first time with this perception the President of Sri Lanka consented to a meeting of his representatives face to face with Tamil militants at Thimpu, the capital of Bhutan, another South Asian state.[19] At the Thimpu talks, neither India nor Bhutan had any direct involvement; a peculiar situation arose when in the earlier All Party Conference, India played the delicate role of a broker or catalyst. The Thimpu meeting was organised to defuse the Sri Lankan internal ethnic conflict. Earlier to the talks at Thimpu, Rajiv Gandhi was the Prime Minister and Parthasarathy's role was assumed by the Foreign Secretary, Romesh Bhandari. The new Foreign Secretary held several parleys with the Sri Lankan authorities which resulted in a summit conference in New Delhi in June 1985 and paved the way for Thimpu talks. In the same month President Jayawardene met Rajiv Gandhi in New Delhi and held discussions over the Tamil problem in Sri Lanka. As a result, a workable compromise appeared to emerge on a political settlement of ethnic problem in Sri Lanka.

At Thimpu in July 1985, two rounds of talks were held between the representatives of Sri Lankan government and the moderate Tamil Party TULF and other five Tamil militant groups including the LTTE who were participating in it. In the first round, the Sri Lankan government delegation merely reiterated the proposals put forward before the aborted APC. The All Party Conference between 10 January 1984 and 21 December 1984 provided for district councils to come together through a referendum and form provincial councils: functional linkages between Provincial Councils was possible but there was no structural linkage. Realising the potentiality of the Tamil Eelam Movement (TEM), the United National Party's government of J.R. Jayawardene formulated the new scheme for devolution of powers in 1978 which was known as the District Development Council (DDC). It consisted of the elected members of the Parliamentary group and the executive committee. The District Development Councils were headed by the district ministers who were under the control of and responsible to the President of Sri Lanka. The district ministers had the authority directed by the President to reject the plan prepared by the DDC at local level. In this provision there were sufficient scope for disagreements between the District Ministers and the Tamil members of Parliament.[20] Consequently, the Tamil were obsessed with frustration and resentment. The DDC become an exercise in deception and had been puppets in the hands of the President. As already known about the proposals of Sri Lankan government, the scheme was not acceptable to the Tamil groups.

Thereafter the Tamil groups announced four cardinal principles as the basic minimum to solve the problems which were reiterated in

Thimpu talks: (i) recognition of the Tamils of Sri Lanka as a distinct identity; (ii) recognition of an identified Tamil homeland and the guarantee of its territorial integrity; (iii) based on the above, recognition of the inalienable right of self-determination of the Tamil nation; and (iv) recognition of the right to full citizenship and other fundamental democratic rights of all Tamils, who look upon the island as their country.[21] These principles too were not acceptable to the Sri Lankan delegation who argued that recognising the above principles was tantamount to conceding Eelam as leader of the Sri Lankan delegation. H.W. Jayawardene said in the opening statement at the second round of talks at Thimpu. 'The third principle of right of self-determination, insofar as it implies the right of secession from and out of the Democratic Socialist Republic of Sri Lanka and the right to create a separate State is totally unacceptable and in this form rejected.[22]

Even the second round of talks at Thimpu collapsed because the Tamil groups staged a walk-out in protest against the violation of the cessation of hostilities and alleged killing of Tamil civilians by the Sri Lankan army. The action of the Tamil groups and their advisers provoked New Delhi and the latter had ordered deportation of several militant leaders within forty-eight hours of the issue of order. Thus, the talks at Thimpu failed miserably. At the end, both sides claimed the intransience of the other led to the breakdown of the talks. To quote Kethesh Loganathan, who represented one of the militant groups at the time said that the Tamil organisations took the position that the burden of presenting a broadly acceptable formula lay with Colombo. The Tamil delegation, instead, subjected the Sri Lankan government delegation to a series of lectures on what constituted the ethic question and as to why the burden lay with Colombo to come out with a solution 'worthy of our consideration'.

However, the talks and deliberations at Thimpu were a major breakthrough for facilitating an accord since there the Tamil demand of Eelam was substituted by a north-east link; having eschewed the quest for Eelam they had indicated willingness to consider a viable, reasonable alternative, and the alternative had emerged. Moreover, their participation in discussions demonstrated that the groups were turning to a solution short of Eelam, and searching for greater autonomy.[23] But it was not the end but start of the residual bitter conflict to resolve the eastern province issue.[24] Thereafter, once again, the ethnic disturbances began to raise its ugly heads which resulted in civilian killings, village burned and other violent activities between the ethnic communities. As a result, the government established new security camps, their homeguard scheme in order to maintain law and order in the eastern region. There were developments after Thimpu talks had hardened attitudes on both sides. In later years, the Sinhala Tamil perceptions conflicted but even in the situation the northeast linkage appeared the one and only way to end further suffering and loss of life on both sides. Even in post-Thimpu periods consultations between the two governments to solve the north-east linkage issue continued which ultimately cleared the desks for signing a peace accord in July 1987, which was considered by many to be the major breakthrough in their relations, from the bilateral, regional and global points of view.

Indo-Sri Lanka Accord of 1987

As a result of the discussions and deliberations between the Sri Lankan government and Indian authorities in post-Thimpu period, an agreement between the two governments was signed namely, the Indo-Sri Lanka Accord, on 29th July 1987. Although the single issue of north-east linkage was left to solve, the ongoing confrontations between the two communities themselves and the government security forces alike witnessed a further deteriorating situation in the island nation. After Thimpu followed the Chidambaram mission in 1986 and government – TULF talks; the Chidambaram proposals resolved virtually all issues concerning the substance of the devolution but left unresolved the issue of the unit of devolution. In December 1986 Chidambaram and Natwar Singh were sent to Sri Lanka to concentrate on the unit but in a later plan the structural linkage was substituted by a common council in which there would be one chief minister and the eastern province was given weightage to obviate northern domination. A year later, the east could decide through a referendum whether they desired linkage or not. However, the developments that took place in the first half of the year had necessitated the accord.[25] In early 1987, retaliating an increasingly bloody insurgent movement Operation Liberation was launched by the Sri Lankan security forces against LTTE strongholds in Jaffna Peninsula, involving nearly four thousand troops, supported by helicopter gunships as well as ground attack aircraft. In June 1987 the Sri Lankan Army laid siege to the town of Jaffna. As civilian casualties grew, calls grew within India to intervene in what was increasingly seen in the Indian and Tamil media as a developing humanitarian crisis, especially with reports of use of aerial support against rebel positions in civilian areas.

In response to Sri Lankan actions in Jaffna and in surrounding areas and with the failure of the naval mission, the decision was made by the

Indian government to mount an airdrop of relief supplies in support of rebel forces over the besieged city of Jaffna. On 4 June 1987, in a blatant show of force, the Indian Air Force mounted Operation Poomalai in broad daylight. Five An-32s under fighter cover flew over Jaffna to airdrop 25 tons of supplies, all the time keeping well within the range of Sri Lankan radar coverage. At the same time, the Sri Lankan Ambassador to New Delhi was also summoned to the foreign office and was informed by the Minister for External Affairs K. Natwar Singh about the ongoing operation. The ultimate aim of the operation was both to demonstrate the credibility of the Indian option of active intervention to Sri Lankan government, as a symbolic act of support for the Tamil rebels as well as to preserve Rajiv Gandhi's credibility. Faced with the possibility of an active Indian intervention and while facing an increasingly war-like situation at home, the Sri Lankan President J.R. Jayawardene offered to hold talks with the Rajiv Gandhi government on future moves.[26] Earlier to this, in the growing involvement of Pakistani and Israeli advisors, it was necessary for Indian to mount a show of force.[27] As a result, the siege of Jaffna was soon lifted.

India had, under Indira Gandhi[28] and later under Rajiv Gandhi provided support to Tamil interests from the very conception of the secessionist movement. This included providing sanctuary to the separatists, as well as supporting the operation training camps for Tamil guerillas in Tamil Nadu of which the LTTE emerged as the strongest force. This was both as a result of a large Tamil community in South India as well as India's regional security and interests which attempted to reduce the scope of foreign intervention, especially those linked to the United States, Pakistan and China. To this end, the Indira Gandhi Government sought to make it clear to the Sri Lankan President, Jayawardene that armed intervention in support of the Tamil movement was an option India would consider if any diplomatic solutions should fail.[29] In fact, Mrs. Gandhi saw in the ethnic crises a golden opportunity to change into a direction she wanted, the Sri Lankan government's pro-Western foreign policy. Also India wanted to ascertain her position of regional security in the South Asian region. Indira Gandhi, in particular, was of the view that United States was engaged in a strategic action designed to sandwich India between China, on the one side, and the smaller pro-Western States of Pakistan, Sri Lanka, and Bangladesh, on the other side.[30] India is the only neighbour of Sri Lanka, separated by the Palk Strait; both nations occupy a strategic position in South Asia and have sought to build a common security umbrella in the Indian Ocean.

However, India desired and did all these but not at the cost of Sri Lankan interests. Mrs. Gandhi while keeping in consideration the regional and global strategic design also declared that India stood for the unity and territorial integrity of Sri Lanka. On 5 August 1983, she took the opportunity of bringing on record before the Lok Sabha..... that the other countries appreciated India's position in respect of the situation in Sri Lanka and acknowledged India's special interest in the whole matter.[31] Not surprising was to in this context that during the height of the ethnic violence in Sri Lanka, the Heads of a large number of foreign missions in New Delhi were called to Foreign Office and asked to tell their respective governments to keep their hands off Sri Lanka.[32] Although the Sri Lankan government denied the fact, it was done by New Delhi as a reaction to Sri Lanka's request for military assistance from the United States, Britain, Pakistan and Bangladesh. By the time President Jayawardene had accepted India's good office but saw no useful role for India until TULF gave up its secessionist demands and thus Colombo now began to give second thoughts on India's role in the Sri Lankan ethnic crisis.

Strategic considerations apart neither before the signing of the peace accord in July 1987 nor thereafter India linked military option to the ethnic crisis and continued its efforts to find a political solution to the issue. Earlier to the agreement, it sent a team to Sri Lanka in May 1986, headed by minister P. Chidambaram whose talks with the Sri Lankan government paved the way for two round of talks in August that year between the TULF and the UNP government. From these two rounds of substantial talks emerged the proposals for the setting up of provincial councils. These proposals also provided for the devolution of power from the centre. President Jayawardene convened a Political Parties Conference (PPC) on 25 June 1986 to discuss the above proposals and sent copies to the Government of India with slight modifications as well as to the Tamil militant groups. All other parties except the TULF participated and welcomed the proposals.[33] Again in mid December an Indian delegation led by Chidambaram and minister of state Natwar Singh visited Colombo and its talks with the UNP ministers evolved a new proposal which came to be known as December 19 proposals. The Sri Lankan President personally supported the proposal; it however, faced some reservations from the Sri Lankan government which halted India to move further in its mediatory efforts. It followed the Colombo's punitive action to teach Sri Lankan Tamils a lesson and as a result direct Indian intervention took place in the name of humanity which ultimately compelled Sri Lanka to agree for the peace accord.

The Indo-Sri Lanka Accord of 29 July 1987 was signed attaching utmost importance to nurturing, intensifying and strengthening the traditional friendship of Sri Lanka and India, and acknowledging the imperative need of resolving the ethnic problem of Sri Lanka, and the consequent violence, and for the safety, well-being and prosperity of people belonging to all communities in Sri Lanka.[34] It contained Articles/ Clauses 1.1 to 1.5, 2.1 to 2.18 and Article 3 except the exchange of letters between the President of Sri Lanka and the Prime Minister of India which also formed an important part of the accord. It has two parts and the first dealt with India's commitment to uphold Sri Lanka's sovereignty and territorial integrity on the condition that Colombo would agree to grant a reasonable amount of autonomy to the Tamils to their satisfaction. The second part of the agreement included the matters regarding Sri Lanka's promise to disallow any extra-regional power to involve in the affairs which had either a known or a potential intention to harm India's security interests in the region. Most importantly the accord was signed between the Governments of Sri Lanka and India, with the Tamil Tigers and other Tamil militant groups having no role in the signing of the agreement. It, and the other political causes gained prominence and consequently the Liberation Tigers of Tamil Eelam (LTTE) had disapproved the Indo-Sri Lanka Accord.

The rejection of the peace accord by the LTTE had cast a long dark shadow over the future of the agreement. As the Indian Peace-keeping Forces (IPKF) landed on the soil of the island nation, as per terms of the peace accord, and the LTTE refused to surrender their arms and ammunition, a direct fight between them became imminent and soon in October 1987 the fight broke out. The confrontation between the IPKF and the LTTE cadres continued unabated till the return of the former to India in March 1990. In the straight fighting they both caused heavy loss of life and arms as well but the LTTE, in particular, became very poor in man power, fund, and armaments. But when we consider the provisions and the Letters of Exchange which accompanied the 1987 agreement, we are confronted by the familiar horns of the security dilemma. The letters represented a big victory for India and a significant enhancement of its prestige and power as the custodian of the security in South Asia. By the same time, it also represented a loss of both power and esteem to Sri Lanka, a small state which had since independence in 1948, pursued an active role in international affairs.[35] The most significant about the Indo-Sri Lanka agreement was the manner in which, by one stroke of the pen as it were, Sri Lanka was squarely brought into the

Indian security fold under its terms whereas no commitment impinging on security had existed on paper in the dyadic relationship before.[36] Thus, there are strong grounds for asserting that India's main objective in signing the agreement was strategic as Prabakaran himself accepted that the Indo-Sri Lanka accord was to prevent involvement of outside forces in Sri Lanka, and tackling the Tamil problem was only a by-product.

After signing the peace accord both the signatories-Rajiv Gandhi and J.R. Jayawardene were bound to explain to the nation the situations that compelled them to write down the terms of the agreement. Sending IPKF on the request of Sri Lankan government was a major issue for both the signatories that needed several clarifications. India's commitment to underwrite and guarantee the implementation of the agreement had been contained in Article 2.14. Article 1.16 (c) had further stated in general terms that if the Government of Sri Lanka requested military assistance from the Government of India for the implementation of the proposals made therein, such assistance would be given by the Government of India when requested. The Indian Prime Minister Rajiv Gandhi explaining presence of the IPKF in Sri Lanka told the Indian Parliament on 31 July 1987, 'President Jayawardene explained that because of the deteriorating situation or as a result of disturbances in the south and the increasing demands that this puts on the Sri Lanka security forces, his Government would need assistance to implement the Indo-Sri Lanka Agreement for ending the ethnic crisis. For this purpose, the Government of Sri Lanka made a formal request for appropriate Indian military assistance to ensure the cessation of hostilities and surrender of arms in the Jaffna Peninsula, and if required, in the eastern province.[37] Hence, in response to this formal request and in terms of our obligations under the just signed agreement, units of the Armed Forces of India landed in Jaffna Peninsula.' But even Rajiv Gandhi's evaluation of the agreement changed very soon and he adopted a two-track approach. In a public meeting in Madras on 2 August 1987, for instance, he declared, 'The Agreement secures everything that the Sri Lanka Tamils had demanded short of breaking Sri Lanka's unity. In fact it goes well beyond the initial demands of the Sri Lanka Tamils. Under the Agreement approximately one-third of Sri Lanka's territory will be made into a single province where the Tamils will have a clear majority. They will have regional autonomy comparable to state governments in India.'[38] He also claimed that now the Tamils in Sri Lanka will continue to live as they have lived in Sri Lanka for hundreds of years as honoured and respected citizens enjoying all the political and civic rights.

After signing the Agreement, Sri Lankan President Jayawardene faced more delicate position and had a different standpoint to explain the nation. After a week of the peace accord he said to the nation keeping in view the presence of the IPKF and devolution issue, 'But this is purely temporary, not forever. Temporary until the Eastern Province by a referendum which I will have to nominate within one year of the election of the Provincial Council, by a referendum and a single majority vote to decide whether they should continue the joinder or they separate. I have no fear of the result of the referendum because all of us can work against the joinder and I intend to ask all those who are against a joinder to come with me and work in the Eastern Province that the joinder should not be made permanent.[39] By this declaration President Jayawardene intended to reassure opinion in the Sinhala south especially in the JVP movement which had taken up arms to denounce the accord, The appeal, however, did not reassure Sinhala opinion about the transient nature of the merger especially since the LTTE terrorism continued to be directed against Sinhala and Muslim inhabitant of the eastern province. Roughly in the eastern province, all the three communities are in equal proportion. As the time went on, the guarantees and undertakings given by Sri Lanka in the Letters of Exchange appeared to have lost much of their force in the context of India's own inability to enforce a ceasefire and bring about a surrender of arms by militant groups.

As a follow up of the Indo-Sri Lanka Accord, the next land marking move of the Sri Lankan government was its passing of the 13th Amendment to the constitution and the Provincial Council Act No. 42 to devolve power for the participation of the Tamil people into the democratic process. The said amendment enabled a scheme of provincial councils, a concept that was anathema to the Sri Lankan state three decades ago, Sri Lanka had the real prospect of converting its political structure into a federal one.[40] According to the amendment three bodies : Provincial Governor, Board of Ministers with Chief Minister, and the Provincial Councils were created to devolve the powers at the Tamil level. Provincial governor was head of all these bodies and was held responsible to the President of Sri Lanka. The Board of Ministers was to aid and advice the governor in the exercise of his powers. But he was not bound to the advice given to him. The Provincial Councils were given with very meager and few of the powers barring the important powers like control of planning, provincial budget, police and public law and order disposition of state land and more importantly the higher education.[41] With the enactment, the Government of Jayawardene hoped that these would fulfil the aspirations of the Tamil people.

The Tamils of Sri Lanka, in general, including the Tamil United Liberation Front (TULF), a political wing of the Tamils, were opposed to the 13th Amendment to the constitution of Sri Lanka and they held all these powers as biased and prejudicial. They did not consider these powers as real because almost all the powers were rested with the Sinhalese. The Tamils were also critical of the amendment as the Provincial Council Act refused the constitutional recognition to the North Eastern province as areas of historical habitation of the Tamils and could not satisfy the recognition of political reality of the Tamil Nation.[42] This 13th amendment also empowers the President to declare an emergency, in any part of the country, for a wide range of reasons. In the past, the Presidents of Sri Lanka have used the emergency powers and the Tamils feared that the 13th amendment would make Tamil autonomy permanently subject to a Sinhalese veto.

However, all these apart, the 13th amendment to the Constitution of Sri Lanka is useful for ever. In November 2005, when Mahinda Rajapaksa became the President of Sri Lanka in mid 2006, he established an All Parties Representative Conference (APRC) to forge a consensus among all parties on a political solution acceptable to all for the resolution of the three-decade-old ethnic conflict. Although the Committee suffered a setback when UNP, the main opposition party withdrew from it and JVP walked out, the APRC, in its four-page interim report titled, 'Action to be taken by the President to fully implement Relevant Provisions of the present Counstitution as a Prelude to the APRC Proposals', the Committee recommended full and faithful implementation of the 13th Amendment to the Constitution, holding of provincial council election in the east and establishment of an interim provincial council in the north.[43] On the northern and eastern provinces, the APRC has recommended special arrangements necessary to permit maximum devolution of power to the Northern and Eastern Provinces under the 13th Amendment. Among other steps, it envisaged province as the unit of power and devolution of power between the centre and the provinces as a solution to the ethnic crisis.[44] It also expressed the view that for a variety of reasons successive governments have not been able to implement various provisions of the 13th Amendment.

In fact, the Indo-Sri Lanka peace accord was signed to resolve the prolonged ethnic civil war. But, the LTTE had not accepted the agreement and under the provisions of the accord, the IPKF was invited by the Sri Lankan government to tackle Tamil militancy. But India could not resolve the issue and had to retreat from Sri Lanka in March 1990. In this mission India had to face very severe opposition from the LTTE. As a result and after the assassination of Rajiv Gandhi in May 1991 by a LTTE suicide bomber, India formulated hands-off policy towards Sri Lanka. Since then, India has remained aloof from any direct intervention in the Sri Lankan internal affairs leaving the entire development on their fate.[45] Although both India and Sri Lanka implemented the accord with political compromises due to internal political compulsions, yet these made them forget three cardinal requirements – openness, transparency, and inclusiveness for any public policy to succeed. These were markedly absent in both India and Sri Lanka from conception to execution of the accord. As a result, the accord conceived to bridge the huge ethnic divide between the Tamils and the Sinhalese actually aggravated the atmosphere of suspicion and distrust about India's intentions among many Sinhalese. They had earlier seen India giving refuge and training to Tamil militants[46] India had laid great emphasis on its regional security interests in Sri Lanka in the accord. Many Sri Lankans, including the LTTE, saw the arrival of Indian troops as a move to make the Indian writ run on the island. While this hurt the national pride of the sections of Sri Lankans, it provided an excuse for the LTTE to denounce the accord as an instrument of Indian hegemony.[47] Thus, the reason why the India-Sri Lanka Agreement did not deliver fully was simple : political expediency took over both the countries.

After a decade of its signing the Indo-Sri Lanka Accord remained in active consideration and the people in general were hopeful about its provisions that were able to provide Sri Lanka peace and prosperity together. Douglas Devanand, leader of the Eelam People's Democratic Party (EPDP) said in July 1997 that both the Sri Lankan government and the LTTE have lost the historical opportunity to work out a durable peace which outlined solution to the vexed ethnic conflict within the framework of the united Sri Lanka.[48] It followed the statement of Ronnie De Mel, leader of the opposition UNP in the Sri Lankan Parliamentary Select Committee (PSC), who praised the accord and said that it had given the war torn and economically ruined country a framework for peace and development. He referred to the 13th constitutional amendment and maintained that if it had been allowed to work, Sri Lanka would be having peace then. The leader of the opposition also blamed the Sri

Lankan Freedom Party (SLFP) for the collapse of the accord and non-implementation of the 13th amendment in its letter and spirit.[49] He laid stress on the need for talks with the LTTE and a genuinely open discussion with all communities so that any set-up brought about would have the support of every section of the country. Apart from it, several defence analysts of India including Major General Ashok K. Mehta, and former Foreign Secretary J.N. Dixit felt that the ground situation in the island nation was no different from what it had been when the IPKF left Sri Lanka. They held the view that there was no possibility for peace in Sri Lanka without bringing the LTTE to the negotiating table.[50] At best the LTTE can be marginalised but can not be eliminated. Decades after its signing the 1987 accord, India and Sri Lanka had kept its relevance alive and in January 2009 when the Sri Lankan forces was to win the final war with the LTTE, the Foreign Minister of Sri Lanka Rohitha Bogallagama had said that the decisive victory against the LTTE will offer a window of opportunity to fully implement the 1987 India Sri Lanka agreement.[51] On the occasion, the Sri Lankan minister also told the visiting Indian Foreign Secretary Shiv Shankar Menon that Colombo perceived the accord as the key to a political solution to the ethnic conflict.

The Ceasefire Agreement of 2002

Like the earlier governments of Sri Lanka, the regime that took over in December 2001 had the real challenge as how to resume negotiations with the LTTE given president Kumaratunga's unequivocal position that military action was the only solution. Still hopeful about the talks, the new government as a gesture of goodwill and with a view to initiate peace talks with the LTTE, the government had announced a month's ceasefire with effect from 24 December which was reciprocated by the LTTE the very next day. In the recent past, the Sri Lankan security forces had mounted significant pressure to compel the LTTE for talks as the latter was at loss of men and arms as well. After the end of a month, the government extended the ceasefire by another month. The confidence building measure and the initial understanding that both had shown resulted in the signing of a long-term agreement on 22 February 2002 between the Sri Lankan government and the LTTE. The Cease Fire Agreement (CFA) was brokered by the Norwegian government and was considered as an essential step towards finding a negotiated political solution to the ongoing ethnic conflict.[52] The basic objective behind the agreement was not a solution but to be a peace interval to move towards a negotiated settlement by pushing the Tigers to come under the security of the international community and to the negotiating table in the presence of international facilitators.[53] The Sri Lankan government had signed the agreement with the LTTE to resolve ethnic war and to safeguard territorial integrity of the country.

According to the Preamble of the Cease Fire Agreement (CFA), the Government of Sri Lanka and the LTTE had recognised the importance of bringing an end to the hostilities and improving the living conditions for all inhabitants affected by the conflict. Bringing an end to the hostilities was also seen by the Parties as a means of establishing a positive atmosphere in which further steps towards a lasting peace could be taken. The Parties further recognised that groups that were not directly party to the conflict were also suffering the consequences of it. This was particularly the case as regards the Muslim population. Therefore, the provisions of this Agreement regarding the security of the civilians and their property would apply to all inhabitants. In the context, the Parties have agreed to enter into a ceasefire, refrain from conduct that could undermine the good intentions or violate the spirit of this Agreement and implement confidence building measures.

The signed Cease Fire Agreement (CFA) contained 4 Articles with several clauses apart from Annextures A and B. Article 1 of the Agreement mentioned modalities of a ceasefire from clauses 1.1 to 1.13. This part of the Agreement has been divided into three sub-parts known as Military operation, separation of forces and freedom of movement. Article 1.2 clearly states that neither Party shall engage in any offensive military operation. This requires to total cessation of all military action but at the same time Article 1.3 envisages that the Sri Lankan armed forces shall continue to perform their legitimate task of safeguarding the sovereignty and territorial integrity of Sri Lanka without engaging in offensive operations against the LTTE. Under the Monitoring Mission scheme (Article 3) and clause 1.6 of the Article 1, the Parties shall provide information to the Sri Lanka Monitoring Mission (SLMM) regarding defence localities in all areas of contention and the monitoring mission shall assist the Parties in drawing up demarcation lines. In Article 2 of the Agreement which extends from 2.1 to 2.13 several confidence-building measures to restore normalcy have been provided with the aim of normal public life to all inhabitants of Sri Lanka. In pursuance of the Article 2.1, the Parties shall as per international law abstain from hostile acts against the civilian population, including such acts as torture, intimidation, abduction, extortion and harassment. The Parties shall also refrain from engaging in activities or propagating ideas that could offend cultural or religious sensitivities (Article 2.2) and places of worship – temples, churches, mosques and other holy sites currently held by the forces of either of the Parties shall be vacated and made accessible to the public.

Both the Government of Sri Lanka and the Liberation Tigers of Tamil Eelam have, with consent, agreed to set up an international monitoring mission in Article 3 of the Agreement which has its detailing from 3.1 to 3.13 with a view to enquire into any instance of the violation of the terms and conditions of the accord. They shall fully cooperate to rectify any matter of conflict caused by their respective sides. The mission shall conduct international verification through on-site monitoring of the fulfilment of the commitments entered into this Agreement. The name of the monitoring mission shall be the Sri Lanka Monitoring Mission (Article 3.1) and subject to acceptance by the Parties. The Royal Norwegian Government shall appoint the Head of the SLMM who shall be the final authority regarding interpretation of this Agreement (Article 3.2). Apart from the SLMM the provision for local monitoring committee was made which shall be established in Jaffna, Mannar, Vavuniya, Trincomalee, Batticaloa and Amparai. Each committee as per Article 3.7 of the Agreement shall consist of 5 members, two appointed by the Government of Sri Lanka, two by the LTTE and one international monitor appointed by Head of the Mission. The international monitor shall chair the committee. The Government of Sri Lanka and the LTTE appointees may be selected from among the retired judges, public servants, religious leaders or similar leading citizens. As per Article 3.11 of the Agreement it shall be the responsibility of the SLMM to take immediate action on any complaints made by either Party to the Agreement, and to enquire into and assist the Parties in the settlement of any dispute that might arise in connection with such complaints.

Likewise Article 4 of the Agreement consists of clauses 4.1 to 4.4 and relates matters – entry into force, amendments and termination of the Agreement. According to Article 4.1 of the accord, each Party shall notify their consent to be bound by this Agreement through a letter to the Norwegian Minister of Foreign Affairs signed by Prime Minister Ranil Wickremesinghe on behalf of the Government of Sri Lanka, and by leader Velupillai Prabakaran on behalf of the LTTE, respectively. It may be amended (Article 4.3) and modified by mutual agreement of both Parties and such amendments shall be notified in writing to the Royal Norwegian Government (RNG). There was also a provision for its termination and the Agreement shall remain in force until notice of termination is given by either Party to the RNG. Such notice shall be given fourteen days in advance of the effective date of termination (Article 4.4). Annexure-A ensures the flow of non-military goods to and from LTTE dominated areas of the Northern and Eastern Province but it will not include non-military arms/ammunition, explosives, remote control devices barbed wire, binoculars/telescopes, compasses, and penlight batteries. While Annexure B ensures an exhaustive list of check posts as agreed in Article 2.7 of the Agreement numbering 17 and included Mandur, Paddirupur, Mamunai Ferry Point, Vanvunateevu, Black Bridge, Kiran Bridge, Valachenai, Muttur, etc.

There are always elements in every society that view the agenda of peaceniks with suspicion. The rights and wrongs of it apart, Sri Lanka could not be expected to be the exception especially given its record of nearly three decades of ethnic disharmony.[54] As such there were several criticisms against the ceasefire agreement and most of them pertained to its structure, provision, and mechanisms. The main charge levelled against the architect of the accord, Ranil Wickremesinghe, was that through it legitimised 'defacto Eelam' and paved the way for a possible dismemberment of Sri Lanka at some stage. Apart from the politically motivated attacks against Wickremesinghe and his approach to the peace process, some of the serious reservations about the agreement had emanated from neutral quarters. These broadly include legitimisation of the LTTE's claim as 'sole representative' of the Tamil people at the expense of other groups that renounced violence and took to parliamentary politics.[55] Besides, the accord sought to freeze the military balance between the Government and the LTTE as of February 2002 but it failed to envisage any mechanism to ensure that non-state actors such as the LTTE do not take advantage of the ceasefire period to indulge in the strategy to rebuild itself.

The Norway-brokered 2002 ceasefire agreement also came as a huge disappointment to the Muslims. Regarding them it was mentioned as a footnote in the CFA that the 'Parties further recognise that group that are not directly party to the conflict are also suffering the consequences of it. This is particularly the case as regards the Muslim population.'[56] As a result within weeks of the CFA, the leader of the Sri Lanka Muslim Congress (SLMC) Rauf Hakeem made it a point to reach out to LTTE leader Velupillai Prabakaran and even signed a significant agreement, promising the right of return for the Muslims to LTTE – controlled areas, an end to LTTE extortion of Muslim businesses in the East and access for Muslims to their lands in LTTE – controlled areas. The International Crisis Group (ICG), a multi-national NGO engaged in reporting on conflict situations, has also, in its report, noted; Muslims have never resorted to armed rebellion to assert their political position, although some have worked with the security forces, and a few were members of early Tamil militant groups. Fears of an armed movement emerged among the Muslims, perhaps with a façade of Islamist ideology, have been present since the early 1990s, but most have remained committed to channelling their frustrations through the political processes and negotiating with the government and Tamil militants of different times.[57] The assessment of the ICG was shared by several independent observers that only a full political settlement of the conflict can allow historical injustices against the Muslims to be addressed and begin a process of reconciliating.

However, in the given circumstances under which the Wickremesinghe Government initiated the ceasefire, it was not possible at that time to have incorporated all these safeguards and address all the apparent inherent weaknesses in the document. The agreement became a reality when Sri Lanka was reeling under a serious economic crisis and the morale of its armed forces had touched the nadir. In fact, the Tiger would not have agreed to any provision that challenged their supremacy and introduced notions such as human rights, democracy, and pluralism. At least without doubt, the ceasefire had resuscitated the economy on oxygen. Prior to 2002, Sri Lanka had registered a negative growth and in 2006 – 2007, the growth was hovering between 7 and 8 per cent. Economists believe the credit entirely goes to the accord. Tourism thrived and people moved from the south to the north and the other way round for the first time in two decades. But to some extent, the problem was not with the agreement but with the ruthless nature of the Tigers' leadership, and the refusal of Prabakaran to negotiate on anything other than Eelam. It was not about the LTTE alone. As a further step the Government should consider re-crafting it in a way that ensures the benefits to the people because easing restrictions on the people and their livelihood is more urgent at that time than ever before.

From the discussions so far it was clear that while, on the one hand, there are inherent contradictions in Sinhalese and Tamil perceptions of ethnicity and nation building, there have been constant efforts too to resolve the conflict through negotiations and political compromises. The CFA of February 2002 was a part of it and it was also supposed to include negotiations. As a part of its goodwill agenda in early September, the government lifted the ban on the Tigers and within a few days the first session of peace talks started (16-18 September) in Thailand with Norwegian facilitation. Perhaps due to the very weakness of the political situation in New Delhi both Sri Lanka and the LTTE were able to get the help of the perennial peace keeping nation of Norway's good help in facilitating and even mediating a peace, making process. Sri Lanka was able to achieve this inspite of a vociferous negative reaction in India in certain quarters to the involvement of western peacemaker within South Asia.[58] These forces were fearful that the peace made in Sri Lanka with the help of the West would end up leading to a just and potentially fissiparous solution in Kashmir. In the first round of talks it was decided that three more rounds would take place namely, between 31 October 2002 and 3 November in Thailand itself, between 2 and 5 December 2002 in Norway and between 6 and 9 January 2003 in Thailand. Other sessions were also held 7 and 8 February 2003 in Germany and the last or sixth session 18-21 March 2003 in Japan. Thus all about 6th sessions of negotiations under the CFA was held between the Parties concerned.

After six rounds of talks in a period of just over a year, the LTTE withdrew from negotiations in April 2003, claiming 'certain critical issues relating to the ongoing peace process.' In the same year, the LTTE proposed an Interim Self Governing Authority (ISGA). This move was welcomed by the international community, but rejected by the Sri Lankan President. In course of the peace talks, the organisation genuinely felt that earlier both Presidents Premadasa and Kumaratunga were not serious in negotiations, but the same could scarcely be said of Prime Minister Wickremesinghe, who was widely believed and certainly so by the Sri Lankan electorate when it voted largely on this issue in April 2004-to be bending over backwards to appease the LTTE. Although the LTTE refused to return to formal negotiations, but they did engage in informal discussions following the December 2004 tsunami regarding a mechanism to deal with aid.

The Ceasefire Agreement of February 2002 was signed for a period of six years and it was widely believed that the LTTE took advantage of this period to attack its Tamil opponents and in acquiring sophisticated arms to strengthen itself. The former militant groups such as the EPDP, PLOTE and the Perumal wing of the EPRLF were almost eliminated by the LTTE. The TULF was now very much under LTTE control and its last independent leader Neelan Tiruchelvam had been killed by the LTTE in 1999. Later in 2005, the LTTE killed Lakshman Kadirgamar, the Foreign Minister of Sri Lanka. The LTTE also used the opportunity of prolonged peace to build its warfare including airforce. It procured advanced arms to fight against government reviving civil war in a more powerful way and even started air attacks. At such juncture, negotiator Norway could not do anything positive in resolving civil war and, therefore, Norway was blamed and criticised for being biased and prejudiced and unnecessarily interfering with government activities.

Particularly, after the withdrawal of the LTTE from the peace negotiation talks in April 2003, the CFA continued for both the Parties as a mere piece of paper and it was witnessed by the assassinations, bomb blasts and huge violations of the accord. In the circumstances the future of the Sri Lanka Monitoring Mission was not bright when ceasefire violations have become the norm. In a candid interaction with foreign correspondents based in Colombo, the SLMM conceded it was not just equipped to deal with the fast deteriorating situation and unless the trend was reversed, the mission members might as well pack their bags and then leave. Which Colombo had indirectly charged them with aiding terrorists. But in the given situation neither the Sri Lankan government nor the LTTE, who keep accusing each other of observing it more in the breach, wanted to call it quits. Both had the choice to walk out after giving 14 days advance notice, yet they were not doing so only for fear of adverse international reactions. According to a statistics of the LTTE Peace Secretariat Website so far about 1,627 have been killed, 2,52,000 displaced, 697 disappeared, and 300,000 evicted since February 22, 2002, the day the agreement came into vogue. As regards to violations the Sri Lanka Monitoring Mission had indicated that from February 22, 2002 to December 31, 2006, the Sri Lankan government had violated 346 times while the LTTE 3,827 times. In other words, the ceasefire was breached 4,173 times or 2.5 violations per day.

The ongoing situation aggravated and worsened further after the killing of Lakshman Kadirgamar, the Foreign Minister of Sri Lanka in August 2005 and coming of Mahinda Rajapaksa as the new President of Sri Lanka by the end of the year. Although the military and the LTTE were engaged in an undeclared war for over a year, the cycle of bloodshed that began with the assassination of foreign minister by suspected LTTE cadres had shown no sign of halting. Apart from this all the killings in Colombo resulted from suicide missions, a dubious technique perfected by the LTTE.[59] But the entire environment began to change when Mahinda Rajapaksa took over as the President of Sri Lanka in November 2005. Not only on devolution of power and the continuing ethnic conflict, but on the Norwegian-brokered Cease Fire Agreement (CFA) of February 2002, the new ruler had a different approach and strategy to deal with. To ensure its success, the Sri Lankan government had chosen to silence dissident voices. Many of those demanding another approach or criticising government actions or policies were accused of being closet LTTE supporters or otherwise sympathetic to terrorists.

Turn and Twists in CFA

Troubles for the CFA in the island nation itself were endless. Since the days of its signing it had remained in controversy and further became an issue in the Presidential election of Sri Lanka in November 2005. Abrogation of the ceasefire agreement and termination of Norway's services as facilitator were two of the main planks of Mahinda Rajapaksa's Presidential election campaign. Rajapaksa, in course of his election campaign, vigorously advocated easing out Norway and disbanding the Sri Lanka Monitoring Mission (SLMM) in view of his belief that both have only helped the LTTE consolidate. Therefore, the CFA of 2002 between the Sri Lankan government and the LTTE virtually broke down with Rajapaksa's victory in Presidential election and soon the new incumbent avowed to step up military campaign against Tamil Tigers. The new government did not miss any opportunity to complain how the Tigers have used the ceasefire to strengthen themselves militarily and politically and subvert the authority of Colombo. Earlier the LTTE had boycotted the November 2005 Presidential election. While the organisation claimed that the people under its control were free to vote, it was alleged that they used threats to prevent the population from voting. Months thereafter, the LTTE stepped-up offensive against the Sri Lankan authorities and it made an attempt on the life of Defence Secretary Gotabaya Rajapaksa, who was a retired military officer of the Sri Lankan Army and brother of the President, on 1 December 2006 in the heart of Colombo.

The incident of attack followed an immediate response of the Government and within hours of the attempt, the President presided over a cabinet meeting to consider a possible ban on the LTTE. Having failed in getting the cabinet nod, the meeting was postponed but Rajapaksa tried to re-define the term terrorism by borrowing some provisions of the dreaded Prevention of Terrorism Act (PTA) which was suspended after the 2002 CFA. On the same night, the President addressed to the nation and referred to the PTA and said that it was being re-introduced to deal with the threat from the LTTE. He was equally apprehensive about the role of NGOs and wanted to tighten the noose around the sector as well. The President was of the view that NGOs have done more harm than good to society. Under the impression, a new diktat from the Government made it obligatory for the NGOs, international and national, to obtain a no-objection certificate from the Department of Defence (DoD) before August 31, 2006, to continue their work in the country.[60] A section in the Government appeared convinced that such a measure was needed to weed out NGOs advocating and advancing the Tigers' goals.

With this motivation Colombo under Rajapaksa, went a step further and told Norwegian Special Envoy Jon Hanseen Bauer that his proposed visit to the LTTE headquarters would not meet with the approval of the Government. The reason preferred was that the Government was reviewing its relations with the LTTE. Implied in the directive was a drastic change in the Government policy of engagement with the Tigers through the Norwegians and the 2002 Cease Fire Agreement. The new government's policies were also criticised by the LTTE and the organisation cried that the measures contemplated by Colombo were a further violation of the CFA and argued that its leader was after all right in saying that talks with the Sri Lankan government were a futile exercise.[61] In this unfavourable situation the visit of Norwegian Envoy Hanseen-Bauer was merely a waste of time and according to diplomatic sources he left Colombo as a very disappointed person and reportedly said, 'Oslo had decided to keep a low profile for the next few weeks before considering any steps towards another round of mediation.'[62] Thus, relations between the Rajapaksa Government and Norway had hit a new low. The Government considered Norway to be pro-LTTE despite the overwhelming backing from the international community for its mediation efforts. The Government appeared to have given legitimacy to those engaged in discrediting forces attempting to mobilise public opinion in favour of peace.

However, despite the killing of Sri Lanka's foreign minister in August 2005 and coming of Rajapaksa Government in November that year, the Cease Fire Agreement in a way remained useful till February 2006 when the two sides expressed their commitment to uphold the Ceasefire Agreement at Geneva meeting which was welcomed by India too. In this respect, the efforts and interests of the international agencies/ mediators have been very encouraging and the very first conference on the issue was organised at Tokyo on 9 and 10 June 2003. The Tokyo

Conference was attended by Ministers and representatives from 51 countries and 22 international organisations. The participating donor countries and international organisations had expressed their willingness to extend assistance to the entire country, to a cumulative estimated amount, of over USD 4.5 billion over the four year period, 2003-2006. But many of them had indicated that actual disbursements of the amounts pledged by them would depend on the progress in the talks between the Government of Sri Lanka and the LTTE. The conference had requested the European Union (EU), the US, Japan and Norway, in their capacity as the co-chairs, to meet periodically to review the progress in the peace talks and make suitable recommendations. The four co-chairs have accordingly been meeting periodically.

In view of the latest developments, a meeting of review of co-chairs was held on 30 May 2006 on the topic 'Reconstruction and Development of Sri Lanka' which was attended by Herve Jouan Jian, the Deputy Director General of the EU Commission, Richard Boucher, the US Assistant Secretary of State for South and Central Asia, Yasushi Akashi, of Japan and Eric Solheim, the Norwegian Minister for International Development. In an important development, a day before the review meeting on 29 May 2006, the EU notified its inclusion of the LTTE in its list of terrorist organisations. But while explaining the decision to include the LTTE in the list, it tried to soften the blow to the LTTE, criticised the Government too. In a statement Australia, in its capacity as the current chairman of the EU Council, added, 'The upsurge in violence is not caused by the LTTE alone. The EU strongly urges the Sri Lankan authorities to curb violence in Government – controlled areas. It notes with concern the growing number of reports of extra-judicial killings'. The EU co-chairs, in a statement issued at the end of the meeting came down strongly both on the LTTE and the Sri Lankan Government for the recent escalation of violence and the lack of progress in the peace talks. The statement also condemned both parties which have failed to deliver upon responsibilities including the commitments made their meeting in Geneva in February 2006. The LTTE is responsible for numerous terrorist attacks. The Government has failed to prevent attacks of armed groups, including Karuna and violent elements of EPDP.

In the period of Ceasefire Agreement Karuna group and Eelam People's Democratic Party (EPDP) had provided the Government with an opportunity to use him in a sophisticated covert action to target and damage the LTTE's military capability, such as its capability for the procurement of arms and ammunition abroad and their transport in its commercial ships. Karuna was a legendary commander of the LTTE, who had deserted from the LTTE in March, 2004, in protest against the allegedly discriminatory policies towards the eastern Tamils followed by its northern leadership. Having served in the LTTE for many years and having been close to Prabakaran, Karuna would have been well informed on the military and procurement capabilities of the LTTE and on how to strike at them. While the Eelam People's Democratic Party (EPDP) is a Tamil Party headed by Douglas Devananda which has been supporting the Government in connection with the attacks on Tamil civilians. The LTTE had been holding the Karuna group and the EPDP responsible for the targeted attacks on Tamil civilians, particularly in the Eastern Province who were suspected to be supporters or sympathisers of the LTTE. Since Rajapaksa took over as the President in November 2005, the security agencies had allegedly been using the Karuna group and the EPDP for carrying out a policy of using Tamils to kill Tamils—particularly in the Eastern Province. Both had been letting themselves be used in the manner without realising that the Government's policy of targeted killings of the Tamil civilians could one day lead to a Sinhalisation of important areas of the Eastern Province, where the strategically important port of Trincomalee is located and where the Tamils now constitute the largest group, if not in a majority. This ill-advised policy has only led to the creation of doubts in the minds of large sections of the international community about the bona fide of the Rajapaksa Government and its Tamil surrogates.

However, the statement issued by the four co-chairs urged the LTTE and the Sri Lanka Government to re-enter the negotiating process. The LTTE must renounce terrorism and violence. It must show that it is willing to make the political compromises needed for a political solution within a united Sri Lanka. This solution should include democratic rights of all peoples of Sri Lanka. The international community will respond favourably to such actions; failure to do so will lead to deeper isolation of the LTTE. On the other hand, the Government must show that it will legitimate grievances of the Tamils. It must immediately prevent groups based in its territory from carrying out violence and acts of terrorism. It must protect the rights and security of Tamils throughout the country and ensure violators are prosecuted. It must show that it is ready to make the dramatic political changes to bring about a new system of governance which will enhance the rights of all Sri Lankans including the Muslims. The international community will support such steps; failure to take such steps will diminish international support. The statement also made it clear that the listing of the LTTE need not mean termination of contacts with it for facilitating the peace process and added, 'The EU sees a need for the LTTE to amend its violent course and return to peace talks and will maintain its dialogue with the LTTE where such contacts, in the pursuit of the peace process, may help to bring about a return to negotiations and an end to violence.' The listing of the LTTE as a terrorist organisation will not prevent Denmark, Sweden and Finland, which are members of the EU, from continuing to interact with the LTTE in their role as members of the Sri Lanka Monitoring Mission. After inclusion of the LTTE as a terrorist organisation by the EU in May 2006, it had rebuffed several conciliatory efforts and refused to accept any rôle for the EU. Its stand was that their presence in the mission has become untenable after the EU ban on the Tigers. The CFA received a further blow to the tottering peace process when Denmark, Finland and Sweden declared that they are pulling out of the Sri Lanka Monitoring Mission, before the September 1, 2006, deadline as set by the Liberation Tigers of Tamil Eelam. It reduced the CFA mere a piece of paper.

Following these national and international developments on the CFA, violence escalated between the LTTE and the Sri Lankan security forces. Several high profile personalities in the Mahinda Rajapaksa regime were either assassinated or had escaped death by a whisker.[63] It succeeded a raid by the security forces and in retaliation caused LTTE's combined attack on 22 October 2007. In the series S.P. Thamilchelvan, LTTE's chief of the political wing, was killed in Sri Lanka Air Force (SLAF) bombing that further escalated the violence in the island nation. On the occasion a brief statement was issued by the Sri Lanka Monitoring Mission (SLMM) which noted that the extensive military operations in the northern region of Sri Lanka, conducted by both parties to the CFA, comprising land, sea and air forces have over the recent weeks reached 'unprecedented proportions.'[64] The SLMM, in its latest report, observed that the extensive military operations in the northern region of Sri Lanka has made credible monitoring exceedingly difficult. But the Mahinda Rajapaksa government had justified the killing.

Gradually, the security situation in Sri Lanka remained delicately poised and there have been repeated violations of the Ceasefire Agreement and a mutual consent on resumption of peace was yet to emerge. Meanwhile, the Sri Lankan Government of Mahinda Rajapaksa decided to terminate the CFA on January 2, 2008, and it officially expired on 16 January. The President in the way blatantly retraced from his country's committed efforts to find a political solution to the conflict between Sri Lanka's majority Sinhalese and minority Tamils that was specifically provided for in the country's constitution.[65] The decision of Rajapaksa administration to withdraw from the Ceasefire Agreement had met with uniformly negative responses from the international community. It had got Sri Lanka isolated from the rights – conscious international support. On the withdrawal of CFA, the LTTE argued, 'we are shocked and disappointed that the Government of Sri Lanka unilaterally abrogated the CFA. The Indian official response on the withdrawal issue was of the same nature and held that there is no military solution to the problem.[66] The shift towards enforcing a purely military solution to an otherwise ethnic conflict appeared illogical. But the President reasoned that 'Army solution should be based on what can be implemented' further adding that unlike his government previous governments have not been bold enough to implement their promises.

On Sri Lanka's withdrawal from the CFA, there was a widely shared view that the ending of the ceasefire will trigger an escalation of hostilities with the armed forces launching a major offensive in the Wanni and the Tigers resorting to guerilla warfare and terrorist strikes in the South and take a fresh toll of civilian lives and welfare. In general, war is not an option and the ceasefire is not sustainable without political dialogue.[67] There is a need for the Government of Sri Lanka to put forward a credible devolution package at the earliest. The much needed consensus on crucial issues is still elusive.

References

1. N. Bhaskara Rao, and P.N. Vasanti, 'Conflict Resolution and Global Peace-Role of Tools of Information and Communication,' *South Asia Politics*, Vol. 5, No. 12, April 2007 (New Delhi : 2007), p. 17.
2. Ibid.
3. Leo E. Rose, 'Nepal, Burma and Ceylon' in Wayne Wilcox, Leo E. Rose and Gavin Boyd (eds.), *Asia and the International System* (Massachusetts : Winthrop Publishers, 1972), pp. 232-33.
4. P. Sahadevan, 'Negotiating Peace in Ethnic Wars,' *International Studies*, Vol. 43, No. 3, July-September 2006 (New Delhi : Sage Publications, 2006), pp. 239-40.
5. Shaukat Hassan, 'Problems of Internal Stability in South Asia', in Shelton U. Kodikara (ed.), *External Compulsions of South Asian Politics* (New Delhi : Sage Publications, 1993), pp. 272-74.
6. Ibid., p. 276.

7. A. Jeyaratnam Wilson, 'Race, Religion, Language and Caste in the Subnationalism of Sri Lanka', in Michael Roberts (ed.), *Collective Identities, Nationalism and Protest in Modern Sri Lanka* (Colombo : Marga Institute, 1979), pp. 462-73.
8. Tilak Gooneratne, 'The Present Situation in Sri Lanka', *Asian Affairs*, Part I, February 1986 (London : 1986), p. 35.
9. Vinod F. Khobragade, 'Ethnic Politics in Sri Lanka – Political Solution to Tamil Cause and Military Solution to LTTE,' *South Asia Politics*, Vol. 7, No. 11, March 2009 (New Delhi : 2009), p. 25.
10. A. Jeyaratnam Wilson, *Politics in Sri Lanka – 1947-1979* (London : Macmillan Press, 1979), pp. 151-52.
11. Ibid.
12. Lucy M. Jacob, 'Regionalism in Sri Lanka', in Ramakant (ed.), *Regionalism in South Asia* (Jaipur : Aalekh Publishers, 1983), pp. 179-80.
13. Vinod. F. Khobragade, 'Re-Thinking Power Devolution in Sri Lanka', *South Asia Politics*, vol. 6, no. 1, March 2007 (New Delhi : 2007), p. 24.
14. Ibid., p. 25.
15. Malini Parthasarathy, 'The Mirage of Eelam', *The Hindu*, 24 April 2009.
16. Bertram E.S.J. Bastiampillai, 'Ethnic Conflict in South Asia and Inter-state Relations Especially in Relation to Sri Lanka', in Shelton U. Kodikara (ed.), *South Asian Strategic Issue – Sri Lankan Perspectives* (New Delhi : Sage Publications, 1990), p. 91.
17. Dayan Jayatilleka, 'A Sri Lankan Analysis – Dixit's Testament : A Critical Review,' *Mainstream*, Annual 1977, p. 107.
18. Vinod Khobragade, 'Sri Lankan Tamil Question – India's Paroxism', *South Asia Politics*, Vol.7, No. 8, December 2008 (New Delhi : 2008), p.37.
19. India Today, 15 December 1985, pp. 74-76.
20. Vinod Khobragade, 'Re-Thinking Power Devolution in Sri Lanka', pp. 24-25.
21. A. Sivarajah, 'Indo-Sri Lanka Relations and Sri Lanka's Ethnic Crisis : The Tamil Nadu Factor', in Shelton U. Kodikara (ed.), pp. 144-45.
22. News Background, 'India Condemns anti-Terrorist Thrust in Jaffna', *Lanka Guardian,* Vol. 10, No. 3, 1 June 1987, p. 9.
23. Bertram E.S.J. Bastiampillai, 'Ethnic Conflict in South Asia and Inter-state Relations Especially in Relation to Sri Lanka,' pp. 108-9.
24. *Tamil Times* (London), Vol. V, No. II, September 1986.
25. *The Island*, 21 January 1987.
26. *The Newyork Times*, 4 June 1987.
27. D.T. Hagerty, 'India's Regional Security Doctrine', *Asian Survey*, Vol. 31, No. 4, April 1991 (New Delhi : 1991), pp. 351-63.

28. S. Mansingh, *India's Search for Power : Indira Gandhi's Foreign Policy 1966-1982* (New Delhi : Sage Publications, 1984), p. 282.
29. D.T. Hagerty, 'India's Regional Security Doctrine'.
30. *The Island*, 25 January and 28 June 1987.
31. Ahsan Ali Khan, 'The Tamil Question in Historical Perspective : Its Impact on Indo-Sri Lanka Relations', *Pakistan Horizon Quarterly*, Vol. 2, pp. 62-63.
32. Ibid., p. 61.
33. A. Sivarajah, 'Indo-Sri Lanka Relations and Sri Lanka's Ethnic Crisis : The Tamil Nadu Factor', p. 147.
34. Shelton U. Kodikara (ed.), *External Compulsions of South Asian Politics* (New Delhi : Sage Publications, 1993), p. 320.
35. Shelton U. Kodikara, 'The Indo-Sri Lanka Agreement of July 1987 : Retrospect', p. 164.
36. Ibid., p. 161.
37. *Foreign Affairs Report*, July-October 1987 (New Delhi : Ministry of External Affairs, 1987), pp. 36 and 208.
38. Ibid., p. 211.
39. Ibid., pp. 36 and 217.
40. Malini Parthasarathy, 'The Mirage of Eelam,' *The Hindu*, 24 April 2009.
41. Vinod F. Khobragade, 'Re-Thinking Power Devolution in Sri Lanka', p. 25.
42. Ibid.
43. *The Hindu*, 24 January 2008.
44. Ibid.
45. Vinod F. Khobragade, 'The Sri Lankan Tamil Question –India's Paroxism', p. 39.
46. R. Hariharan, 'The Discarded Accord and the Unwanted War,' *The Hindu*, 7 August 2007.
47. Ibid.
48. *The Times of India*, 30 July 1997.
49. *The Hindustan Times*, 25 October 1997.
50. Ibid., 2 November 1997.
51. *The Hindu*, 17 January 2009.
52. Arti Bali, 'Enforcing Military Solutions to Ethnic Conflict,' *South Asia Politics*, Vol. 7, No. 2, June 2008 (New Delhi : 2008), p. 49.
53. B. Muralidhar Reddy, 'In Sri Lanka, a Ceasefire Under Siege', *The Hindu*, 16 March 2007.

54. B. Muralidhar Reddy, 'Not a Good Time For Advocates of Peace in Sri Lanka', in Ibid., 12 September 2006.
55. B. Muralidhar Reddy, 'In Sri Lanka, A Ceasefire Under Siege', in Ibid., 16 March 2007.
56. B. Muralidhar Reddy, 'Sri Lanka's Muslims : Out in the Cold', in Ibid., 31 July 2007.
57. Ibid.
58. Rajkumar Singh, *Relations of NDA & UPA with Neighbours* (New Delhi : Gyan Publishing House, 2010), p. 364.
59. *The Hindu*, editorial, 6 November 2007.
60. B. Muralidhar Reddy, 'Not a Good Time For Advocates of Peace in Sri Lanka.'
61. B. Muralidhar, 'Sri Lanka : Uncertainty as De-merger Nears'.
62. Ibid.
63. Ibid., editorial, 6 November 2007.
64. Ibid., 4 November 2007.
65. Arti Bali, 'Enforcing Military Solutions to Ethnic Conflict'.
66. *The Hindu*, 10 January 2008.
67. Ministry of External Affairs' *Brief on India –Sri Lanka Relations*, 26 February 2007 (New Delhi : 2007), p. 2.

5

LTTE'S LAST FIGHT AND FALL

Premonitions of Eelam War IV

Sufficient ground and background have been prepared for the Eelam war IV before the coming of Mahinda Rajapaksa as the new President of Sri Lanka in November 2005. In this context there is no exaggeration to say that the LTTE's demise as a military machine began in March 2004 when it was rocked by a stunning and unprecedented rebellion by thousands of its cadres in the eastern province of Trincomalee, Batticaloa, and Amparai districts. Unlike the predominantly Tamil north, the eastern wing was multi-racial where Tamils, Sinhalese and Muslims lived in mostly equal numbers. The development shook the Tamil Tigers at their very roots. At the head of the epochmaking event was Vinayagamurthy Muralitharan, widely known as Karuna Amman or Karuna, the LTTE's longest serving regional commander and in charge of Batticaloa and Amparai districts. Although an estimated 4,000 -5,000 guerillas had left the LTTE from the early 1980s and lived mostly in the West, the group had never faced a mass revolt.[1] The LTTE was too stunned by the initial turn of developments to know how to respond and it attempted to brush off the unexpected challenge as an individual problem and an internal matter but it became soon clear that the unthinkable had happened and its confidence was misplaced. In addition, the passionately anti-LTTE Eelam People's Democratic Party (EPDP) headed by Douglas Devananda, a militant turned cabinet minister, threw its lot with Karuna and some Muslim traders of the east also backed Karuna and refused to pay taxes to the LTTE for the first time in years.[2] While for Colombo, the split was a divine gift. The Tigers knew this but Prabakaran waited for the opportune moment to strike back.

What began with the killing of Foreign Minister Lakshman Kadirgamar on 12 August 2005 was a tide pushing Sri Lanka towards another war. It was a cold-blooded assassination who for a long time figured high on the Tamil Tigers' hit list and certainly a death blow to the already floundering peace process. Kadirgamar was a Jaffna Tamil married to a Sinhalese, knew he was living on borrowed time because, the LTTE had a long time ago branded him as a 'traitor' for the Tamil cause. In the LTTE blood-soaked dictionary a 'traitor' deserves to die. It was one of those meticulous killings the LTTE was notorious for. It irrevocably turned the West against the Tigers and eventually killed the ceasefire pact. At least three features stand out in the killing : one, the LTTE's ability to kill, and kill anyone anywhere, to achieve its goal of Tamil Eelam; two, the persisting inability of the Sri Lankan political establishment to understand the sheer determination of its foe; and three, now the very visible failing of Norway and the West to herald genuine peace in the island nation.[3] The LTTE had not only boycotted the Presidential election of November 2005 but in the same month he declared in his annual speech that he would give Rajapaksa a year to prove his sincerity vis-à-vis the Tamil. It helped to convince Rajapaksa that the assessment of the LTTE provided by his aides was right.

After assuming office, President Mahinda Rajapaksa worked hard to end the prolonged civil war by employing sundry mechanisms. Rajapaksa was not only a determined and calculating politician but also a lucky one. One of his predecessors, Ranasinghe Premadasa, had been blown up by the LTTE in 1993 after trying to make peace with the group. Another head of state who had been a long-standing sympathiser of Tamil grievances, Chandrika Kumaratunga, lost an eye during a suicide bombing aimed at killing her. Yet another, Junius Jayawardene, otherwise considered a wily fox, had earlier gone politically bankrupt fighting the Tigers. Fortunately for Rajapaksa, even before he took over the reigns of Sri Lanka, luck had slowly begun to desert Prabakaran, after being on his side for an unusually long, long time.

The new President of Sri Lanka and his core group had made a political resolve in August 2006 to launch a 'fight-to-finish campaign against the Tigers'. The Presidential core team in the campaign included his younger brother and Defence Secretary, Gotabaya Rajapaksa, and the army chief, Lt. General Sarath Fonseka, both of whom had scores to settle with the Tigers. Fonseka survived an assassination attempt when a woman suicide bomber of the LTTE blow herself up at the army hospital inside the army headquarters complex in April 2006. In December that year, Gotabaya Rajapaksa, who had retired as a colonel for the Army almost two decades ago and settled down in the US only to return as the Defence Secretary in his brother's government, was the target of a suspected suicide bomber attack on a trishaw in the heart of Colombo.[4] The Defence Secretary and the army chief proved to be a lethal combination for the LTTE. On the political front, Rajapaksa government adopted a shrewd strategy, borrowing some of the LTTE's own tactics, such as continuing to make politically correct statements on matters of peace, development and steps towards conflict resolution while meticulously planning operations for an all-out war. The façade of the Cease Fire Agreement (CFA) brokered by the Norwegian government was kept alive until January 2008 despite the fact that hostilities between the military and the Tigers had reached a point of no return in early 2007.[5] Perhaps to impress upon the international community that it was keen on keeping the door open for negotiations, the government did not ban the LTTE as a terrorist outfit until the first week of January 2009.

However, the first of Rajapaksa's initiatives was All Party Representative Committee (APRC) in mid-June 2006 to find political consensus on Power sharing between the conflicting communities, under the chairmanship of honourable Minister Tissa Witharana, leader of the Lanka Sama Samaja Party (LSSP). Its mandate was to reach consensus on a package of measures to guarantee the rights of Tamils. The Government of Rajapaksa publicly proclaimed that a politically negotiated settlement is the objective and put forward the CFA and the All Party Representatives' Committee process as evidence of this.[6] But the genuine efforts of the President could not confer affirmative result due to the traditional rivalry of major political parties and lack of participation of Tamil parties. In this matter both parties showed their obstinacy. They could not learn anything from the history of mutual hatred and mistrust.[7] The Sri Lankan political establishment is not just a badly divided house; any democratic society is bound to see sparring divisions. Now it is clear that the top political leaders have, despite two decades of blood and gore, not understood the LTTE's cold-blooded will to break up the island and achieve a free state called Tamil Eelam.

Subsequently, Rajapaksa continuing his efforts, appointed a group of multi-ethnic experts to evolve a political package acceptable to all and in line. In October 2006, both the UNP and SLFP signed a Memorandum of Understanding (MoU) to cooperate in all the spheres of national interest. This pact was first of its kind in the Sri Lankan political history which was long-awaited and much desired consensus of the major political parties. It was an important milestone in this process. But the timing of the understanding was not suitable because Rajapaksa was heading the United People's Freedom Alliance (UPFA) Government and the coalition faced the problems of a minority government. Several of the UNP's had crossed over to the ruling alliance and in the House of 225, the count of Ministers became over 90. President Rajapaksa inducted a sixth UNP rebel into the Government which gave the opposition UNP to criticise and oppose the government move on the issue of consensus in the name of national interest.[8] Even under normal circumstances, the arch rivals – the ruling Sri Lanka Freedom Party (SLFP) and the UNP – had difficulty in working together. The way the SLFP is poaching UNP Members of Parliament did not make for an atmosphere conducive to cooperation.

In fact, President Rajapaksa had embarked on a laudable and ambitious mission to work towards a national consensus, or to be more precise, a southern coming together, on the touchy subject of power sharing with the Tamils and other minorities and the move should have gone a long way in sending a clear message on the determination of the ruling combine and the polity to find a solution to the ethnic conflict. But after initial enthusiasm, it strengthened the opinion that the President is pursuing personal interest and not national agenda. For the gain of the ruling coalition, he continued the efforts to woo the disgruntled elements in the UNP despite warnings of adverse consequences. Political observers including Jayadeva Uyangoda, Professor of Political Science at Colombo University, saw the expansion spree of the Government as a sad development when the island nation is faced with an undeclared war. Professor Uyangoda said 'The past Governments too indulged in such antics but the Rajapaksa has broken all records. Conceded that it is a problem of a minority government but would not augur well for consensus on crucial issues between main opposition Party and the Government. It strengthens the opinion that the President is pursuing personal not agenda and national the one.[9] Fortunately, for a variety of reasons the then UNP was a divided house and faced with a plethora of problems.

At the juncture, the international community, India in particular had been an ardent advocate of revival of the political dialogue on the ethnic issue at the earliest to pave the way for isolation of the LTTE. And everyone within and outside Sri Lanka is agreed that an earnest effort towards a political process cannot commence without harmony and understanding between the SLFP and the UNP. All peaceloving constituencies were of the view that the need of the hour was for the ruling combine and opposition to close ranks and demonstrate that they are ready to work on a solution that satisfies all reasonable sections, defeating the designs of the LTTE. The steps taken by the Rajapaksa government in this regard was also criticised by Ranil Wickremesinghe,

UNP leader, Leader of Opposition, and former Prime Minister who was of the view that if the MoU had been proceeded with as planned, with an agreed agenda of action, the sufferings of economy, tourism, and foreign investment could have been avoided, 'Regrettably, the government let go of this opportunity for the short-term advantage of increasing its majority. The nation is now at a decisive crossroads. In this perilous situation—political and economic—for this nation and the wider world, the government cannot hide its head in the sand like the proverbial ostrich.[10] He charged the government that it continued to make out that it was always ready to resolve the North-East conflict through negotiations and that its doors were always open, but it die absolutely nothing to follow up with concrete actions through its Peace Secretariat. The government's actions had divided the people – not united them. Only a negotiated political settlement could bring peace to our country.

The multi-ethnic experts' panel which consisted of 17 members of which eleven members - six from the majority Sinhalese community, four Tamils and one Muslim prepared the 37 - page report which came up with four ways of deciding the future of the Tamil majority of the northeastern province. The experts, in course of preparing the report, studied several constitutions including India's to frame suggestions to act as a viable alternative to Tamil separatism and had admitted that the failure of minorities to have their due share of power has alienated them from the Sri Lankan state. The report covered all areas of governance including constitutions, provinces, unit of devolution, judiciary, national security, law and order, relations between Colombo and provinces, local governments, public services, language, land as well as safeguards for provincial powers.

Among the suggestions of the experts' panel, the important as well as the relevant ones were –bicameral legislature, two vice Presidents from among the minorities, creation of an Autonomous Zonal Council, and a single northeastern province with two internally autonomous units to address the concerns of the Muslims and Sinhalese who live in the Tamil majority region. The report noted that as a form of genuine power sharing between the different ethnic and religious communities, provincial institutions and local authorities would be set up and all communities shall share power in the central government, integrating them into the body politic and strengthening national integration.[11] The group had suggested that the country would be called "Republic of Sri Lanka" and described as "one, free, sovereign and independent state", avoiding any contentious tags such as unitary, federal or union of regions or provinces.

The Committee, in its report, recommended that there should be two houses in the legislature and all legislations, with the exception of Money Bills may be initiated in the second chamber. It wanted that the cabinet should reflect the pluralistic character of Sri Lanka and be representative of all provinces. The experts suggested that two directly or indirectly elected vice presidents for Sri Lanka who shall belong to two different ethnic communities distinct from that of the President, who has always been a Sinhalese since the country became independent in 1948. There was a significant suggestion to create an Autonomous Zonal Council (ANC) and an Indian Tamil Cultural Council (ITCC) to cater to the needs of what in Sri Lanka are known as "Indian Tamils" employed in the country's tea industry. It also suggested a single northeastern province with two internally autonomous units to address the concerns of the Muslims and Sinhalese who live in the Tamil majority region.[12] It added in the report that Sinhala and Tamil shall be the official languages and languages of administration while Sinhala, Tamil and English shall be the national languages of Sri Lanka. It wanted Sinhala, Tamil and English to be made compulsory subjects at the school leaving examination over a period of time. But unfortunately President Rajapaksa, fearing a storm in the majority Sinhalese community, conveniently buried it.

Having initial attempts failed in getting a negotiated political settlement to solve the decades long ethnic conflict in the country from the second quarter of 2006 onwards, President Rajapaksa was a changed man and the island nation a country with different approach to deal with the ethnic issue. In an earlier decade, the Rajapaksa had passionately battled human rights abuses by security forces when thousands of youths were butchered in the wake of an insurrection launched by the Sinhalese – Marxist group, Janatha Vimukti Peramuna (JVP). The times were now different and he was presiding over a conflict-torn country whose fortunes seemed wedded to the whims and fancies of a Tamil man called Prabakaran. Like the newly elected President, Prabakaran too was a determined man but his aim was different. Especially after the killing attempts made by the LTTE to finish Sarath Fonseka and Gotabaya Rajapaksa, the president now was more than convinced that Prabakaran and the band of men and women who made up the LTTE could never be trusted.

Subsequently, on account of frustration, lack of cooperation from fellow parties and failures in all initiatives, the President was left with no option but to wage a powerful military attack on LTTE. Commenting on the feasibility of military solution that could retard the country's economic growth in an era of globalisation promising new goals and horizons, Rajapaksa reiterated that though economic growth was important he would not betray the motherland while achieving growth.[13] In the same vein the army chief Fonseka also said later using the terminology of cricket, a game that united Sri Lanka like perhaps nothing else, the government concluded that it would play for certain victory, not for a draw, Rajapaksa and his core group had made a political resolve in August 2006 to launch a "fight to finish" campaign against the Tigers.[14] With the President in charge of the Defence portfolio and his brother as the Defence Secretary, war budget was no constraint though the economy of Sri Lanka was in dire stage. The President and his team tapped all possible sources for defence supplies, at times causing discomfort to India. When the domestic, regional and international community and almost all the confidence building measures faded, the only mechanism left with the state was to fight the complex network of terrorism and use the full-fledged command of the military might of the nation without responding to the pressures around.[15] The political solution was held as the supreme mechanism to resolve ethnic crises in Sri Lanka and in this direction plenty of measures and efforts were put in so far, but in vain.

From then on, Sri Lanka rejected the parrot-like suggestions that there could only be a negotiated end to the conflict. In the process, for the first time, Colombo took on not only Western countries but also international institutions, at times accusing them of bias towards the LTTE. Human rights activists were treated with contempt. To ensure its success, the Sri Lankan government had chosen to silence dissident voices. Many of those demanding another approach or criticising government actions or policies were accused of being closet LTTE supporters or otherwise sympathetic to terrorists. On the face of it, the logic of those criticising the advocates of peace and resolution appeared simple. The anti-war and pro-rapprochement campaign was considered as an obstacle in the state's war against terrorism. Worse, peace chants and yagnas were supposed to be giving much-needed breathing space for the terrorists to regroup.[16] In the situation, the Government appeared to have given legitimacy to those engaged in discrediting forces attempting to mobilise public opinion in favour of peace. Further, the Government and institutions, such as, the military had their own grievances and complaints against those in the business of peace-making. In addition, Eymard de Sila Wijeyeratne wrote in the *Sunday Standard*, dwelt at length on how mediatory efforts by international groups and volunteerism (NGOs) are nothing but elaborate efforts to gobble up Sri Lanka. 'The peace-process was an argued assumption based on an ideology that generates violence. It was never a genuinely reciprocal response between two parties to settle grievances.[17] In a nutshell, peaceniks, mediators, and non-governmental organisations (NGOs), indigenous and foreign, in Sri Lanka were all increasingly coming under attack from several quarters.

Not only that in the year 2006, Sri Lanka was one of the most militarised societies of South Asia. A Mumbai based think-tank Strategic Foresight Group (SFG) had conducted a study on the effects on Sri Lanka of decades-old ethnic conflict. The study, 'Cost of Conflict in Sri Lanka, had found that in previous years owing to the ongoing conflict the island nation has emerged as the most militarised society in the region. In 2006 it had 8,000 military personnel per one million population. Even Pakistan of which it is said while every country has an army, the Pakistan army has a country, has only half that number, 4000 military personnel per one million population. The figures for other South Asian countries are : Nepal 2700; India 1,300; and Bangladesh 1,000.[18] In terms of military expenditure as a percentage of Gross Domestic Product (GDP), too, Sri Lanka spent the most 4.1 per cent. In the case of Pakistan it is 3.5 per cent; 2.5 per cent in the case of India and Nepal; and 1.5 per cent in the case of Bangladesh. Thus, Sri Lanka's defence expenditure as a percentage of its GDP is the largest not only in South Asia but is also higher than other conflict-ridden countries such as Colombia, Myanmar, Sierra Leone, Sudan, the Philippines, and Uganda.

Apart from this the study group established a direct linkage between the ongoing ethnic conflict and the steep rise in defence spending. It noted that from an allocation of 0.5 per cent of the GDP in the 1970s to as high as 6.3 per cent in 2000. But it supposed to have declined to 4 per cent of the GDP after the 2002 Cease Fire Agreement (CFA) brokered by Norway. Likewise there was an unexpected rise in the strength of the Sri Lankan Army and war materials. In the early 1970s it was 15,000 while now 1.5 lakh. Its arsenal included multi-barrel rocket launchers, long range artillery, mortars, battle tanks, and armoured personnel carriers. In comparison, the navy is smaller; it has 20,000 personnel and used fast attack craft with 23 mm guns, inshore and offshore patrol vessels, landing crafts, etc. The Air Force used Kfir supersonic fighter bombers, MIG-23s, and choppers, including MI - 24s.

The SFG study group also studied the war strength of the LTTE which was essentially a military outfit and whose expenditure on weapons and the maintenance of a war economy got top priority. Its estimated strength was 10,000 but this did not reflect its actual capability given its use of suicide bombers and guerilla tactics. Its navy had about 2,000 personnel. The LTTE had no functioning air force and no anti-aircraft defences but it is said to have acquired two to five small aircrafts and built one or two airfields. The LTTE's annual income was anywhere between USD 175 million and USD 385 million. It spent minimum on its cadres and the maximum on sustaining a war economy and its support base internationally. Of the total income USD 100 million to USD 250 million was believed to come from drug trafficking although there was no direct evidence of the outfit's involvement in that trade. Local taxation and extortion were said to contribute about USD 30 million; human smuggling and funds siphoned off from NOGs gave USD 3-5 million; contributions from the Tamil expatriate community fetched USD 40-50 million; and profits from businesses USD 35-50 million.[19] The conflict and the consequent militarisation meant enormous human sufferings in social, economic, and political terms. By the end of 2005, about 65,000 persons had died. Life was subjected to never-ending checkposts and security drills. Inflation in 2006 hovered around 15 per cent and the struggle went on, the study findings added.

Phase of Restricted Fight 2006-2007

Since 2006, when both sides resumed major military operations, the conflict had killed and wounded thousands of civilians and displaced hundreds of thousands, leaving many suffering from disease and hunger. After the breakdown of the peace process, the Sri Lankan military launched a major offensive against the Tigers, brought the entire country under their control and gradually defeating the LTTE militarily. In June 2006, the Deputy Chief of Army, Major General Parami Kulatunga, who was filling in for the recuperating Army Commander, was killed.[20] In the same month, pursuing the LTTE's technique and planning on the propaganda front the government borrowed liberally from its tactics and created the Media Centre for National Security (MCNS) with the sole aim of countering the pro-LTTE portal TamilNet. The Defence Ministry revamped its own website and kept up a relentless campaign not only against the Tigers but against anyone and everyone who was critical of the war. On the battle front, the motto, in the words of the army chief, was : Go for the kill, maximum casualties and destruction of infrastructure of the enemy with minimum possible damage to the troops.[21] The current phase of hostilities witnessed the maximum use of air power.

By July 2006, fighting had reached its worst level since the period before the 2002 ceasefire. Hundreds had been killed in the most recent wave of violence and in the United Nation's reports tens of thousands of people had been forced to flee their homes. With the deterioration of the security situation in the North and East of Sri Lanka since the beginning of this year, and particularly after the suicide bomb attack on the Sri Lankan Army Commander in Colombo in April 2006 resulting in bombings of the LTTE controlled areas in the East by the Sri Lankan Armed Forces, there was a fresh influx of Sri Lankan Tamil refugees to India. The 'water war' that started in the Eastern Sri Lanka in July 2006 and spread to the Northern Sri Lanka resulted in further deterioration in the security situation leading to the exodus of Sri Lankan Tamils towards India. Since January 12 that year, more than 16,000 refugees had arrived in India.[22] Majority of the refugees were from Trincomalee area followed by Mannar, Vavuniya and Jaffna areas of Sri Lanka. As many as 6000 refugees arrived in India during the month of August 2006 alone.

Once the large scale fighting broke out in 2006, it dawned on Prabakaran that Colombo too had psychologically prepared itself for war. Rajapaksa was ready to pay back in a fitting manner, whatever the consequences. Half-hearted peace talks held in Norway and Switzerland that year collapsed as quickly as they started. They were perhaps not meant to succeed. The Sri Lankan forces after six attempts to negotiate had launched this war against a terrorist group, who killed one hundred thousand people and disabled thousands, destroyed billions worth property and infrastructure; murdered almost all the Tamil leaders, many Sinhalese leaders and two world leaders; made the entire country and economy suffer for more than three decades. Like in earlier times, capital Colombo became a fortress. The LTTE meant business. Bombs went off in areas far removed from the conflict threatre, killing innocents. Sri Lanka unleashed its air force and artillery barrage on LTTE areas like never before. For once, the state decided that it needed to be an LTTE to defeat the LTTE. Anyone with the slightest of suspected links with the LTTE got picked up. Abductions in government areas became rampant as the government embraced unconventional methods to break the LTTE's very deadly sleeper network. Many victims simply disappeared. The bodies of others turned up in unlikely places, at times with their hands tied and with bullets in their head.

Gotabaya Rajapaksa, a retired Sri Lankan army officer and younger brother of the President, had a clear vision as much as the insurgent outfit was concerned. A no-nonsense man, he had firmed up much earlier that the only language the LTTE understood and respected was that of force. And that is what Colombo would now employ. On the otherhand, with the fighting going on had realised correctly that New Delhi's military training to Tamil militant groups, the LTTE included, was not meant to break up Sri Lanka but to pressure Colombo to talk peace. He also concluded accurately that New Delhi would apply the squeeze one day, leaving the Tamil groups high and dry. So without fanfare, the LTTE boss put in place a well-oiled network to source arms and ammunition from around the world with money donated by the growing number of Tamil expatriates, so that the Indian brakes, when applied, would not halt the Eelam war.[23] However, in this connection the change of guard proved to be a monumental blunder for the LTTE. Prabakaran felt the absence of Karuna group, once the war started and picked up lethal speed from 2006 and the LTTE started losing one ship after another and suffering unprecedented battlefield reverses. After the death of his aide Anton Balasingham in December 2006, Prabakaran's loneliness only increased.

By early 2007, it was clear that the LTTE was using Tamil Nadu to source and to ship war materials to Sri Lanka. It was also evident from the seizures in Tamil Nadu that the Tigers were preparing for a long war. Tamil Nadu became vitally important for the LTTE after Sri Lanka began to decimate Tamil Tiger ships involved in long distance arms smuggling. In the last three months, authorities in Tamil Nadu have taken into their possession equipment and vast quantities of materials that can be used to make bombs meant for the LTTE.[24] The latest find took place in Chennai on 24 January 2007 when five Sri Lankan Tamil and three Indian men were taken into custody with two tonnes of iron ball bearings, following a strong lead from the Indian security establishment. A day later three more tonnes were seized and another Indian was arrested. 'It was clear the LTTE's reliance on Tamil Nadu was slowly increasing.[25] Earlier in January 2006, the Sri Lankan Navy intercepted a boat that had sailed from Tamil Nadu with 60,000 detonators and five Indian fishermen. After a long gap, in November 2006, a lathe machine, which can be used to make shells for bombs, was found in the seabed near the Indian coast. Officials say the increasing dependence on Tamil Nadu could reflect one or two things : that some other supply line has been cut off or that the LTTE has decided to use its finances judiciously by doing for purchases in a place close to the war threatre.

The seizure of war materials in huge quantity in the Indian state of Tamil Nadu concerned directly to the bilateral relations of the two sovereign countries – India and Sri Lanka and New Delhi's security agencies promptly went after the LTTE activists and supporters in Tamil Nadu and succeeded in preventing tonnes and tonnes of arms, explosives and related stuff from being smuggled out. M. Karunanidhi, the then Chief Minister of Tamil Nadu, in an alarming tone, declared that he would not tolerate any illegal activity even as he sympathise with the suffering of the island's Tamil community. The officials of Home Ministry have also admitted that for every tonne of material seized, much more may have gone past the Tamil Nadu coast and those arrested say that they have clear-cut instruction from the top LTTE leadership to avoid any skirmish with Indian security forces.[26] Further, a Tamil Nadu police officer disclosed that the material is being brought from places like Andhra Pradesh and Maharashtra while Tamil Nadu is used as a transit point. The most notable of the finds were arms and ammunition, including a 7 kg suicide belt from an explosives – packet boat off the Tamil Nadu coast in February 2007.

The LTTE's dependence for war materials on the Indian State of Tamil Nadu was viewed by several analysts as organisation's mounting difficulty in Western countries many of which have outlawed LTTE as a terrorist outfit. 'With violence rising in Sri Lanka, Tamil Nadu's importance has naturally gone up.' As the island nation slid towards war, the international community overseeing the tottering peace issued one of its most important statements ever. They made it abundantly clear to the LTTE that an independent Tamil Eelam was an absolute no-no. This was done so as to remove any suspicion in the minds of the people in Sri Lanka vis-à-vis the West. Especially, the co-chairs have declared that solutions to Sri Lanka's problems cannot be brought through conflict and that war is not winnable for either side.[27] Both the LTTE and the Sri Lankan government have been reminded that they have agreed to the basic principles of any future peace during the successful period of negotiation in 2002-03 and asked to recommit to these principles as well as to the Geneva peace talks of February 2006. Further, in early 2007 Robert Blake, the US envoy to Sri Lanka, who took over the charge in

September 2006, had made it clear that it is only devolution of powers that satisfy the legitimate aspirations of the Tamil minority could be the basis for any negotiations between the Sri Lankan government and the LTTE. 'The situation is serious but there is light at the end of the tunnel.' He said a majority in the southern part of Sri Lanka, populated mainly by the dominant Sinhalese community, felt that a military solution is possible. We respectfully disagree. The LTTE cannot be defeated militarily without a parallel political strategy to address the grievances of the Tamil community.[28] The assumption that the LTTE can not be defeated militarily was widely shared in the international community.

The ongoing struggle between the LTTE and the Sri Lankan forces intensified by the daredevil aerial raids carried out by the Tamil Tigers in a span of over a month from March 26 to April 29, 2007. Earlier the threats emanated either from land or sea but now even the skies are a source of horror. The current escalation of hostilities resulted in rebels staging a dramatic demonstration of their air-strike capabilities by using Czech - built Zin Z-143 aircraft in March 2007, they attacked the country's largest air force base at Katunayake. Another attack on the air base at Anuradhapura, a staging area for the Northern threatre of military operation, damaged or destroyed more than USD 30 million worth assets.[29] For the first time the LTTE had carried out an air attack. This meant it now possessed the capability to select a target anywhere in the country – access it by air – unopposed and destroy it. The LTTE air raid had raised fundamental questions about the strategy employed by the government. While publicly proclaiming that a politically negotiated settlement is the objective – and putting forward the Cease Fire Agreement and the All Party Representatives' Committee process as evidence of this, the government has clearly chosen the military option with the avowed aim of annihilating the LTTE. It is this option that is being seriously challenged by the air attack. The government's contradictory policy demands an explanation.[30] Even after this air attack, the government has not received the envisaged support of international community to prosecute the military option. Ban Ki-moon, the Secretary General of the United Nations, said that he 'deeply regrets the air raids, military confrontations on the ground, and suicide bombings which have become a daily occurrence prompting massive displacement and suffering for civilians.'[31] He called for both the government and the LTTE to return to the negotiating table. Many friendly countries, all of whom are opposed to terrorism and support human rights, have issued statements similar to this.

The security implications of the air attack were best described in an editorial in *The Hindu*. 'The first-ever air raid by the Liberation Tigers of Tamil Eelam targeting the main Sri Lanka Air Force (SLAF) base near the Colombo International Airport is a dangerous development for the strife-torn country. It not only worsened the prevailing volatile security environment but also posed a new challenge in the fight against terrorism. Clearly, with the daring midnight attack, the ongoing undeclared war between the Sri Lanka military and the LTTE seems to have entered a perilous phase.[32] From the government side it was said that the two LTTE bomber planes were able to get through unscathed because the radar system was out of order. As the country's principal air base and airport from which regular bombing raids are carried out was left unprotected at a time when the government was knowing that the adversary had airplanes. The attack took place at a time when the government had claimed daily military victories, and the Defence Secretary has stated that the LTTE has been cleared from the East and the LTTE war machine has been put out of action.

In fact the Sri Lankan security forces too in the year 2007 achieved some success. The Sri Lankan government took effective control of the Sri Lanka's eastern province, though it has had trouble defeating LTTE combatants in the north. On its website, the Sri Lankan Ministry of Defence catalogues alleged victories against the LTTE. The United States had helped train Sri Lankan forces in agencies that relate to counterterrorism. According to the State Department, the Government of Sri Lanka cooperated with the United States to implement both the Container Security Initiative and the Megaports programme at the port of Colombo. In the east, the Sri Lankan forces recaptured almost all including large areas of rebel – dominated territory south of the strategic eastern port city of Trincomalee. This area served as the lifeline for some 40,000 government troops deployed in the Northern Jaffna Peninsula. The port city in question was used for ferrying all supplies and troops to the northern capital.

Despite the success in the battle field, the Sri Lankan government had attracted widespread criticism for its alleged human rights abuses. Like the LTTE it had been accused of engaging in extrajudicial killings, abductions, extortion, conscription, and the use of child soldiers. In August 2007, Human Rights Watch released a report that catalogues the various human rights abuses conducted in Sri Lanka by both the LTTE and the Sri Lankan military. Earlier Ranil Wickremesinghe, the Leader of Opposition and former Prime Minister, also criticised the Rajapaksa government for human rights violations. He charged the government for the loss of support of the international community on the count as the island nation is being treated like a beyond - the - pale nation because the government has failed to protect its people. Human rights violations occur daily with abductions and disappearances going on unchecked. People live in fear of white vans. Institutions are harassed with non-existent inland revenue violations, and visits by the CID.[33] In the situation, it makes nonsense of the government's claims of defending the integrity of our country and protecting its people – the primary duty of any government of Sri Lanka. We as a country are living in an interdependent world respecting human rights that are globally accepted.

On the otherhand, no significant gain was registered on the progress of peace process held in the year 2007. Most of the times, the Government had sought a resumption of talks with the LTTE, but was told by the Norwegian Ambassador, who visited Kilinochchi in August, that the LTTE was unwilling. Attempts at informal talks, through calls from the Peace Secretariat to the LTTE's Peace Secretariat, and through messages sent via the Sri Lanka Monitoring Mission, were also repulsed. By then, the Sri Lanka Monitoring Mission was down to a shadow of its former self, and was unable to issue rulings on violations of the Ceasefire Agreement, since the LTTE had refused to allow nationals of European Union (EU) states to interfere. It had also fired on a vessel bearing Sri Lanka Monitoring Mission representatives which led to the cessation of naval monitoring. In these circumstances, the Government pressed ahead with negotiations with other parties, focussed on Tamilgroups committed to pluralism and democracy. While the opposition had withdrawn from the All Party Representative Committee by this time, parties representing Tamils, Up-country Tamils and Muslims were all participating. The political situation on which they were attempting to reach agreement could no longer be held back by the intransigence of a single organisation, and one that had not demonstrated the slightest interest in coexistence.

Although the LTTE made several devastating attacks on the Sri Lankan security forces, mainly the air raids in the year 2007, its overall position in the war was on decline. Since its ouster from the east in August, the terrorist organisation has failed to conduct any military operation of significance notwithstanding the fissures within the Karuna group and general unrest in the east. According to the Sri Lankan Navy, the LTTE has lost all of its ten ships, ferrying supplies from various clandestine sources, in one-sided sea battles. Eight of these losses were in 2007 and other two ships were sunk in Indonesian waters. As per informed estimates, which were not contested by the LTTE, 200 of its cadres were killed in the past one month. For the first time in years, the Sri Lankan army made territorial gains in the north by capturing a Tiger base in Mannar.[34] In mid-October, the security forces launched several pre-emptive strikes near their forward defences in Wanni and Jaffna in which at least 30 LTTE Tigers and eight soldiers were killed. As claimed by the Defence Ministry on the Wanni front, troops launched their first strike at a terror hideout at Mullikulama, killing 15 cadres and injuring 15. Troops found seven bodies of young women and seized six T-56 machine guns and one Multi Purpose Machine Gun (MPMG). The military said one soldier was killed and seven were injured as the terrorist used artillery and heavy mortar fire.[35] It added further that infantrymen killed eight more LTTE cadres in two separate attacks at Vilathikulama. Separately, six soldiers at the Thalgasmankada military post in the Ampara district were killed following an attack by the LTTE. The Air Force claimed to have destroyed an LTTE's military and logistic base in Mullaittivu.

In the circumstances once again the LTTE demonstrated its air power and on 22 October 2007 attacked the Anuradhapura air base in the North Central Province leaving four military helicopters destroyed and 14 soldiers dead was in reality a suicide operation by an organisation on the run. It was the fifth aerial foray since the Tigers made their debut in the skies in March 2007 targeting the air base near the only international airport of the country at Kalunayaka and the first after the Sri Lanka government put in place a revamped air defence system. With this act the LTTE hoped to bolster the sagging moral of its cadres.[36] According to the Defence Ministry two Russian - built MI 24 helicopter gunship and a K/8 aircraft on ground were severely damaged in the Tiger attack. Besides a Bell 212 helicopter which was pursuing the Tiger aircraft crashed into Doramadalawa in the Mihinthale area due to technical fault. Categorising LTTE, as per the photograph released by the organisation was in the age group of 13 to 16 and said that no further proof was required of its callousness to humanity.

LTTE, the opposite number of Sri Lankan security forces, in its version said that at 3.20 a.m. a special LTTE Black Tiger team of 21 men and women attacked the Anuradhapura base and destroyed and burnt down eight planes and helicopters, including reconnaissance planes and training. The destroyed Sri Lankan aircraft belonging to the Sri Lankan Air Force included one training plane, two MI - 24 helicopters, one MI

- 17, one PT - 6, one Bell - 212, one reconnaissance plane and one CTH - 748.[37] The LTTE operation showed up continuing weaknesses in Sri Lanka's intelligence machinery and in the capability of the armed forces to secure the air space even against sub-military threats. However, in retaliation, as claimed by the Defence Ministry, the air sorties were carried out around 5.30 a.m. by both MIG and Kfir jets and they destroyed the identified targets.[38] The supersonic fighter jets of Sri Lanka Air Force pounded on LTTE airstrips located at Iranamadu area in the north.

Further, the death of S.P. Tamilchelvan, LTTE's political wing chief on 2 November 2007 in Sri Lanka Air Force bombing was a huge blow to the outfit because many diplomats and the world community in general, considered him the friendly face of Tamil Tigers. Hailing from a poor family in Chavakachcheri in Jaffna, Tamilchelvan, like many young Tamil men of his era drifted to militancy and later teamed up with LTTE founder leader Velupillai Prabakaran. Although he joined the LTTE as a fighter while in his teens, it was his growing importance as a negotiator in peace talks that fetched him a larger than life image.[39] The death was sure to hit the morale of the LTTE, which was still celebrating last week's crippling attack on the Sri Lankan Air Force base in Anuradhapura that wiped out military helicopters and planes worth millions of dollars. After his death, Prabakaran went a step further and said that he did not desire enmity with India. B. Nadesan, who succeeded Tamilchelvan, conveyed this message to a Tamil National Alliance (TNA) MP. The LTTE, Nadesan went on, would never accept weapons from any country inimical to Indian interests even if the Tigers felt choked.[40] He also added that their leader Prabakaran wanted this conveyed to the Indian government and the Indian people.

While President Rajapaksa justified the killing of Tamilchelvan and praised the armed forces as 'the most disciplined' in the world. Rajapaksa asserted that the 'war heroes were fighting for a cause, with a vision and a mission'.[41] Separately, the Army media spokesman Udaya Narayakkara said the death of Tamilchelvan was a great loss to the LTTE as he was one of the top members involved in many of the recent operations conducted by the organisation. A report posed on the Defence Ministry website under the charge of Defence Secretary Gotabaya Rajapaksa said, this is a message to all those who use violence, killings, suicide bombing and devastation to disrupt the life of the Tamils and other Sri Lankans to rethink within themselves before it is too late.[42]

He also noted further : 'They should stop now. They should renounce violence immediately while there is still time.'

Tamilchelvan's death was not only a setback to the institutional memory of the peace talks but a fear of escalating the violence appeared imminent as held by many including Sri Lanka Monitoring Mission (SLMM) and National Peace Council, an NGO. After the killing of LTTE's chief negotiator a diplomat in Sri Lanka said, 'who are the Sri Lankans going to talk to now. This is the real problem' while another diplomat added, 'It is a huge blow to negotiations. With Balasingham dead in December 2006, Tamilchelvan would have played a key role in any future negotiations.'[43] The Sri Lankan Monitoring Mission (SLMM) after watching the ground situation said that the death could only further escalate the conflict. In line, the National Peace Council in a statement said that the killing is likely to lead to more severe escalation of the present phase of war. 'It deepens the crisis of violence that confronts the country and serves to remind us of the tens of thousands of lives that have been lost including a large number of democratically elected leaders of the government and other political actors.[44] Although some of those killings seemed very significant at the time they took place, none of them led to a solution to the conflict, but only served to generate more hatred and determination to retaliate and fight back.

As feared after the death of Tamilchelvan, the LTTE leader Velupillai Prabakaran vowed to continue the liberation struggle with renewed determination. He blamed the Sri Lankan government that despite the repeated and continuous calls from the international community to find a peaceful resolution to Tamil national question, we have not seen any goodwill from the Sinhala nation.[45] In response to the Prabakaran's statement Ratnasiri Wickremanayake, the Prime Minister of Sri Lanka, had asserted that the force will continue to track down the hiding places of LTTE leaders and launch attacks. He also made it clear that the government was not in favour of a fresh ceasefire though it was ready for unconditional talks, as it had always been. As reported by the state-run English paper *Daily News* Wickremanayake had said, 'It is not the government that left the negotiating table. It is the LTTE which spurned the peace drive. Nevertheless, the government will be ready if they want to negotiate. But we will not stop retaliating terror attacks even while discussions are going on.[46] He noted that the terrorists had not only attacked security personnel, southern targets and Sinhala politicians but also their own brethren. Tamilchelvan was responsible for the death of thousands and vested interests were attempting to create the false impression that his death would derail the peace process.

Amid claims and counterclaims, the upper hand of Sri Lankan security forces continued in the conflict. In a public opinion survey by the Centre for Policy Alternatives (CPA), a Colombo based think-tank 48.5 per cent of the Sinhala community felt that the war can be ended and peace restored in the country only by the government defeating the LTTE. There were the views expressed by three communities : Tamils 62.3 per cent, Upcountry Tamils 96.7 per cent, and Muslims 85.2 per cent had opted to stop the war and conduct peace negotiations. The objective of the survey was to gauge the level of public confidence in the peace process and capture the public mood on the politics in the nation.[47] It covered the Sinhala, Muslim and the Upcountry Tamil communities in the areas outside the North and East.

In the circumstances, the world community in general and peace-loving countries, in particular, feared further security deterioration in the island nation at the close of the year 2007. The rest of the world was tightening its screws on the terrorist organisation, with Washington in the lead, banning the activities of Tamil Rehabilitation Organisation, one of the major fund raisers of the Liberation Tigers of Tamil Eelam. The US had also suspended the issuance of licenses for the sale or transfer of military equipment and services to Sri Lanka with effect from 26 December 2007, as per Department of State Foreign operations and Related Programmes Appropriation Act, though it had relaxed the grant of such licenses for equipment connected with the limited purpose of maritime and air surveillance and communication.[48] The internationally backed peace process collapsed in 2007. India remained an active though not a successful player via-a-vis Sri Lanka, where violence since President Rajapaksa took over power in late 2005 has left thousands dead.[49] Also there was no indication, only hope, that the All Party Representative Committee (APRC) would prepare a new document acceptable to everyone in a country badly divided on ethnic and political lines.

At the close of the year, the overall position of the LTTE appeared on decline. Although Velupillai Prabakaran, in his Heroes Day (2 November 2007) speech concluded, 'Thousands of Tamil guerillas were standing ready to fight and we will overcome the hurdles before us and liberate our motherland' yet it did not carry much weight as a few minutes before the LTTE supremo began his speech, the Sri Lankan

Air Force demolished the building that housed the Voice of Tiger.[50] In the situation Prabakaran's speech was not illustration of characteristic defiance but an expression of a significantly weakened position on the ground and increasing international isolation.[51] Perhaps it was delivered with the intention to boost the sagging morale of the cadres and supporters.

Again on 23 December 2007, the Sri Lankan Navy and terrorist from the Tamil Sea Tigers had faced one another in a fierce sea battle off the coast of Sri Lanka's northern Jaffna peninsula south off Delft island. According to military spokesman Udaya Nanayakkara, the sea battle started around 11.00 a.m. when 12 naval fast attack crafts intercepted a Sea Tiger flotilla, composed of 16 boats, trying to smuggle arms into the country. The sea battle lasted for four hours claiming the lives of at least 40 Tamil Tiger terrorists and one naval officer. At this time the Sri Lankan Navy had destroyed at least nine LTTE Sea Tiger boats while loosing one of its own when two LTTE suicide boats of the LTTE black sea tiger ramped one of the FACs. The Sri Lankan Navy called upon the Air Force in order to win this sea battle against the LTTE.

Thus, recently the LTTE had received remarkable reversal. Carefully coordinated action by the Sri Lankan security forces had seen the Tigers being targeted at many difficult levels. From destroying LTTE ships carrying arms to ambushing LTTE operatives in landmine attacks, the forces had been hitting hard consistently. The military establishment was gearing up to use a purely military approach. The LTTE was also committed to escalating the war. Tamil civilians were bearing the brunt of the conflict. Minorities fearing the resurgence of Sinhala Buddhist nationalism ... Sri Lanka could well be in another protracted cycle of war and the year ahead looked very bleak.[52] After decades of see-saw fighting, Colombo took a visible upper hand vis-à-vis the LTTE, driving it away from the country's eastern province and crippling its shipping network.

Fighting and Political Developments in Post - CFA

In the first week of January 2008, the Government of Mahinda Rajapaksa decided to withdraw from the Cease Fire Agreement (CFA) brokered by Norway in February 2002. Although the decision had met with negative responses from the international community and as a result it had got isolated, yet over the past year, with the rout of the Liberation Tigers of Tamil Eelam in the Eastern Province and the serious losses inflicted by an increasingly aggressive Sri Lankan army and air force in the North, the military balance in Sri Lanka had shifted significantly in favour of the state. The Tigers had lost territory, ships carrying arms, and a large number of fighters. They have scored some terrorist hits in the South including a dramatic ground and air attack on the Anuradhapura air base and the assassination of the Minister for Nation Building in the vicinity of Colombo.[53] But the military remained offensive and relentless and in the circumstances the ending of the ceasefire will trigger an escalation of hostilities in the near future.

By abrogating the Ceasefire Agreement with the Liberation Tigers of Tamil Eelam, the Sri Lankan government had finally proclaimed what had been a reality for two years – the effective end of the ceasefire brokered by the Norwegians six years ago. The Sinhala dominated government and the Tamil Tigers have had decided that war is not only inevitable but also required before any fresh political process can emerge.[54] From the current situation three scenarios are expected to emerge. The LTTE can emerge defeated, weakened or emboldened from this fighting. The Tigers will be defeated if the government succeeds in ejecting them from the territory they control and in eliminating their leadership. They will be weakened if the government ejects the Tigers from territory they control but they can still continue as an insurgent organisation capable of guerilla operations and terrorist attacks. The LTTE will be emboldened, of course, if it succeeds in bringing the government offensive to a standstill.

Is before in 2008, the Government of Sri Lanka was determined to give a decisive blow to the LTTE, ejecting it from territory under its control a and eliminating its leadership. The hope in this is that a Sri Lanka liberated from war will find the will to seek peace. This will create the opportunity for a new politics of co-existence among all communities on the island.

With this objective in view at the start of the year, the foreign policy of Sri Lanka was directed at upgrading contacts with governments that can substantially augment the military procurement efforts of the island nation so as to enhance its capabilities at crushing the rebels. It had acquired armaments, multi-barrel rocket launchers, heavier artillery, precision guided missiles, and bunker busters and had recruited 30,000 new recruits into its armed forces. In line Sri Lanka had also included those countries that have scant consideration for harmonising the ground situation in the island neighbourhood. Many of these countries deal in arms sales with purely commercial purpose and are often found supplying arms to terrorist groups/organisations.[55] Recently, Symon Hill spokesman from the Campaign Against Arms Trade (CAAT) while commenting on 10,000 military missiles that are designed to be dispatched from Slovakia said that the sale was 'exactly what Sri Lanka does not need at the moment' adding that the country has been engaged in civil war for 25 years and the CAAT fears that the weapons may be used against civilians. 'There are many instances of Sri Lanka army being accused of killing of civilians as often happens in civil war' he added.[56] The military solution infact has resulted in stirring up ethnic hatreds and branding of striking workers, protesting farmers and media critics as Tiger sympathisers and terrorists.

In the meantime the LTTE leader had proclaimed that only military force will work to change the government's policy. Prabakaran had directed attacks against hard military targets such as Air Force bases and soft political targets like ministers and civil guardsmen. The Tamil Tigers were using a combination of hit and run attacks, bombings and assassinations to deter and delay the government's impending assault. They had developed an air wing, an effective sea wing and have heavily infiltrated population centres in the Sinhala-dominated South. The next round of violence will lead to the deaths of thousands, and the destruction of property on a large scale than what we have ever witnessed before in Sri Lanka. Thus in the light of preparations done by the Sri Lankan security forces and the LTTE it was not possible to negotiate the political settlement. Dayan Jayatilleka, a political analyst and academic who enjoyed a close rapport with Mahinda Rajapaksa, was of the view that 'with Prabakaran there can be no peace. A peaceful negotiated settlement is possible only if it recognises that any solution has to be within a single, united Sri Lanka and the Tigers are verifiably demilitarised and democratised.'[57] The diplomat Jayatilleka in an interview when asked how the war in Sri Lanka will end, asserted prophetically and said :

It will all end the way it all ended in Angola after decades of conflict when (rebel leader) Jonas Savimbi was killed by the Angolan armed forces. It will all end the way it did in Chechnya when the Russian army got Djokar Dudayev, defeated the Chechen separatist militia in fierce combined arms warfare ... Angola and Chechnya are peaceful and prosperous now. It cannot end while Prabakaran has not been demilitarised one way or another.[58]

As a result of the fighting between the Sri Lankan forces and the

LTTE, the latter's held territory dramatically shrunk. In the year 2005 the LTTE controlled a vast area in Sri Lanka's north and east. In the context President Chandrika Kumaratunga once told an Indian journalist that the LTTE controlled a third of Sri Lanka's land territory and two-third of its winding coast. At the time it was a *de facto* Tamil Eelam. But soon after President Mahinda Rajapaksa took over, the LTTE took the offensive, stoking a war that rages to this day.[59] In 2008 the LTTE was appealing to Tamil families to contribute at least one member each, irrespective of age and gender, to take on the advancing military. Now it controlled about 4,000 sq. kilometre – or just six per cent of Sri Lanka's land territory with population under its control about 2,50,000 – a mere 1.25 per cent of the country's total.

The year 2008 proved a decisive one in the struggle between the LTTE and the Sri Lankan security forces and the latter had continued its all-out offensive against the Tamil militant groups. It made several successful land air and navy attacks on LTTE strongholds and destroyed its training camps. In the month of March and April the LTTE had received heavy beating during clashes along the Wanni and the Jaffna forward Defence Lines (FDLs). According to a Defence Ministry statement at Colombo in the Wanni clashes continued on the Vavuniya, Mannar and Welioya battlefronts. Meanwhile, it was informed by the United States Embassy in Sri Lanka that the State Department's Bureau of Diplomatic Security, Office of Antiterrorism Assistance has donated equipment worth of $220,000 to the Sri Lankan National Police. The purpose of the help was to sustain and enhance the critical capabilities of the security forces of the country in their efforts to fight terrorism.[60] The donated materials included three Explosives Incident Counter measures, kits, two Post-Blast Investigation kits and two Hostage Negotiations kits, which was divided between the Sri Lankan National Police (SLNP) and the Special Task Force (STF). In the ongoing struggle both sides had suffered casualties, it however was costlier for the LTTE due to its limited cadres and war materials and in a desperate act the terrorists triggered a train blast at Dehiwela in which nine people were killed and 70 injured.

However, during the fight the LTTE announced its decision to observe a unilateral ceasefire from July 26 to August 4, 2008, to coincide with the SAARC Summit scheduled at Colombo on August 2 and 3. On 22 July, the Political Wing of LTTE, in a statement announced that as a sign of goodwill towards the SAARC, the LTTE would observe a unilateral ceasefire that is devoid of military actions during the period of the SAARC conference and extend its cooperation for the success of the conference, but added that if the occupying Sinhala forces, disrespecting our goodwill gesture of our people and our nation, carry out any offensive, our movement will be forced to take defensive actions.[61] Later on July 12, the leader of its Political Wing in an interview expressed its readiness for a ceasefire and holding talks but Rajapaksa said that his government is ready for talks only if the LTTE gives up arms. According to political and diplomatic observers the announcement of the outfit was another attempt to embarrass the Rajapaksa government and score brownie points vis-à-vis the international community. The air force attacks on LTTE fortifications in northern Sri Lanka continued further and as a result the troops had broken through the rebels' defences and seized a series of key towns and bases. On the basis of intelligence reports, the military claimed to have killed at least 11,000 LTTE cadres since the current phase of hostilities in July 2006. The military believed that the Tigers' strength was down to below 5,000.

The LTTE having failed to garner the required support for itself tried to insulate the Tamil Nadu politicians as a last attempt to solve this vexed issue and stop the war. Evidently, the game plan of the LTTE and its supporters was to rally Tamil chauvinist sentiment and translate that into pressure on New Delhi to signal its disapproval to Colombo, thereby weakening its moral authority in the eyes of the Sri Lankan Tamil community. The political parties of Tamil Nadu had launched a campaign in the State ostensibly to express solidarity with the Sri Lankan Tamils trapped in the war zone in northern Sri Lanka but the timing of this campaign which appeared to have materialised overnight was a dead giveaway. At the time, the Sri Lankan army was just two kilometres away from the LTTE's administrative capital, Kilinochchi and it had been successfully encircled the Tigers and their leaders who were virtually trapped in their bunkers. For the first time in years, the Sri Lankan government was on the brink of a major success in its battle with terrorism.[62] In the situation, the general mood of Indian public was not in favour of Tamil Nadu and held the view that the latest campaign in the State was masterminded by a desperate LTTE and it must not be allowed to undermine the sound policy decision upheld by successive Indian governments since 1991 to stay out of Sri Lanka's internal affairs.

In November 2008, the Sri Lankan security forces got major success in destroying the outfit's several training camps including the capture of LTTE's sea base Ponneryn which was considered the last strategic stronghold. The Air Force spokesperson Janaka Nanayakkara said that it raided a suspected hideout of senior LTTE leader Prabakaran and Soosai. As claimed by the Sri Lanka Air Force, it had pounded an LTTE training and logistic base located in the Iranamadu area in Mullathivu district. A Defence Ministry statement said sporadic fighting was reported close to the 12th mile post along the A-32 Mannar-Ponneryn Main Road on the Western Kilinochchi battlefront. Fighting was reported between troops and LTTE at Kovilkoduttavil, Podimuruppukulama and Urutirapurankulama. It added that this phase of the military surge has forced the LTTE to retreat with heavy casualties. The LTTE is on the verge of losing its supply line along the western coast.[63] The terrorists are faced with fierce multi-prolonged attacks from the military, which has left scores of terrorists killed and many bankers abandoned. In the same month, President Rajapaksa while presenting the budget proposals for 2009 with a record provision of Rs. 200 billion for defence expenditure, called on the LTTE to lay down arms and join the democratic process 'even at this last moment'. Responding to a query from a member on media reports quoting the LTTE that it had always been in favour of a ceasefire, the government stated in the Parliament that a ceasefire with the LTTE could be considered only if the Tigers were ready to lay down arms and agree to sit across the negotiating table along with other stakeholders.

The capture of Ponneryn by the Sri Lankan security forces had turned the war in favour of Sri Lanka's military and also paved further the way for a fresh land route to Jaffna. The statement of Defence Ministry characterised the fall of Ponneryn as the greatest feat against terrorists by the forces in their courageous march along the northwestern coast of the island. At the moment the Jaffna peninsula is accessible only through sea route after the military shut down the A-9 highway in August 2006 on grounds of security. Gain of Ponneryn, a strategic land that runs parallel to the neck of the northern Jaffna Peninsula across a narrow lagoon, will enable the military to strike the LTTE administrative capital of Kilinochchi from three sides. Lieutenant-general Sarath Fonseka, the chief of Sri Lanka Army, told the media that it has been liberated after 20 years and it has opened a land route to Jaffna. 'We have eliminated a large number of terrorists during this battle; the remaining terrorists are now running for their lives across the Kilali Lagoon.'

As expected, the next move of Sri Lankan military was to try to gain control over Kilinochchi and as per Defence Ministry statement, heavy clashes were continuing along Kilinochchi's outskirts in the last week of November 2008. Terrorists had suffered serious damages in the fighting and unable to resist the military onslaught, terrorist had fled leaving the dead and a cache of weapons behind. The intense military assaults and the small-group operations had confined major movements of terrorists in the area. In line the Sri Lankan troops captured Kokavil - an LTTE strategic location in Mullathivu. This was the first time after 18 years that the Army had gained full control over this area. In Sri Lankan context Kilinochchi was considered to be a vital battle terrain and the most valued trophy for the security forces who were determined to flush out LTTE during the world's most effective duel tasked counterterrorist-cum-humanitarian operation in modern time.[64] The defence observers also expected the fall of other LTTE-dominated towns soon in the current phase of fighting.

The year 2008, apart from fighting the Sri Lankan security forces and the cadres of the terrorist outfit LTTE, witnessed some progress in the political field and the island nation went a step ahead in this direction. Earlier, in mid-2006 the Rajapaksa government established an All Parties Representative Committee (APRC) to forge a consensus among all parties on a political solution acceptable to all for resolution of the three-decade-old ethnic conflict. The APRC submitted its interim report to the President of Sri Lanka on 23 January 2008 in which it recommended full and faithful implementation of the 13th Amendment to the constitution, holding of provincial council elections in the east and establishment of an interim provincial council in the north. Under the circumstances, the APRC taking into consideration its own proposals had identified a course of action to achieve maximum and effective devolution of powers to the provinces in the short term.[65] On the northern and eastern provinces, the APRC had recommended special arrangements necessary to permit maximum devolution of power to the Northern and Eastern Provinces under the 13th Amendment. The Committee was of the view that conditions in the Eastern Provinces are conducive for holding elections to the provincial council and that elections should be held immediately. It also noted that an alternative arrangement is required in the Northern Province to enable the people of that Province to enjoy the fruits of devolution. This measured political intervention helped put things in perspective in the post-ceasefire period by reminding everyone that there can be no military solution to the island nation's ethnic conflict.

After receiving the proposals from APRC, Rajapaksa said that the government and the political parties that supported it, undertook the responsibility to fully implement the proposals. He noted that they all had a responsibility to ensure the rights of all people to enjoy freedom without fear irrespective of race, religious, political and other differences.[66] In the light of APRC's recommendations, the Rajapaksa government had taken a significant step forward in their project of finding a political solution to Sri Lanka's ethnic conflict by going in for Provincial Council elections in the Eastern Province in May 2008. This was the first democratic exercise of its kind in nearly two decades and as a prelude the ground for this was prepared by the peaceful conduct of local body elections in March 2008 in Batticaloa district. Rohitha Bogollagama, the Foreign Minister in Rajapaksa had characterised these local bodies' elections as a first step proceeding from the proposals of the APRC in a continuing process for greater devolution of power with the objective of achieving a final and durable political settlement.[67] The results of local bodies elections went in favour of the Tamil Makkal Viduthalai Puligal (TMVP), the breakaway Karuna group, now led by Pillian. Through this successful conduct of local body elections, the government had exposed the LTTE's pretence to be the sole representative of the Tamils of the North-East.

Later the Foreign Minister of Sri Lanka termed the local bodies elections in the ethnically mixed Eastern province a "major" and "singular achievement, surpassing all other peripheral successes we have had" as it had led to the empowerment of the people politically. The first ever election to the Eastern Provincial Council (EPC) was won by the ruling United People's Freedom Alliance (UPFA), which teamed up with the breakaway LTTE faction led by Pillian by securing 20 of the 35 seats. After the declaration of results, President Rajapaksa said the people had given a clear mandate for peace through the defeat of terrorism, the strengthening of democracy and development of the country.[68] He maintained, 'The voters of the Eastern Province who participated in this election peacefully and in large numbers have demonstrated their interest in protecting their democratic rights which were denied to them for nearly two decades by the force of terror.

Afterwards on a number of occasions, President Mahinda Rajapaksa reiterated his government's readiness for talks with the LTTE and its co-commitment to power devolution. In an effort to seek opposition support, Rajapaksa made it clear that there was no ethnic conflict in the country, and that the present operations of the security forces were designed to disarm the LTTE, which is posing a challenge to democracy.

This would enable the empowerment of the people in the process of evolving a viable and durable political solution. He, in a *suo motu* statement on the floor of the Parliament in October 2008 requested all to marginalise the LTTE and consider it in correct perspective. 'The LTTE does not represent the Tamil community in Sri Lanka. Therefore, military action against the LTTE should never be perceived as action against our brethren, the Tamil community. We are concerned about them and will work with them to ensure their welfare, security and aspirations since they are our fellow citizens, he added.

As the hostilities between the Sri Lankan security forces and the LTTE escalated and reached a point of no return by June 2008, the Tamil civilians in the areas which were under LTTE clutches for more than two decades began to flee and continuously reaching towards the government-controlled side. With the capture of almost all the terror strongholds, the rate of influx increased gradually. Although there was no accurate estimates of number of civilians in LTTE-held areas, UN agencies estimated that over 1 lakh people could have been displaced in Wanni due to the recent fighting. On the issue, the Government of Rajapaksa had a clear and positive policy and its agents of Kilinochchi and Mullaithivu had been asked to provide temporary accommodation in schools to internally displaced Persons (IDPs). In the circumstances government's plans were also under way to settle them in shelters located in safe areas. In this context, the government alleged that while it encouraged civilians to move from the conflict zone to safe areas, the LTTE has hindered thousands from moving to safer places by imposing a pass system and in some instances, forcing some family members to stay behind to ensure the return of the rest of the family.[69] The LTTE measures seem designed to use civilians as a buffer against the government forces which was a serious violation of international humanitarian norms. On September 1, the Sri Lankan government proposed a 'humanitarian corridor' to enable civilians trapped in battle zones to flee from the Tiger-held territories.

To help Sri Lanka solved the daily needs problems of Internally Displaced Persons (IDPs) as a result of the ongoing war, several countries of the world including the United States of America and India along with the UN agencies and NGOs supplied tonnes of relief materials to Sri Lanka for tens of thousands of people displaced due to fighting. An Indian ship containing 1,700 metric tonnes of food and relief material for displaced Sri Lankan citizens arrived at Colombo in the third week of November which was to be distributed at the disposal of the

International Committee of Red Cross (ICRC). This was the biggest Indian humanitarian intervention in Sri Lanka after the 2004 tsunami.[70] Meanwhile, V. Anandasangaree, the leader of Tamil United Liberation Front (TULF) had written a letter to Chief Minister of Tamil Nadu M. Karunanidhi on the Wanni situation and urged him to prevail upon the LTTE to let people trapped in the war zone go wherever they wished. In his letter the TULF leader said that the Tamil people of Sri Lanka were glad that Tamil Nadu had started showing interest in Sri Lankan ethnic problem but were disappointed that the concerns of the trapped Tamil people had been ignored. At the juncture, the LTTE was using them as human shield to protect them. Considering gravity of the situation, Rajapaksa served an ultimatum on LTTE to free the citizens stranded in the war zone by January 1, 2009, or face a formal ban by the government.

Decisive Fight and Fall of LTTE

At the dawn of the year 2009, the Sri Lankan Army (SLA) captured the island nation's northern town Kilinochchi – the administrative and political capital of LTTE. The military had crossed into Kilinochchi district on August 4, 2008 and had since been engaged in pitched battles with the Tigers. It was a major blow to the Liberation Tigers of Tamil Eelam and the military victory came after a phase of intense fighting that lasted several weeks. Kilinochchi had been under Tiger control for over a decade. The LTTE took control of it in 1990 when the SLA withdrew its garrisons after the departure of the India Peace-keeping Force. The SLA gained control of the town following operations Sathjaya I, II and III in September 1996. The town again fell into LTTE hands in September 1998 and ever since it had been under outfit's control.[71] It was stated that the loss of Kilinochchi had caused a substantial dent in the LTTE's image. It was also stated that after the fall of Kilinochchi, the LTTE was likely to collapse soon under unbearable military pressure on multiple fronts. It marked a turning point in the Tamil Tiger history.

Kilinochchi is a small but strategically located town that served as the political hub of the once sprawling LTTE territory in the north and east of the island. It was where LTTE leaders met diplomats and government representatives during congenial times. Most important Kilinochchi town sat on a winding highway known as A-9 that linked Jaffna in the northern tip to the rest of Sri Lanka. Once A-9 fell to the Tigers, the government had no option but to keep feeding supplies to the military in Jaffna by sea and air, making the war extremely costly.[72]

However, militarily, the LTTE had taken a continuous battering over the past two years. President Mahinda Rajapaksa did give it a window of opportunity to return to the peace talks. But after the success of the Mavil Aru operation there was no stopping of Sri Lankan armed forces. In 2007 they rapidly evicted the LTTE, which had been fractured and weakened by the Karuna revolt, from the province. More surprisingly, over the past year the Sri Lankan army backed effectively by air force and navy, had made dramatic inroads into LTTE – held territory in the northern province.[73] In August 2006, the LTTE controlled 1,500 square kilometre and at the start of the year 2009, it curtailed to 350 square kilometres with its fighting cadre strength believed to be down to about 1,000.

On January 2, 2009, the President of Sri Lanka, Mahinda Rajapaksa, announced that the Sri Lankan troops had captured Kilinochchi, the city which the LTTE had used for over a decade as its *de facto* administrative capital. In a special address to the nation on state television described it as a major victory in the world's battle against terrorism. With the loss of Kilinochchi and all major bases in the district, the Tigers have now been confined to the jungles of Mullaithivu district. 'What our heroic troops have achieved is not only the capture of the great fortress of the LTTE, but a major victory in the world's battle against terrorism.'[74] But on the occasion he added that the capture of Kilinochchi should not be viewed as the victory of one community or region over the other. He maintained that it was a dream of all Sri Lankans who are opposed to separatism, racism and terrorism and strived for peace, freedom and democracy. Rajapaksa reiterated the resolve of his government to continue the fight till the LTTE was fully and finally defeated, and asserted it was the final message to the LTTE, to lay down their arms and surrender. The President of Sri Lanka had termed the victory as the decisive one over savage terrorism that was playing around with the blood, muscle and sinews of humans. It is a victory over venomous separatism that sought to divide people on grounds of race and religion.

After Kilinochchi, the armed forces were all set to zero in, on the bases of the Tigers in Elephant Pass and Muhamalai across the Jaffna peninsula. On January 8, 2009, the LTTE was abandoning its positions on the Jaffna peninsula to make a last stand in the jungles of Mullaithivu. With the fall of Elephant Pass the Sri Lankan security forces were now poised to capture the remaining LTTE strong points at Mulliyan,

Chempiyanpattuwa, Chundikulama and Kaddaikadu. The Elephant Pass was earlier occupied by the Dutch during the colonial rule in the island, who had built a fort in 1760, identifying its strategic value in maintaining vital military cum logistic supply with the Jaffna mainland. After independence of the country in 1948, the late Prime Minister S.W.R.D. Bandaranayake maintained a small military detachment which was turned into a permanent Army transition base following the July 1983 unrest.[75] The surge of calamity in Jaffna forced the military to shift its presence from Jaffna to the more remote Elephant Pass.

In line the entire Jaffna peninsula was captured by the Sri Lanka Army by January 14 and in a major success on 25th of this month the island's troops completely captured Mullaithivu town, the last major LTTE stronghold. It is an strategic town and capital of the district with the same name and the last bastion of the Tamil Tigers. It is situated in a narrow stretch of land between Nanthikandal lagoon and the Indian ocean, Mullaithivu is inhabited largely by fishermen and had been under control of the LTTE since 1996 after a bloody battle in which more than 1,200 Sri Lankan Army soldiers were killed. With the capture of the town, the Tamil rebels were now said to be cornered in an area some 200 to 230 square kilometres in size in the district. The area has the coast on one side and lagoons and forest on the other. Karuna, who had also served the LTTE as the commander for the eastern region of Sri Lanka, said that the only major place they still control is Puthikkudiyirippu, a small town located on the A - 35 highway that links Paranthan and Mullaithivu. In this area the army's offensive had come on several fronts. It currently involved five offensive divisions and three task forces rapidly closing in on the top LTTE leaders and fighting cadres who had nowhere to escape.[76] At the juncture there was little doubt that politically speaking the game is up for Prabakaran and his organisation which is banned or designated as terrorist in about 30 countries, including India, United States, the United Kingdom, and in the latest instance Sri Lanka. It was certainly too late for any bailout package, if there was ever on anybody's practical agenda.

Now, it appeared that the moment of truth had come for the Liberation Tigers of Tamil Eelam and meanwhile the outfit received two jolts further. In Chennai, Dravida Munnetra Kazagham leader and Chief Minister M. Karunanidhi reiterated that he does not support the LTTE that had weakened the Tamil resistence. In addition the European Union, Japan, Norway, and the US, the four co-chairs of the Oslo peace process

2002, called upon the LTTE to lay down weapons and surrender after accepting the amnesty offer put forth by the Sri Lanka government and prevent further loss of civilian life.[77] In previous years the outfit, instead of vigorously pursuing the objective of getting the best devolution package through the talks, the LTTE focussed on building its armed strength with the trappings of a government – its own police, judiciary and administration. The time has come for the LTTE to give up war. The EU call to lay down arms and renounce terrorism was welcomed by the Government of Sri Lanka and as a response the government claimed that it suspended hostilities for a 48- hour period and designated no-fire zones to allow safe passage to the civilian population fleeing the conflict areas. The government also added : 'If the LTTE was ready to heed the call of the European Union to lay down arms, the need for immediate ceasefire to protect the interests of stranded civilians does not arise.'[78] Earlier, hours before the EU Foreign Ministers statement, the Tigers in a letter to the Co-chairs of Sri Lanka argued why it was not helpful to ask the LTTE to give up arms and said it was ready for an internationally supervised ceasefire.

As a result of the offensive, there was increasing belief that the final military defeat of the LTTE was near. After capturing Mullaithivu, the Sri Lankan troops, amid intense fighting further advanced into LTTE's remaining stronghold Puthukkudiyiruppu. In the area heavy fighting took place between the troops of I Sinha Regiment (ISR) and 9 Field Engineers intercepted a group of terrorists trying to infiltrate army forward boundary east of the Nathikadal lagoon. In this war in a major set-back for the Tigers, the LTTE's financial wing chief Subarathnam Selvalureiy alias Thamilendi alias Ranjith Appa, who handled the outfit's bank accounts, tax collection and all other financial matters, was killed in the confrontation. In the first week of April 2009, the Sri Lankan Defence Ministry claimed that it had gained total control over Puthukkudiyirippu. In the battle field LTTE's intelligence wing leader Pottu Amman, Theepan and Bhanu had led the LTTE fighting formations. It claimed that LTTE's artillery wing head Manniwannan was killed in the fighting and Adithyan, LTTE's former in-charge of Welioya, was also among the dead.

By the end of April, the combat operations against the LTTE had reached their conclusion and in the light of developments, the Sri Lanka government announced that the combat operations against the LTTE had reached their conclusion and the troops instructed to end the use of heavy weapons, which could harm civilian population. The brief statement titled, "Statement by the Government on the Security Situation" issued by the Presidential Secretariat said,' Our security have been instructed to end the use of heavy calibre guns, combat aircraft and aerial weapons which could cause civilian casualties.'[79] Earlier, President Rajapaksa while addressing workers of the Sri Lanka Freedom Party (SLFP) he said that the leaders trapped in the few square kilometres of the No-Fire Zone (NFZ) had reached their Waterloo. He added, 'They have only three alternatives. Either they have to surrender to our armed forces, eat the cyanide capsule and commit suicide or plunge into the sea.'

As the intense fighting for decisive war was going on between the LTTE and the Sri Lankan security forces, the islands government faced the most sensitive humanitarian challenge of the time. The immediate priority was to ensure the safety of Tamil civilians, officially reckoned to be in the range of 100,000 to 200,000, whom the LTTE evidently had no compunction in using as a human shield. In this period President Rajapaksa adopted the "Zero Civilian Casualty Policy" and he expressed satisfaction when the Sri Lankan forces captured Kilinochchi, claimed that the army had implemented perfectly the government's policy during the operation to liberate the areas. Under a policy, the Sri Lankan government created several safe zones and no-fire zone in the war regions to protect and provide safe passage to civilians. According to military in mid February, the Tigers were confined to 140 square kilometres and were engaged in a no-holds-barred combat to halt the military advance. In spite of governmental efforts for civilian safety, the independent observers of the country were of the view that safe zone was a misnomer for two reasons. Firstly, there was no agreement between the forces and the Tigers on the no fire areas. Secondly, the citizens caught in the crossfire had little knowledge about the zones. 'It is a no-win situation for the ordinary citizens stranded in the fast – shrinking Tiger - held territory. We only hope and pray that better sense prevails and the Tigers keep out of the areas where the majority of the innocent citizens are struck.'[80]

The international community including the UN and some big powers had also shown equal interest in the safety of Sri Lankan citizens in war zones. Apart from expressing concern over the safety of Sri Lankan citizens, Sir John Holmes, UN Undersecretary General for Humanitarian Affairs, at a briefing on the situation in Sri Lanka in Newyork criticised Rajapaksa's order for two-day halt to military offensive and said that very few civilians could cross over during the 48-hour humanitarian pause observed by the Sri Lankan security forces. In another development, Richard Boucher, the US Assistant Secretary of State for South Asian & Central Asian Affairs also telephoned Rohitha Bogollagama, the Sri Lankan Foreign Minister and expressed US concern over the wider implications for Sri Lanka's security. In the talks Bogollagama assured Boucher that the security forces had always respected the sanctity of safe zones designated by the government, where the civilian population has been herded by the LTTE and would continue to desist from directing retaliatory fire at such areas. Further, Ban Ki Moon, UN Secretary General, too appealed on LTTE that children should not be held hostage, recruited as child soldiers or put in harms way. Claude Heller of United Nations Security Council said, 'We demand that the LTTE immediately lay down arms, renounce terrorism, allow a UN-assisted evacuation of the remaining civilians in the conflict area, and join the political process.'

By the end of April 2009 the Government of Sri Lanka had made several no-fire zones and civilians were coming in government – controlled zones in large numbers which, on the other side, presented before the authority the gigantic task of providing them immediate shelter and basic facilities. President Rajapaksa in an interview to CNN – IBN in Colombo made it clear that his government's key objective now was getting the civilians out from the clutches of the LTTE. Noting that the military operations were "almost over", he said the choice before the LTTE was either surrender or face the Army. About the current phase of war, he disclosed that what he had ordered was not a ceasefire but it was proceeding almost like a ceasefire….. our are moving forward …it looks like a real war but we are not using our heavy weapons.[81] The government termed the unilateral cessation of offensive military operations a "joke" and said that the remaining LTTE cadres had no option but to surrender with their weapons and release the civilians they were using as human shield. 'It is a joke and cheap publicity stunt. They were not fighting but are on the run from the military.' However, the LTTE's declaration came in the face of an unprecedented humanitarian crisis and in response to the calls made by the UN, EU, the governments of the USA, India and others. Before the finishing days of war nearly 2,00,000 civilians had crossed over into the government territory in the last few months and had been accommodated in 44 temporary camps, spread over the districts of Vavuniya, Mannar and Jaffna.

For the LTTE beginning of May was a decisive one that proved a debacle and it accepted the defeat in principle. Now, the Sri Lankan military was less than a kilometre from the remaining part of the No-Fire Zone (NFZ) where the LTTE top brass and cadre had been holed up holding an estimated 20,000 civilians as hostage. When about 80,000 civilian were to flee the LTTE - occupied Zone on May 10, 2009, the Tigers made a determination that they have lost the war and that no purpose would be achieved by holding on to the civilians. The very next day the Tigers seemed to have deserted the sentry points, dismantled the defence lines and destroyed every thing they could. The exodus of the last batch of civilians started on 12/13 and perhaps by the night of May 15 there was no civilians left in the 1.5-square – kilometre area the Tigers were boxed into. On the other hand, the Sri Lankan military was hopeful of neutralising the military capabilities of the Liberation Tigers of Tamil Eelam in the next 48 hours and was poised for a major breakthrough. In fact a significant aspect of the confrontation between the Sri Lankan army and the LTTE for over eight weeks now was the total absence of any diversionary attack by the LTTE in other parts of Sri Lanka. The last successful diversionary attack was on a Muslim procession in Matara in the southern province on March 10. One would have expected easily that facing severe pressure from the army, the LTTE would have tried to organise more diversionary attacks outside the Tamil areas. But the fact was that it was not able to do so for want of human and material resources left to organise diversionary attacks. The loss of its capabilities in the Tamil and non-Tamil areas was immense.

Decisive debacle for the LTTE started on May 16, 2009, and lasted for two more days although President Rajapaksa declared on that very day at the G - 11 Summit in Jordan that the LTTE had been defeated, even as troops moved in to flush out the remaining Tiger cadre and leaders holed up in the area. The endgame inside the war zone began early on May 16, with soldiers freeing the last remaining coastal stretch that the LTTE held. The link-up marked the first time that the military had total control of the island's coastline in three decades. On May 17, the military and the Tigers were engaged in one of the most intense battles witnessed during the 33 - month - old Eelam War IV. The military operations began at 5 a.m. and loud explosions could be heard in the battle zone throughout the day.

However, the curtain came down on Eelam War IV in the early hours of May 18 with the decimation of the LTTE's military capabilities in a 22 - hour battle, which also resulted in the death of at least 18 of its top leaders. The intensity of the battle in the final hours to end the war could be gauged from the fact that the military collected at least 250 bodies of the Tiger cadres. The first sign that the military had completely overwhelmed the last remaining cadres and leaders of the LTTE were evident to the correspondent of *The Hindu* around 10 a.m. at the headquarters of the 58 Division. Around the same time confirmation of the news that it was all over for the LTTE came on the pro - LTTE web site, Tamil Net titled, 'Long live human dignity, shame on the international community.' It read, 'While the so-called international community is exposed by its shameful conning, thousands of Tamil civilians and combatants are laying down their lives to uphold Tamil dignity and human dignity.'[82] The fighting with Prabakaran and his men erupted at 4 a.m. and was over within 90 minutes, leaving the man who had terrorised the country for over a quarter century dead near a lagoon in Mullaithivu district.[83] On the same day in the evening, the three chiefs of the Sri Lanka Army, Navy and the Air Force called on President Rajapaksa and informed him that the war against the LTTE had concluded and the forces had been successful in wiping out its entire leadership and either destroyed or captured its arms and ammunitions.

At the G-11 Summit Rajapaksa told the gathering that the defeat of the LTTE heralded a new era in Sri Lanka and provided all Sri Lankans with a brand new opportunity for peace and development. 'Many in the world believed that the LTTE is invincible, but, I am proud to announce at this august gathering that my government with the total commitment of our armed forces, has in an unprecedented humanitarian operation finally defeated the LTTE militarily.'[84] 'This freedom comes after 30 long years. My government's precise and well coordinated humanitarian operation has so far succeeded in rescuing over 2,10,000 civilians who were being used as human shields by the LTTE. The liberation of the regions hitherto controlled by the LTTE, which amounted to a fourth of Sri Lanka's land mass, paves the way for democracy to root itself and development to march ahead after decades of conflict,' he added. Later, the President in an address to Parliament said that the island nation had been freed from the clutches of separatist terrorism and the need of the hour was to ensure full rights to the Tamils in the country, with a home-grown solution acceptable to all.[85]

The death of Velupillai Prabakaran, the LTTE chief, was announced officially by the Sri Lankan government when the island's military had recovered his bullet-ridden body laying on the bank of the Nanthikadal lagoon and after it was identified by Karuna, a minister in Rajapaksa's government and former Tiger commander who broke ranks with the LTTE in 2004. Sri Lanka's decisive victory over the LTTE is the biggest success story in the world of anti-terrorism. It is in sharp contrast to the dragging military campaign the US leads against the Taliban and Al Qaeda in Afghanistan and Pakistan. It also outshines the collapse of the Maoist Shining Path movement in Peru. And it came about despite emerging evidence that a section of the West tried to save at least some LTTE leaders before the war ended. The Tigers' biggest blunder after Rajiv Gandhi's killing was the 2005 appeal to Tamils to boycott the presidential election. In the process, Ranil Wickremesinghe, who signed the 2002 truce with Prabakaran, was defeated narrowly, after losing Tamil votes that would have gone to him. This led to the victory of Mahinda Rajapaksa, who proved to be the LTTE's nemesis.

The dramatic collapse of the Tamil Tigers, accompanied by white flags and surrenders, is a sad commentary on the politics of uncompromising mayhem the rebels pursued for so long in Sri Lanka. When they were repeatedly called to go for negotiations, they decided to settle for nothing less than independence. Those who wanted to shake hands with the Sri Lankan state were dubbed traitors and killed. The LTTE set out to form an independent Tamil state by breaking up the north and east of Sri Lanka. They never fought any elections but prided themselves as the sole and authentic representatives of the Tamils. By the time a quarter century of unceasing bloodletting passed, more than 90,000 people lay dead, many thousands were injured and maimed, the Tamils were in ruins, and there was no trace of Tamil Eelam. The dominant thinking now in Colombo is that the Tamil community needs relief and rehabilitation, particularly in the northern and eastern provinces, nothing more; a region that saw nothing but war for over two decades needs economic development to merge it with the larger Sri Lanka. It is highly unlikely that this assessment would change in the near future.

References

1. M.R. Narayan Swamy, *The Tiger Vanquished LTTE's Story* (New Delhi : Sage Publications, 2010), p. xxxvii.
2. Ibid., pp. xli-xlii.
3. Ibid., p. 24.
4. B. Muralidhar Reddy, 'The War is Over', *Frontline*, Vol. 26, No. 12, 6-19 June 2009 (Chennai : 2009), p. 7.
5. Ibid., p. 8.

6. Ranil Wickremesinghe, 'The Way to Resolve Sri Lanka's Political Crisis,' *The Hindu*, 6 April 2007.
7. Vinod F. Khobragade, 'Ethnic Politics in Sri Lanka –Political Solution to Tamil Cause and Military Solution to LTTE', *South Asia Politics*, Vol. 7, No. 11, March 2009 (New Delhi : 2009) p. 26.
8. B. Muralidhar Reddy, 'War Clouds Darken the Outlook for Peace,' *The Hindu*, 4 August 2006.
9. Ibid.
10. Ranil Wickremesinghe, 'The Way to Resolve Sri Lanka's Political Crisis.'
11. M.R. Narayan Swamy, *The Tiger Vanquished LTTE's Story*, p. 64.
12. Ibid., pp. 65-66.
13. Arti Bali, 'Enforcing Military Solution to Ethnic Conflict,' *South Asia Politics*, Vol. 7, No. 2, June 2008 (New Delhi : 2008) p. 49.
14. B. Muralidhar Reddy, 'The War is Over', p. 7.
15. Vinod F. Khobragade, 'Ethnic Politics in Sri Lanka – Political Solution to Tamil Cause and Military Solution to LTTE,' p. 27.
16. B. Muralidhar Reddy, 'Not a Good Time for Advocates of Peace in Sri Lanka', *The Hindu*, 12 September 2006.
17. Ibid.
18. B. Muralidhar Reddy, 'South Asia's Most Militarised Society,' in Ibid., 27 September 2006.
19. Ibid.
20. Ibid., editorial, 6 November 2007.
21. B. Muralidhar Reddy, 'The War is Over,' p. 8.
22. Ministry of External Affairs, BSM Division, '*Brief on India –Sri Lanka Relations*, 26 February 2007 (New Delhi : 2007) p. 4.
23. M.R Narayan Swamy, *The Tiger Vanquished LTTE's Story*, p. 1.
24. *Indo-Asian News Service* (New Delhi), 30 January 2007.
25. Ibid.
26. Ibid., 27 February 2007.
27. Ibid., 31 May 2006.
28. Ibid, 25 February 2007.
29. Arti Bali, 'Enforcing Military Solutions to Ethnic Conflict,' p. 49.
30. Ranil Wickremesinhe, 'The Way to Resolve Sri Lanka's Political Crisis.'
31. Ibid.
32. As quoted in Ibid.
33. Ibid.

34. *The Hindu*, editorial, 24 October 2007.
35. Ibid., 17 October 2007.
36. Ibid., editorial, 24 October 2007.
37. Ibid., 23 October 2007.
38. Ibid.
39. M.R. Narayan Swamy, *The Tiger Vanquished LTTE's Story*,' pp. 112-13.
40. Ibid., *Introduction*, p. lv.
41. *The Hindu*, 4 November 2007.
42. Ibid.
43. *Indo-Asian News Service*, 2 November 2007.
44. *The Hindu*, 5 November 2007.
45. Daily News as quoted in Ibid., 6 November 2007.
46. *The Hindu*, 19 December 2007.
47. Arti Bali, 'Enforcing Military Solutions to Ethnic Conflict,' p. 49.
48. *Indo-Asian News Service*, 31 December 2007.
49. V. Suryanarayan, 'Explaining Prabakaran's Persistent Defiance,' *The Hindu*, 21 December 2007.
50. Ibid.
51. Ibid., 25 December 2007.
52. *Indo-Asian News Service*, 31 December 2007.
53. *The Hindu*, editorial, 10 January 2008.
54. Ram Manikkalingam, 'Will War Lead to Peace in Sri Lanka?' Ibid., 21 January 2008.
55. Arti Bali, 'Enforcing Military Solutions to Ethnic Conflict,' p. 50.
56. Ibid.
57. *Indo-Asian News Service*, 1 June 2008.
58. Ibid.
59. M.R. Narayan Swamy, *The Tiger Vanquished LTTE's Story*, pp. 132-33.
60. *The Hindu*, 19 March 2008.
61. Ibid., 23 July 2008.
62. Malini Parthasarathy, 'The Danger of Tamil Chauvinism', Ibid., 14 October 2008.
63. Ibid., 3 November 2008.
64. Ibid., 8 December 2008.
65. Ibid., 24 January 2008.
66. Ibid., 25 January 2008.

67. Ibid., editorial, 31 March 2008.
68. Ibid., 12 May 2008.
69. Ibid., 1 September 2008.
70. *Indo-Asian News Service*, 6 November 2008.
71. *The Hindu*, 3 January 2009.
72. M.R. Narayan Swamy, *The Tiger Vanquished LTTE's Story*, p. 147.
73. *The Hindu*, editorial, 5 January 2009.
74. Ibid., 3 January 2009.
75. Ibid., 10 January 2009.
76. Ibid., editorial 27 January 2009.
77. R. Hariharan, 'The Movement of Truth for the LTTE', in Ibid., 5 February 2009.
78. Ibid., 25 February 2009.
79. Ibid., 28 April 2009.
80. Ibid., 4 February 2009.
81. See the text of Rajapaksa's *interview given to CNN – IBN* in Colombo in Ibid., 29 April 2009.
82. *Frontline*, 19 June 2009, p. 14.
83. *Indo-Asian News Service*, 20 May 2009.
84. *The Hindu*, 17 May 2009.
85. Ibid., 20 May 2009.

6

SRI LANKA : TODAY AND TOMORROW

Post-LTTE Scenario

There was a time and not long ago when it looked that there would be no return of peace in Sri Lanka minus Prabakaran. But the rebel chieftain slipped on the political art of compromise and accommodation so badly that Sri Lanka concluded that his elimination was necessary to unlock the knot it was in, ever since Prabakaran vowed to settle for nothing less than an independent Tamil Eelam.[1] The security forces claimed that the LTTE lost around 22,000 cadre, while 9,100 of them have been apprehended. These figures might be exaggerated, but the LTTE had probably lost between 12,000 and 15,000 cadre in Eelam War IV. After suffering a crushing defeat and left leaderless in isolated pockets, many of these cadre including the sleeper cells, are likely to be a demoralised lot. Prabakaran's death has left a big void in the LTTE leadership. His successor will find it very difficult to meet the high expectations of supporters particularly after the organisation has been so grievously maulded.[2] However, as KP's statement said, 'There is not a person who can doubt the LTTE's fearless and unending commitment to this cause, with which we have been entrusted by our people. Know that the Tamils are a people deeply rooted in culture and history. No force can prevent the attainment of justice for our people. Our sons and daughters have taken up this call without question and without hesitation or fear of death.'[3] The LTTE had for almost three decades fought the Sri Lankan military and defended its right to carry arms as a means of protecting the Tamil people living in the island.

After defeating the LTTE militarily at the G-11 Summit in Jordon and later in his address to the Parliament, Rajapaksa reiterated that the island had been freed from the clutches of separatist terrorism and the need of the hour was to ensure full rights to the Tamils in the country with a home grown solution acceptable to all. 'At this victorious moment, it is necessary for us to state with great responsibility that we do not accept a military solution as the final solution ...the responsibility that we accept after freeing the Tamil people from the LTTE is a responsibility that no government in the history of Sri Lanka has accepted. It is necessary that we give these people the freedom that are the right of people in all other parts of the country. Similarly, it is necessary that the political solution they need should be brought closer to them faster than any country or government in the world would bring.[4] The President had blamed the LTTE for this position of Tamil community. Those who raised their voices for the protection of terrorists, and all who helped the terrorists should now fall at the feet of these Tamil mothers and seek their pardon. Those who live abroad and supported the terrorists with funds, if they have any love for their own people should leave no room for terrorism again. But as the end of LTTE is not the end of the humanitarian problem. It will be the beginning of a new phase of it. In his address Rajapaksa admitted that having defeated the most ruthless terrorists of the world, another powerful challenge was the task of restoring the rights and dignity of the Tamil people destroyed by the LTTE. The state of the Sri Lankan economy may not enable the Sri Lankan government to deal with it adequately. Earlier keeping in view the fact mainly India and the International Committee of the Red Cross had been allowed by the Sri Lankan Government to undertake humanitarian relief work.

Developments over Sri Lanka's ethnic problem and the ongoing Eelam War IV were watched and analysed by the countries of the world — international organisations including India, US, Cuba, Serbia, Vietnam, the EU, UN and NAM Summit held in mid - July 2009. Indian Prime Minister Manmohan Singh said that President Mahinda Rajapaksa had won the war against the LTTE and its terrorism, and can now win the peace. His enormous talent should help solve the long drawn out issue in Sri Lanka permanently. Rajapaksa also met several leaders of Cuba, Serbia, Vietnam, Malaysia, Egypt, South Africa, Philippines and Nepal on the sidelines of the 15th Non-Aligned Summit and they all welcomed Sri Lanka's success in defeating the LTTE and the extended period of terror in the country. They held the view that the end of terrorism in the country had opened new opportunities for investment in Sri Lanka.

Earlier, during the war the US, UN Security Council and Amnesty International had condemned strongly the LTTE for its use of civilians as human shields and called on the government to take urgent action to ensure the safety of civilians. Barack Obama, the US President, condemned the LTTE's use of civilians as 'human shields' and urged the Sri Lankan government to stop the indiscriminate shelling' in the area and asked for access by humanitarian agencies to the civilians who are trapped between the warring parties and those displaced people within Sri Lanka so that they can receive additional support needed. In addition, Gregg Sullivan, a senior US State Department office, termed the post – LTTE phase a real opportunity to get Sri Lanka back to its status in the 1980s as one of the "Asian Tigers" with vigorous economic growth. 'If the Sri Lankan Government moves forward with policies that embrace the civilian Tamil community, bring the Tamils into the reconstruction process, empower responsible Tamil leaders through implementation of the 13th Amendment, and foster a new political and economic integration of the Sinhala and minority communities, it can be an example for all other countries that have suffered ethnic conflict. In line the UN Security Council, in a statement called for an end to the use of heavy calibre weapons, while Irene Khan, the Secretary General of Amnesty International, called on the Security Council to ensure that attacks on civilians by the Sri Lankan army or the LTTE be stopped, that the LTTE allow all civilians to leave the conflict area; and that the Sri Lankan government stop using heavy artillery in a very densely populated area and provide immediate access to international monitors and humanitarian agencies.

On number of occasions, Mahinda Rajapaksa, the President of Sri Lanka, reiterated that the whole country has been liberated from LTTE terrorism and his intention was to save the Tamil people from the cruel grip of the LTTE and we all must now live as equals in this island nation. Commenting on the prevailing situation in Sri Lanka, *The Times of India* wrote editorially on 2 June 2009, 'The war against the LTTE has been won but Colombo has a battle ahead to win the minds of the Tamils. A beginning has been made but there are disturbing questions that need answers. The alleged massacre of civilians is just one such. Backing from countries like China, Pakistan, Russia and regrettably, India, may help Colombo override the international community's apprehensions about the way the war was won and how refugees are treated. Colombo needs to engage constructively with criticism and respect the right to dissent. It should collaborate with international agencies to rehabilitate and rebuild the Tamil areas.[5] Two days after the military operations against the LTTE ended, on 21 May Rajapaksa announced a 180-day resettlement plan which was elaborated further in the meeting of the newly constituted All Parties Committee (APC) for Development and Reconciliation held in the first week of July 2009 and chaired by the President himself.

At the end of Eelam War IV, the Government of Sri Lanka was confident of resettling and providing a new lease of life to the Tamils displaced by war in the north. President's G - 11 Summit confirmed that efforts were under way to complement the humanitarian mission with a political solution, 'History has taught us that solutions externally prescribed, with little understanding of the complexity of the problem on the ground are prone to failure. My government is, therefore, firmly committed to seeking a home-grown solution acceptable to all.'[6] Emphasis on resettlement was reiterated by the President in the third week of May when India's National Security Advisor M.K. Narayanan and Foreign Secretary Shiv Shankar Menon visited Colombo just after the end of war. He also revealed further that his government also intends to begin a broader dialogue with all parties, including the Tamil parties, in the new circumstances, for further enhancement of political arrangements to bring about lasting peace and reconciliation.[7] Amid continuing international concern, Basil Rajapaksa, the President's brother and overall in-charge of the rehabilitation, while outlining his government's thinking on the rehabilitation of the displaced Tamils talked about government's experience and ability to undertake the massive exercise.[8] He said that the government had already resettled a similar number in the eastern province, which the military captured from the Tamil Tigers in 2007. The issue of resettlement of war displaced Tamils emerged as one of the trickiest as well as thorniest problems for the Sri Lankan government.

As a follow up of his promise to address the grievances of the Tamil community and resettle the displaced people in the north, Rajapaksa convened an All Party meeting on 2 July 2009. However, it was aimed at getting rid of several charges levelled by the international community in general. At the moment, the Rajapaksa government was seen in many world capitals as an almost authoritarian regime with a shoddy record on human rights. Media freedom was restricted and scores of people, including journalists and human rights activists, had been killed or had disappeared in extraordinary circumstances. State agencies had been blamed in several cases.[9] For instance, following the war the, European Union nations called for an independent war crimes investigation into the killing of civilians in Sri Lanka. David Miliband, the British foreign secretary had also said that there had been "very grave allegations" of war crimes on both sides of the conflict and they should be properly investigated. Taking a humanitarian approach, the EU foreign ministers, in a statement, appealed to the Sri Lankan government to let UN aid groups into the country to help provide food and medical care to civilians caught in the fighting and to seek reconciliation with the country's minority Tamil population.

For the first time since a section of the Tamil groups in Sri Lanka took to arms 30 years ago to fight for their rights, representatives of all political parties came together in the first meeting of the newly constituted All Party Committee on Development and Reconciliation chaired by President Mahinda Rajapaksa. It was attended by 22 political parties along with representatives of the opposition United National Party (UNP), pro-LTTE Tamil National Alliance (TNA) and the break-away LTTE political party Tamil Makkal Viduthalai Pulikal (TMVP). Besides discussing development and reconciliation, the APC focussed on speedy resettlement and rehabilitation of the nearly 3,00,000 war - displaced sheltered in government-run relief camps in the northern province. In his remarks at the opening session Rajapaksa told the party representatives that the operation to free people from terror was now over and now it was time for a humanitarian mission to address new challenges. He appealed the gathering to set aside the past and look ahead. 'It is necessary to bring peace and tranquility to the minds of the people in the North whose lives had been so badly shattered in the recent past, and restore their democratic rights and self-respect.'[10] He noted that it is more important to search for the commonalities that existed among the political parties gathered than seek the causes that divided them.

In the meeting the pro-Tamil parties, in particular, requested the President for speedy resettlement and rehabilitation of the war-displaced. N. Srikantha of the Tamil National Alliance, the single largest party of the Tamils in Parliament, expressed the gratitude of his party to Rajapaksa for the opportunity to participate in the forum. He said in the conference that TNA believed the country now had the political will to solve the national question. Srikantha assured the President of his Party's support in achieving democratic solutions. Likewise, Nimal Siripala De Silva, Minister of Healthcare and Nutrition, representing the ruling Sri Lanka Freedom Party (SLFP) and Kabier Hashim, UNP MP, offered their cooperation and held the view that the present situation required positive attitude towards development and reconciliation to ensure lasting peace.[11] The Eelam People's Democratic Party stressed the need to give priority to resettlement of Internally Displaced Persons (IDPs) as well as opening the A - 9 highway for civilian traffic. In a nutshell, the first APC fully assured the President of their cooperation and support in this ambitious project. It had strengthened the government's confidence and raised hope all round that the rehabilitation process will be fast-tracked and implemented smoothly.

Even earlier to the first meeting of All Party Committee (APC), in an interview to *The Hindu* in Colombo on 30 June 2009, Rajapaksa highlighted his determination to re-settle as soon as possible the Tamil civilians displaced by the conflict with the LTTE. He laid out his road map of what needed to be put in place to ensure the safety and meet the basic needs of those who are to be sent back to their villages. In Rajapaksa's sketched vision in post-conflict Sri Lanka there was no place for racism and anything that creates a disturbance among our three communities – Sinhala, Tamil and Muslim. In course of the interview he also talked about the political solution –"the 13th Amendment Plus" – he had in mind but made it clear that he wanted to get that from the people or after re-election as President. He insisted that all parties, and especially the Tamil National Alliance representatives should participate in discussions on the political solution.[12] He also took the opportunity to reiterate his belief, 'in my theory there are no minorities in Sri Lanka, there are only those who love the country and those who don't'.

In a further clarification on approach to the political settlement of The Tamils, a senior Sri Lankan official and Rajiva Wijesinha, Secretary to the Ministry of Disaster Management and Human Rights, disclosed that Colombo wanted to adopt a cautious approach to the issue of political settlement of Tamils. 'We need to move forward on the process of empowerment. But one problem with federalism in a small country is that it is subject more to splitting. Quoting the development in Kosovo, the secretary said that we have to be careful.[13] He acknowledged that unfortunately, there was discrimination and violence against the Tamils in the 1970s and early 1980s. Colombo believed that the settlement of 1987 should have helped to resolve several issues, but it did not happen, largely due to the intransigence of the Liberation Tigers of Tamil Eelam as also to internal Sri Lankan politics. In the post-LTTE phase what the displaced Sri Lankan Tamils returning home wanted was empowerment – the ability to decide all non-security aspects of government such as the social and educational systems. The secretary underlined that we have solved some initial problems but have not been implementing the provisions fast enough due to tension of the last 20 years.

Mahinda Rajapaksa after defeating the LTTE President, did not miss any opportunity to assure the Tamils of their safety, security and equal treatment. Having got fresh mandate by the people in the Presidential election held on 26 January 2010, at a function organised to mark the 62nd Independence Day on February 4, Rajapaksa urged minorities in general and Tamils in particular to come forward for discussions on the resolution of all issues with an open mind and assured that every one would be treated equally. 'Anyone can go anywhere freely. That is very important. This is our motherland. All of us are children of one mother. All of us are kings today. We all should live together as brothers with equal rights and dignity. Let us discuss our issues among ourselves and resolve them. Everyone will receive all facilities in an equal manner. That is called equality and equal rights. One country, one people, one law, That is our way, the only way'.[14] He assured the public to use the fresh mandate to re-establish all that was lost over the past 30 years due to war.

In course of the Eelam War IV, the United Nations had been critical of Sri Lanka's approach towards the humanitarian issues. According to UN figures, an estimated 7,000 ethnic Tamil civilians were killed between 20 January and 7 May 2009, when a military offensive pushed the rebels into a tiny enclave in the north-east. Earlier too the UN secretary-general Ban Ki-Moon had called for the protection of trapped civilians, asking the LTTE to allow civilians to leave the conflict area of their own free will and reminded the Sri Lankan government of its responsibility to protect civilians, and to avoid the use of heavy weapons in areas where there were civilians. Recently in the year 2010 the Secretary General Ban Ki-Moon decided to appoint a panel of experts to advise him on Sri Lanka and the vociferous objections raised by Colombo to the proposal. The decision of Secretary – General to appoint a panel of experts was termed as uncalled for and unwarranted by President Rajapaksa and condemned by the chair of the Coordinating Bureau of the Non-Aligned Movement. Its Ambassador and Permanent Representative Maged A. Abdelaziz in his letter to Ban said, 'The Non-Aligned Movement strongly condemns selective targeting of individual countries which it deems contrary to the Founding Principles of the Movement and the United Nations Charter.'[15] Since the defeat of the LTTE, Colombo had been countering demands for a commission to investigate alleged human rights violations in the 34-month long Eelam War IV and repeatedly pointed to the resolution by the Human Rights Commission lauding Sri Lanka on the issue.

In the circumstances, Sri Lankan President Mahinda Rajapaksa decided in March 2010 to appoint a committee to study the root cause of the ethnic conflict, lessons learnt since sections of Tamils took to military to gain their rights in the mid-seventies and challenges faced since the military defeat of the LTTE in May 2009. It would be a comprehensive study and would cover the circumstances leading to the deployment of the IPKF and the 1989 Janatha Vimukthi Peramuna (JVP) second insurgency[16] as said by Mahinda Samarasinghe, Minister of Disaster Management and Human Rights. Particularly, in the light of UN objections, Rajapaksa, in May 2010, constituted a eight-member Sri Lankan Lessons Learnt and Reconciliation Commission (LLRC) to probe the incidents from early 2002 and the end of the war in 2009. The said Commission submitted its interim report in September 2010 in which it suggested measures to better the lot of resettled Internally Displaced Persons and people living in the former conflict areas. As it had been asked to fix responsibility and recommend ways for reconciliation between the majority and minority communities, its suggestions also include the measures to enable people to use their own language in official dealings, especially making statements to the police.[17] President Rajapaksa discussed the rehabilitation of the Tamils and other bilateral issues with Manmohan Singh, Indian Prime Minister when he visited New Delhi in mid-October 2010.

Re-settlement of Internally Displaced Persons

Every calamity presents an opportunity for progress. The war has ended, but the struggle for economic survival is just beginning for the Tamil people of the Northern Province of Sri Lanka. Peace has come, but for it to last a union of hearts is essential. A complex interplay of war and politics in Sri Lanka had led to a situation where national reconciliation appeared a distant and difficult proposition. There exists now in Sri Lanka a government wedded to a mindset that there never was an ethnic conflict, only a terrorist problem, now that the LTTE has been crushed beyond recognition, the menace of terrorism is over, although security concerns remain.[18] Thus the Tamil population of Sri Lanka needs both peace and bread with human dignity to become proud citizens of the beautiful country that is linked spiritually to India through Buddhism. Speaking at a seminar on "Post Conflict Sri Lanka and India's Role' organised by the Observer Research Foundation in Chennai in the first week of July 2010 C. Romesh Jayasinghe, Sri Lanka's High Commissioner to India, said that Colombo would also draw on the UN agencies, the International Committee of the Red Cross (ICRC) and reputed international non-governmental organisations (INGO) for assistance in coping with those displaced and affected by the conflict.

As we all are aware New Delhi is bound to take lively interests in Sri Lankan affairs, particularly on Tamil problems due to various reasons known to all. Organisation of the seminar had provided several eminent scholars and experts an opportunity to express their views on the issue. Apart from Sri Lankan envoy, it was attended by N. Ram, Editor-in-Chief, of *The Hindu*, R. Swaminathan, President, International Institute of Security and Safety Management, V.R. Raghavan, President, Centre for Security Analysis and N. Sathiya Moorthy of the Observer Research Foundation, the seminar organising institution among others. N. Ram, describing the nature of relations between New Delhi and Colombo said that India-Sri Lanka relations were tied closely to the principal national question of the status of Sri Lankan Tamils for a long time and quoted the statement of M. Karunanidhi, the Chief Minister of Tamil Nadu in State Assembly asking the Tamils to focus on autonomy and devolution of powers. Tamil politicians should adjust themselves to this reality, and they would do well to participate in the political process and fight for the Tamils right from within the constitutional framework.'[19] Economic expert R. Swaminathan was of the view that in spite of the military victory, terrorism could not be eliminated until the grievances of the Tamils were addressed and resolved, but V.R. Raghavan hinted at military excesses and said that it was up to the government to make sure the people did not treat the military as an "occupying force". N. Sathiya Moorthy suggested to remain watchful on Tamil diasporas.

Following the end of Eelam War IV in Sri Lanka, India pledged Rs. 500 and Rs. 25 crore granted by Tamil Nadu for the rehabilitation of Internally Displaced Persons in government transit facilities. In October 2009, a 10-member delegation of Members of Parliament from Tamil Nadu visited Sri Lanka to assess the state of the internally displaced persons in the hill region of the island nation for an interaction with Indian-origin Sri Lankans working in the plantation sector. T.R. Baalu, leader of the delegation said that the team was there on the instructions of Tamil Nadu Chief Minister M. Karunanidhi in consultation with the Union government and that it would visit the IDP camps and urge the government of Sri Lanka to expedite resettlement process.[20] Another team member and Rajya Sabha MP Kanimozhi reportedly said that the team would extend assistance through the Government of India to the Sri Lankan Tamils to help them to live with equal and legitimate rights. The Sri Lankan government assured the delegation that 58,000 internally-displaced Sri Lankan Tamils in camps will be sent back to their native places in 15 days. In the same month Preneet Kaur, India's Minister of

State for External Affairs met Sri Lankan Foreign Minister Rohitha Bogollogama in a meeting on the sidelines of the 8th Asia Cooperation Dialogue (ACD) Ministerial Meeting at Colombo and the former had expressed New Delhi's readiness to provide further humanitarian assistance for the welfare of nearly 2.5 lakh war-displaced people housed in the refugee camps of Sri Lanka's Northern Province. Bogollogama told his Indian counterpart that from the perspective of his government, everything possible was being done to improve conditions in the IDP welfare villages.

At this juncture India's help is needed particularly in the spheres of agricultural research and education. Over 80 per cent of the population of the Northern Province, comprising the districts of Jaffna, Kilinochchi, Mullaithivu, Mannar and Vavuniya, depend on farm enterprises for work and income security. Prior to the conflict, the province had a cultivable area of about 300,000 hectares, of which over 100,000 hectares were under rice. The rest had onion, chillies, mungbean, sesame, groundnut, yams, fruits, vegetables and coconut. There had been much damage to the ecological foundations of agriculture, such as soil, water and biodiversity, due to planting of mines, erection of protective structures and other security measures.[21] The Northern Province was an agricultural paradise before the conflict. Currently, it is estimated that crop production may be of the order of 150,000 tonnes, as against 800,000 tonnes earlier. In addition to agriculture, Indian investors could focus on construction, infrastructure and railways. With tourism expected to resurge now that the conflict had ended, Indian players were expected to invest in building tourism infrastructure in the northern province.

By October-November 2009, more than 50,000 war-displaced had been sent to their original villages in Vavuniya, Mannar, Kilinochchi and Mullaithivu district. Remaining 2.50,000 Tamil refugees were in camps and the government was planning to release them gradually. Progress on their release was linked to de-mining work, certification by the UN and creation of basic infrastructure for people to return to normal life. At a function in Mannar town in the last week of October 6,631 displaced persons were released. Each of them was given Sri Lankan Rs. 5,000 in cash and a saving bank account with a deposit of Rs. 20,000. A packet containing rations to last six months, an emergency kit, roofing and bed sheets were supplied to each. Island's officials in general felt that it would be difficult for the government to engage in a constructive dialogue on a political solution until the resettlement issue had been dealt with. 'It is hard to think those in welfare camps will be too keen to discuss a political solution before they get settled. To engage in a constructive dialogue, it is best to get this out of the way.[22] The government had estimated that $1.5 billion per year must be spent in the northern province reconstruction process, Ajith Nivard Cabraal, governor of the Central Bank of Sri Lanka, in an interview with *The Hindu*, stated that in order to encourage restoration of livelihoods, the Central Bank had set aside $ 2 billion for quick loans. Cabraal felt that the resurgent post-war economy would return to a 6.5 per cent rate and catch up with India's growth rates in a few years.

In the meantime, keeping ahead of the coming Parliamentary and Presidential election, President Rajapaksa directed the authorities to resettle the war displaced Tamil civilians from the transitional camps by January 31, 2010. As a further concession, the government had lifted the restrictions imposed on the movement of the camp dwellers from 1 December. Major General Kamal Gunaratne, Competent Authority (CA) for the government - run camps in the north said, 'Those wanting to travel out of the relief camps, can get into the convoy of buses from Vavuniya to Jaffna and visit their relatives, friends and well-wishers in the north. They can return to the camp by the same convoys'.[23] Rajapaksa had also announced a package under which each of the resettled people would be provided with Sri Lankan Rs. 5,000 in cash, a saving bank account with Sri Lankan Rs. 50,000, six months of ration and an emergency kit with roofing material and bed sheets. By the end of the year, the number of IDPs had also come down. According to the Human Rights and Disaster Management Minister Mahinda Samarasinghe of the 2.8 lakh war displaced, the total number of IDPs remaining in the welfare centres in Vavuniya, Jaffna Mannar, Trincomalee and the hospitals had come down to 1,36, 328. The Sri Lankan government announcement also claimed that more than 70 per cent had returned to their original places.

Indian help to the war displaced Tamil persons continued and in line in February 2010, New Delhi handed over a consignment of galvanised corrugated sheets worth $ 2.7 million to Sri Lanka as part of its commitment to help Colombo in providing relief and re-settlement of the nearly three lakh war displaced in the north. The first lot of the second consign of 2,600 metric tonnes of sheets would be distributed among 20,000 families being resettled in Jaffna, Kilinochchi, Mullaithivu and Vavuniya districts. Ashok K. Kantha, India's High Commissioner to Sri Lanka, at the ceremony also said that India would send another 2,65,000 sheets in the next two weeks. He recalled it was as a follow-up of

Manmohan Singh's announcement made weeks after the military defeat of the LTTE that India would provide $ 100 million to help in the relief, rehabilitation and resettlement of the civilians.[24]

In addition, India had also announced a line of credit of $ 425 million for the reconstruction of railway infrastructure and is committed to assist the parts and aviation sector to include the Kankesanthurai Port, the Point Pedro Harbour and the Palaly airfield. India's Foreign Secretary Nirupama Rao when visited Sri Lanka in March 2010, also conveyed Rajapaksa India's willingness to continue assisting Sri Lanka in the resettlement of the IDPs. The issue of India's help and its monitoring was also raised in the Lok Sabha and responding to the call attention motion S.M. Krishna, India's Minister for External Affairs, assured the House that India was heavily dependent on the International Red Cross and the UN Commission on Refugees for monitoring aid.[25] On the basis of periodic assessment received from these two agencies and, based on the feedback received, we take it up with Sri Lanka, he added.

On the issue of resettlement of war displaced Tamil civilians more hopes were pinned when President Mahinda Rajapaksa was re-elected President of the island nation in January 2010 and took the oath on 19 November that year. On the occasion, he recalled the same date five years ago when he first assumed the office and got the country divided facing a threat to its existence. Following his assumption in the last week of November, India's External Affairs Minister S.M. Krishna paid a four-day visit to Sri Lanka to discuss the whole gamut of relations including the re-settlement of three lakh war displaced and the quest for a political solution to the ethnic strife.[26] Rajapaksa appreciated the offer of India to build 50,000 houses for war displaced Tamil civilians in the North and East and announced that his government would build 80,000 more houses for nearly three lakh IDPs in the next three years. In this trip Indian Foreign Minister was said to have announced a grant of $1.7 billion for developing the north and east of the island nation over the next three years. Since the end of the war between the Sri Lankan security forces and the LTTE, India had been engaged in a major way in initially helping Colombo in relief operations and later in re-settling the internally displaced civilians.

Second Inning of Mahinda Rajapaksa

Mahinda Rajapaksa assumed the office of the President of Sri Lanka for his first term on 19 November 2005 for the period of six years. But it was cut short and advanced by two years for the next presidential election which the constitution of the island nation allows. In the Presidential election held on January 26, 2010, Rajapaksa had scored a stunning victory with a margin of 17.73 per cent in which the opposition candidate Sarath Fonseka, retired Army Commander General, who was widely regarded as a brilliant commander, was defeated. Bringing forward the Presidential election was a shrewd political move to cash in on the popularity gained from the total military victory over the Liberation Tigers of Tamil Eelam in May 2009. However, preliminary analysis of this magnificent triumph indicated clearly that it was the mixed nature of result. Quantitatively, the mandate was overwhelming but qualitatively it appeared fractured. The ethnic divide in the voting was impossible to overlook. Both candidates received support from the three main ethnic groups – the Sinhalese, the Tamils, and the Muslims.[27] But there was ethnic polarisation, with the Sinhala majority preponderantly voting for the incumbent and the Tamils and Muslims for the challenger. With such a sharp ethnic divide it was imperative that President Rajapaksa address the legitimate aspirations as well as the real grievances of the Tamil and Muslim people. According to preliminary assessment, Rajapaksa received overwhelming support in Sinhala rural region while his opponent performed better in urban and semi urban areas. All this demonstrated that the electoral verdict, although conclusive on the whole had some cracks in parts. As the President of the whole country, Mahinda Rajapaksa must take the initiative and reach out to those sections of the people who have been alienated in terms of ethnicity, class, and the urban-rural divide.[28]

After President Rajapaksa's big victory in the January 26 Presidential election, Parliamentary elections were held in April 2010 which too went in favour of the President. In the 225 - seat House, Rajapaksa's ruling United Progressive Freedom Alliance (UPFA) led by Sri Lanka Freedom Party got 144 and scored a decisive victory with a vote share of 60 per cent. Within hours of the contours of the new Parliament becoming known, Rajapaksa described the outcome of the general election as a re-statement of people's faith in him and his policies.[29] Earlier Mahinda Rajapaksa during the campaigning had repeatedly sought a mandate for a strong Parliament to enable his government to go ahead with the necessary changes in the constitution to evolve a political solution to redress the legitimate grievances of minorities in general and the Tamils in particular. Now with his political stock enormously boosted, President Rajapaksa must turn his attention to the urgent task of reconciliation with Sri Lanka's Tamil minority and the development of the North and the East. Under his leadership, the government must quickly articulate a set of comprehensive political reforms that would devolve power to the Tamils in genuine and far-going way.[30] What Sri Lanka's Tamils badly need is a responsible democratic leadership that can engage meaningfully with the Sinhala majority to resolve all aspects of the Tamil questions on the basis of equality and devolution of power within a united Sri Lanka.

At a grand ceremony in Colombo, President Mahinda Rajapaksa was sworn in for his second term on November 19, 2010. Earlier Rajapaksa, winner in the January 26 Presidential poll had sought the opinion of the Supreme Court on the date due to differing views on the constitutional provision and it said that his second term in office would commence on November 19, 2010. Before taking the oath for his second term talking to a delegation from the Commonwealth Parliamentary Association in October, Rajapaksa was emphatic that what the LTTE wanted could not be given. But any reasonable aspect of devolution, for which all parties had consensual agreement, can be granted by Parliament. On the day of assumption of office, speaking to a large gathering outside the Presidential Secretariat, Rajapaksa promised to transform the island nation into an economic wonder of Asia. Unlike the first term, which was dominated by the war with the LTTE, the focus during his second term was expected to be on revival of economy and working towards consensus for a political solution to the ethnic conflict.[31] Recently in an important constitutional amendment, the two-term limit on holding the office of President had also been lifted.

Following the oath of the President on 22 November a 90 - member Cabinet was announced in which 18 new faces were added. As Sri Lanka follows the system of Executive Presidency, Prime Minister and other ministers are nominated by the President. In the newly-formed team Rajapaksa had kept the crucial portfolios of Defence and Finance. Hours after naming the government, the President presented the 2011 budget to Parliament that aimed at giving a boost to the economy in the post conflict situation. A statement by the government on the occasion said the President in his budget unveiled plans for major investments in making Sri Lanka a trilingual country, increasing computer literacy by 75 per cent by 2016, improving educational research and educational facilities in universities, and expanding the tourism industry.[32] In a letter addressed to the President, the Indian Prime Minister extended felicitations and was confident that his second term in office would usher in a new era of peace, reconciliation and development for the people of Sri Lanka.

Around the sametime, in an interview given to N. Ram of *The Hindu* at Temple Trees in Colombo, President Rajapaksa talked about his vision of Sri Lanka in post-conflict situation. Elaborating his three-language initiative he said that last year was the year of English and Information Technology. In accordance with, the people started to learning English. So, now the best thing was that all Sinhalese must learn Tamil, the Tamil must learn Sinhala, and they all must learn English and acquire knowledge, international knowledge.[33] The new President in his second term in office gave a development-oriented message to the people and said that he wanted to make Sri Lanka a hub for the development of knowledge, energy, commerce, naval transportation, and aviation. He also extended a message for the international community and requested them to understand the situation. Sri Lanka had defeated terrorism but not freedom fighters. They must help us not to widen the gap between the communities but to bring them closer. The past is past. We must think positively, not negatively.

References

1. M. R. Narayan Swamy, *The Tiger Vanquished LTTE's Story* (New Delhi : Sage Publications, 2010), p. 181.
2. R. Hariharan, 'Succession Squabble', *Frontline*, Vol. 26, No. 12, 6-19 June 2009 (Chennai : 2009), p. 20.
3. *The Hindu*, 18 May 2009.
4. Ibid., 20 May 2009.
5. *The Times of India*, editorial, 2 June 2009.
6. *The Hindu*, 17 May 2009.
7. Ibid., 22 May 2009.
8. *Indo-Asian News Service*, 22 May 2009.
9. *The Times of India*, editorial, 2 June 2009.
10. *The Hindu*, 3 July 2009.
11. Ibid.
12. Ibid., 6 July 2009.
13. Ibid., 7 November 2009.
14. Ibid., 5 February 2010.
15. Ibid., 14 March 2010.
16. Ibid.
17. Ibid., 16 September 2010.
18. M.R. Narayan Swamy, *The Tiger Vanquished LTTE's Story*, p. 183.

19. *The Hindu*, 8 July 2009.
20. Ibid., 13 October 2009.
21. M.S. Swaminathan, 'Sri Lanka : Task of Livelihood Rehabilitation', in Ibid., 16 June 2009.
22. Ibid., 6 November 2009.
23. Ibid., 2 December 2009.
24. Ibid., 4 February 2010.
25. Ibid., 26 August 2010.
26. Ibid., 26 November 2010.
27. D.B.S. Jeyaraj : A Resounding But Fractured Verdict', in Ibid., 29 January 2010.
28. Ibid.
29. Ibid., 10 April 2010.
30. Ibid., editorial.
31. Ibid., 20 November 2010.
32. Ibid., 23 November 2010.
33. Ibid.

APPENDICES

Appendix I : Bandaranaike – Chelvanayakam Pact, July 1957

Part A

Representatives of the Federal Party had a series of discussions with the Prime Minister in an effort to resolve the differences of opinion that had been growing and creating tension.

At the early stages of these conversations, it became evident that it was not possible for the Prime Minister to accede to some of the demands of the Federal Party.

The Prime Minister stated that, from the point of view of the Government, he was not in a position to discuss the setting up of a Federal Constitution, or regional autonomy or any step which would abrogate the Official Language Act.

The question then arose whether it was possible to explore the possibility of an adjustment without the Federal Party abandoning or surrendering any of its fundamental principles or objectives.

At this stage the Prime Minister suggested an examination of the government's Draft Regional Council Bill to see whether provisions can be made under it to meet, reasonably, some of the matters in this regard which the Federal Party had in view.

The agreements so reached are embodied in a separate document.

Regarding the language the Federal Party reiterated its stand for parity but in view of the position of the Prime Minister in this matter they came to an agreement by way of an adjustment. They pointed out that it was important for them that there would be a recognition of Tamil as a national language and that the administrative work in of the Northern and the Eastern Provinces should be done in Tamil.

The Prime Minister stated that as mentioned by him earlier, it was not possible for him to take any steps that would abrogate the Official Language Act.

Use of Tamil; After discussions it was agreed that the proposed legislation should contain recognition of Tamil as the language of a national minority of Ceylon and that the four points mentioned by Prime Minister should include provision that, without infringing on the position of the Official Language as such, the language of administration of the Northern And Eastern Provinces be Tamil, and any necessary provision be made for non-Tamil speaking minorities in the Northern and Eastern Provinces.

Regarding the question of Ceylon citizenship for the people of Indian descent and the Citizenship Act, the representatives of the Federal Party forwarded their views to the Prime Minister and pressed for an early settlement.

The Prime Minister indicated that this problem would receive early consideration.

In view of these conclusions the Federal Party stated that they were withdrawing their proposed Satyagraha.

Part B

1. Regional areas to be defined in the Bill itself by embodying them in the Schedule thereto.
2. That the Northern Province is to form one regional area whilst the Eastern Province is to be divided into one or more regional areas.
3. Provision is to be made in the Bill to enable two or more regions to amalgamate even beyond provincial limit; and for one region to divide itself subject to ratification by Parliament. Further provision is to be made in the Bill for two or more regions to collaborate for specific purposes of common interests.

Direct Elections

4. Provision is to be made for the direct election of Regional councillors. Provision is to be made for a delimitation commission or commissions for carving out electorates. The question of MPs representing districts falling within regional areas to be eligible to function as chairman is to be considered. The question of Government Agents being Regional Commissioners is to be considered. The question of supervisory functions over larger towns, strategic towns and municipalities is to be looked into.

Special Powers

5. Parliament is to delegate powers and specify them in the Act. It was agreed that regional councils should have powers over specified subjects including agriculture, cooperatives, lands and land developments, colonisation, education, health, industries, fisheries, housing, social services, electricity, water schemes and roads. Requisite definition of powers be made in the Bill.

Colonisation Schemes

6. It was agreed that in the matter of colonisation schemes the powers of the regional councils shall include the powers to select allottees to whom land within their area of authority shall be alienated and also power to select personnel to be employed for work on such schemes. The position regarding the area at present administered by the Gal Oya Board in this matter requires consideration.

Taxation And Borrowing

7. The powers in regard to the Regional councils vested in the Minister of Local Government in the draft bill to be revised with a view to vesting control in Parliament wherever necessary.
8. The Central Government will provide block grants to the regional councils. The principles on which the grants will be computed will be gone into. The regional councils shall have powers of taxation and borrowing.

S.J.V. Chelvanayakam	*S.W.R.D. Bandaranaike*
Leader of the Federal Party of Sri Lanka	The Prime Minister of Sri Lanka

Appendix II : Dudley Senanayake – Chelvanayakam Pact, March 1965

Mr. Dudley Senanayake and Mr. S.J.V. Chelvanayakam met on the 24-3-1965 and discussed matters relating to some problems over which the Tamil-speaking people were concerned, and Mr. Senanayake agreed that action on the following lines would be taken by him to ensure a stable government:

1. Action will be taken early under the Tamil Language Special Provisions Act to make provision of the Tamil Language to be the language of Administration and of Record in the Northern and Eastern Provinces.

   Mr. Senanayake explained that it was the policy of his party that a Tamil-speaking person should be entitled to transact business in Tamil throughout the island.

2. Mr. Senanayake stated that it was the policy of his party to amend the Language of Courts Act to provide for legal proceedings in the Northern and Eastern Provinces to be conducted and recorded in Tamil.

3. Action will be taken to establish District Councils in Ceylon vested with powers over subjects to be mutually agreed upon between two leaders. It was agreed, however, that the government should have power under the law to give directions to such councils under the national interest.

4. The Land Development Ordinance will be amended to provide that citizens of Ceylon be entitled to the allotment of land under the Ordinance.

   Mr. Senanayake further agreed that in the granting of land under colonisation schemes, the following priorities be observed in the Northern and Eastern provinces.

   (a) Land in the Northern and Eastern provinces should in the first instance be granted to landless persons in the district.

   (b) Secondly, to Tamil-speaking persons in the Northern and Eastern provinces.

   (c) Thirdly, to other citizens in Ceylon, preference being given to Tamil residents in the rest of the island.

S.J.V. Chelvanayakam
Leader of the Federal Party
of Sri Lanka

Dudley Senanayake
The Prime Minister
of Sri Lanka

Appendix III : Indo-Sri Lanka Accord, 29 July 1987

The Prime Minister of the Republic of India, His Excellency Mr. Rajiv Gandhi and the President of the Democratic Republic of Sri Lanka, Mr. J. R. Jayawardene having met at Colombo on 29 July 1987.

Attaching utmost importance to nurturing, intensifying and strengthening the traditional friendship of India and Sri Lanka and acknowledging the imperative need of resolving the ethnic problem of Sri Lanka, and the consequent violence, and for the safety, well-being and prosperity of people belonging to all communities of Sri Lanka,

Having this day entered into the following agreement to fulfil this objective,

In this Context

1. desiring to preserve the unity, sovereignty and territorial integrity of Sri Lanka;
2. acknowledging that Sri Lanka is a multi-ethnic and multi-lingual plural society consisting, *inter-alia*, of Sinhalese, Tamils, Muslims (Moors) and Burgers;
3. recognising that each ethnic group has a distinct cultural and linguistic identity which has to be carefully nurtured;
4. also recognising that the Northern and the Eastern provinces have been areas of historical habitation of Sri Lankan Tamil speaking peoples, who have at all times hitherto lived together in this territory with other ethnic groups;
5. conscious of the necessity of strengthening the forces contributing to the unity, sovereignty and territorial integrity of Sri Lanka, and preserving its character as a multi-ethnic, multi-lingual and multi-religious plural society, in which all citizens can live in equality, safety and harmony, and prosper and fulfil their aspirations;

Resolve that

1. Since the Government of Sri Lanka proposes to permit joining Provinces to join to form one administrative unit and also by a Referendum to separate as may be permitted to the Northern and Eastern provinces as outlined below:
2. During the period, which shall be considered an interim period (i.e. from the date of the elections to the provincial council, as

specified in para 2.8 to the date of the Referendum as specified in para 2.3), the Northern and Eastern provinces as now constituted, will form one administrative unit, having one elected Provincial Council. Such a unit will have one Governor, one Chief Minister and one Board of Ministers.

3. There will be a referendum on or before 31st December 1988 to enable the people of the Eastern Province to decide whether:
   (A) The Eastern province should remain linked with the Northern province as one administrative unit, and continue to be governed together with the Northern Province as specified in para 2.2 or:
   (B) The Eastern Province should constitute a separate administrative unit having its own distinct provincial council with a separate governor, chief minister and board of ministers. The president may, at his discretion, decide to postpone such a referendum.
4. All persons, who have been displaced due to ethnic violence or other reasons, will have the right to vote in such a Referendum. Necessary conditions to enable them to return to areas from where they were displaced will be created.
5. The Referendum, when held, will be monitored by a committee headed by the Chief Justice, a member appointed by the President, nominated by the Government of Sri Lanka, and a member appointed by the President, nominated by the representatives of the Tamil speaking people of the Eastern province.
6. A simple majority will be sufficient to determine the result of the Referendum.
7. Meetings and other forms of propaganda, permissible within the laws of the country, will be allowed before the Referendum.
8. Elections to Provincial Councils will be held within the next three months, in any event before 31st December 1987. Indian observers will be invited for elections to the Provincial Council of the North and East.
9. The emergency will be lifted in the Eastern and Northern provinces by 15 August 1987. A cessation of hostilities will come into effect all over the Island within 48 hours of signing of this Agreement. All arms presently held by militant groups will be

surrendered in accordance with an agreed procedure to authorities to be designated by the Government of Sri Lanka. Consequent to the cessation of hostilities and the surrender of arms by militant groups, the army and other security personnel will be confined to barracks in camps as on 25 May 1987. The process of surrendering arms and the confining of security personnel moving back to barracks shall be completed within 72 hours of the cessation of hostilities coming into effect.

10. The Government of Sri Lanka will utilise for the purpose of law enforcement and maintenance of security in the Northern and Eastern Provinces the same organisations and mechanisms of Government as are used in the rest of the country.

11. The President of Sri Lanka will grant a general amnesty to political and other prisoners now held in custody under The Prevention of Terrorism Act and other emergency laws, and to combatants, as well as to those persons accused, charged and/or convicted under these laws. The Government of Sri Lanka will make special efforts to rehabilitate militant youth with a view to bringing them back into the mainstream of national life. India will cooperate in the process.

12. The Government of Sri Lanka will accept and abide by the above provisions and expect all others to do likewise.

13. If the framework for the resolutions is accepted, the Government of Sri Lanka will implement the relevant proposals forthwith.

14. The Government of India will underwrite and guarantee the resolutions, and cooperate in the implementation of these proposals.

15. These proposals are conditional to an acceptance of proposals negotiated from 4.5.1986 to 19.12.1986. Residual matters not finalised during the above negotiations shall be resolved between India and Sri Lanka within a period of six weeks of signing this agreement. These proposals are also conditional to the Government of India cooperating directly with the Government of Sri Lanka in their implementation.

16. These proposals are also conditional to the Government of India taking the following actions if any militant groups operating in Sri Lanka do not accept this framework of proposals for a settlement, namely:

(A) India will take all necessary steps to ensure that Indian territory is not used for activities prejudicial to the unity, integrity and security of Sri Lanka.

(B) The Indian Navy/Coast Guard will cooperate with the Sri Lankan navy in preventing Tamil militant activities from affecting Sri Lanka.

(C) In the event that the Government of Sri Lanka requests the Government of India to afford military assistance to implement these proposals the Government of India will cooperate by giving to the Government of Sri Lanka such military assistance as and when requested.

(D) The Government of India will expedite repatriation from Sri Lanka of Indian citizens to India who are resident there concurrently with the repatriation of Sri Lankan refugees from Tamil Nadu.

(E) The Governments of Sri Lanka and India will cooperate in ensuring the physical security and safety of all communities inhabiting the Northern and Eastern Provinces.

17. The Government of Sri Lanka shall ensure free, full and fair participation of voters from all communities in the Northern and Eastern Provinces in electoral processes envisaged in this Agreement. The Government of India will extend full cooperation to the Government of Sri Lanka in this regard.

18. The official language of Sri Lanka shall be Sinhala. Tamil and English will also be official languages.

This agreement and the annexure thereto shall come into force upon signature.

In witness whereof, we have set our hands and seals hereunto. Done in Colombo, Sri Lanka, on this the twenty-ninth day of July of the year one thousand nine hundred and eighty-seven, in duplicate, both texts being equally authentic.

Junius Richard Jayawardene
President of the Democratic
Socialist Republic of
Sri Lanka

Rajiv Gandhi
Prime Minister of the
Republic of India

Annexure to the Agreement

1. His Excellency the President of Sri Lanka and the Prime Minister of India agree that the Referendum mentioned in paragraph 2 and its sub-paragraphs of the Agreement will be observed by a representative of the Election Commission of India to be invited by His Excellency the President of Sri Lanka.
2. Similarly, both heads of Government agree that the elections to the Provincial Council mentioned in paragraph 2.8 of the Agreement will be observed by a representative of the Government of India to be invited by His Excellency the President of Sri Lanka.
3. His Excellency the President of Sri Lanka agrees that the Home guards would be disbanded and all paramilitary personnel will be withdrawn from the Eastern and Northern Provinces with a view to creating conditions conducive to fair elections to the Council.

   The President, in his discretion, shall absorb such paramilitary forces, which came into being due to ethnic violence, into the regular security forces of Sri Lanka.
4. The President of Sri Lanka and the Prime Minister of India agree that the Tamil militants shall surrender their arms to authorities agreed upon to be designated by the President of Sri Lanka. The surrender shall take place in the presence of one senior representative each of the Sri Lankan Red Cross and the Indian Red Cross.
5. The President of Sri Lanka and the Prime Minister of India agree that a joint Indo-Sri Lankan observer group consisting of qualified representatives of the Government of India and the Government of Sri Lanka would monitor the cessation of hostilities from 31 July 1987.
6. The Prime Minister of India and the President of Sri Lanka also agree that in the terms of paragraph 2.14 and paragraph 2.16(c) of the Agreement, an Indian Peace Keeping contingent may be invited by the President of Sri Lanka to guarantee and enforce the cessation of hostilities, if so required.

Exchange of Letters

President of Sri Lanka

29 July 1987

Excellency,

Please refer to your letter dated 29th of July 1987, which reads as follows:

Excellency,

1. Conscious of the friendship between our two countries stretching over two millennia and more, and recognising the importance of nurturing this traditional friendship, it is imperative that both Sri Lanka and India reaffirm the decision not to allow our respective territories to be used for activities prejudicial to each other's unity, territorial integrity and security.
2. In this spirit, you had, in the course of our discussions agreed to meet some of India's concerns as follows:
   (i) Your Excellency and myself will reach an early understanding about the relevance and employment of foreign military and intelligence personnel with a view to ensuring that such presences will not prejudice Indo-Sri Lankan relations.
   (ii) Trincomalee or any other ports in Sri Lanka will not be made available for military use by any country in a manner prejudicial to India's interests.
   (iii) The work of restoring and operating the Trincomalee oil tank farm will be undertaken as a joint venture between India and Sri Lanka.
   (iv) Sri Lanka's agreements with foreign broadcasting organisations will be reviewed to ensure that any facilities set up by them in Sri Lanka are used solely as public broadcasting facilities and not for any military or intelligence purposes.
3. In the same spirit India will:
   (i) Deport all Sri Lankan citizens who are found to be engaging in terrorist activities or advocating separatism or secessionism.
   (ii) Provide training facilities and military supplies for Sri Lankan forces.

4. India and Sri Lanka have agreed to set up a joint consultative mechanism to continuously review matters of common concern in the light of the objectives stated in para 1 and specifically to monitor the implementation of other matters contained in this letter.
5. Kindly confirm, Excellency, that the above correctly sets out the agreement reached between us.

Please accept, Excellency, the assurances of my highest consideration.

Yours sincerely,

(Signed Rajiv Gandhi)

Prime Minister of India

29 July 1987

Excellency,

Conscious of the friendship between our two countries stretching over two millennia and more, and recognising the importance of nurturing this traditional friendship, it is imperative that both Sri Lanka and India reaffirm the decision not to allow our respective territories to be used for activities prejudicial to each other's unity, territorial integrity and security.

In this spirit, you had, in the course of our discussions agreed to meet some of India's concerns as follows:

(i) Your Excellency and myself will reach an early understanding about the relevance and employment of foreign military and intelligence personnel with a view to ensuring that such presences will not prejudice Indo-Sri Lankan relations.

(ii) Trincomalee or any other ports in Sri Lanka will not be made available for military use by any country in a manner prejudicial to India's interests.

(iii) The work of restoring and operating the Trincomalee oil tank farm will be undertaken as a joint venture between India and Sri Lanka.

(iv) Sri Lanka's agreements with foreign broadcasting organisations will be reviewed to ensure that any facilities set up by them in Sri Lanka are used solely as public broadcasting facilities and not for any military or intelligence purposes.

In the same spirit India will :

(i) Deport all Sri Lankan citizens who are found to be engaging in terrorist activities or advocating separatism or secessionism.

(ii) Provide training facilities and military supplies for Sri Lankan forces.

India and Sri Lanka have agreed to set up a joint consultative mechanism to continuously review matters of common concern in the light of the objectives stated in para 1 and specifically to monitor the implementation of other matters contained in this letter.

Kindly confirm, Excellency, that the above correctly sets out the agreement reached between us. Please accept, Excellency, the assurances of my highest consideration.

Yours sincerely,

(Signed J. R. Jayawardene)

President of Sri Lanka

Appendix IV : Ceasefire Agreement, 22 February 2002

Preamble

The overall objective of the Government of the Democratic Socialist Republic of Sri Lanka (hereinafter referred to as the GOSL) and the Liberation Tigers of Tamil Eelam (hereinafter referred to as the LTTE) is to find a negotiated solution to the ongoing ethnic conflict in Sri Lanka.

The GOSL and the LTTE (hereinafter referred to as the Parties) recognize the importance of bringing an end to the hostilities and improving the living conditions for all inhabitants affected by the conflict. Bringing an end to the hostilities is also seen by the Parties as a means of establishing a positive atmosphere in which further steps towards negotiations on a lasting solution can be taken.

The Parties further recognize that groups that are not directly party to the conflict are also suffering the consequences of it. This is particularly the case as regards the Muslim population. Therefore, the provisions of this Agreement regarding the security of civilians and their property apply to all inhabitants.

With reference to the above, the Parties have agreed to enter into a ceasefire, refrain from conduct that could undermine the good intentions or violate the spirit of this Agreement and implement confidence-building measures as indicated in the articles below.

Article 1: Modalities of a ceasefire

The Parties have agreed to implement a ceasefire between their armed forces as follows:

1. A jointly agreed ceasefire between the GOSL and the LTTE shall enter into force on such date as is notified by the Norwegian Minister of Foreign Affairs in accordance with Articlc 4.2, hereinafter referred to as D-day.

Military operations

2. Neither Party shall engage in any offensive military operation. This requires the total cessation of all military action and includes, but is not limited to, such acts as:

   (a) The firing of direct and indirect weapons, armed raids, ambushes, assassinations, abductions, destruction of civilian or military property, sabotage, suicide missions and activities by deep penetration units;

(b) Aerial bombardment;

(c) Offensive naval operations.

3. The Sri Lankan armed forces shall continue to perform their legitimate task of safeguarding the sovereignty and territorial integrity of Sri Lanka without engaging in offensive operations against the LTTE.

Separation of forces

4. Where forward defence localities have been established, the GOSL's armed forces and the LTTE's fighting formations shall hold their ground positions, maintaining a zone of separation of a minimum of six hundred (600) metres. However, each Party reserves the right of movement within one hundred (100) metres of its own defence localities, keeping an absolute minimum distance of four hundred (400) metres between them. Where existing positions are closer than four hundred (400) metres, no such right of movement applies and the Parties agree to ensure the maximum possible distance between their personnel.
5. In areas where localities have not been clearly established, the status quo as regards the areas controlled by the GOSL and the LTTE, respectively, on 24 December 2001 shall continue to apply pending such demarcation as is provided in article 1.6.
6. The Parties shall provide information to the Sri Lanka Monitoring Mission (SLMM) regarding defence localities in all areas of contention, cf. Article 3. The monitoring mission shall assist the Parties in drawing up demarcation lines at the latest by D-day + 30.
7. The Parties shall not move munitions, explosives or military equipment into the area controlled by the other Party.
8. Tamil paramilitary groups shall be disarmed by the GOSL by D-day + 30 at the latest. The GOSL shall offer to integrate individuals in these units under the command and disciplinary structure of the GOSL armed forces for service away from the Northern and Eastern Province.

Freedom of movement

9. The Parties' forces shall initially stay in the areas under their respective control, as provided in Article 1.4 and Article 1.5.

10. Unarmed GOSL troops shall, as of D- day + 60, be permitted unlimited passage between Jaffna and Vavuniya using the Jaffna-Kandy road (A-9). The modalities are to be worked out by the Parties with the assistance of the SLMM.
11. The Parties agree that as of D-day individual combatants shall, on the recommendation of their area commander, be permitted, unarmed and in plain clothes, to visit family and friends residing in areas under the control of the other Party. Such visits shall be limited to six days every second month, not including the time of travel by the shortest applicable route. The LTTE shall facilitate the use of the Jaffna-Kandy road for this purpose. The Parties reserve the right to deny entry to specified military areas.
12. The Parties agree that as of D-day individual combatants shall, notwithstanding the two-month restriction, be permitted, unarmed and in plain clothes, to visit immediate family (i.e. spouses, children, grandparents, parents and siblings) in connection with weddings or funerals. The right to deny entry to specified military areas applies.
13. Fifty (50) unarmed LTTE members shall as of D-day + 30, for the purpose of political work, be permitted freedom of movement in the areas of the North and the East dominated by the GOSL. Additional 100 unarmed LTTE members shall be permitted freedom of movement as of D-day + 60. As of D-day + 90, all unarmed LTTE members shall be permitted freedom of movement in the North and the East. The LTTE members shall carry identity papers. The right of the GOSL to deny entry to specified military areas applies.

Article 2: Measures to restore normalcy

The Parties shall undertake the following confidence-building measures with the aim of restoring normalcy for all inhabitants of Sri Lanka:

1. The Parties shall in accordance with international law abstain from hostile acts against the civilian population, including such acts as torture, intimidation, abduction, extortion and harassment.
2. The Parties shall refrain from engaging in activities or propagating ideas that could offend cultural or religious sensitivities. Places of worship (temples, churches, mosques and other holy sites, etc.) currently held by the forces of either of the Parties shall

be vacated by D-day + 30 and made accessible to the public. Places of worship which are situated in "high security zones" shall be vacated by all armed personnel and maintained in good order by civilian workers, even when they are not made accessible to the public.

3. Beginning on the date on which this Agreement enters into force, school buildings occupied by either Party shall be vacated and returned to their intended use. This activity shall be completed by D-day + 160 at the latest.
4. A schedule indicating the return of all other public buildings to their intended use shall be drawn up by the Parties and published at the latest by D-day + 30.
5. The Parties shall review the security measures and the set-up of checkpoints, particularly in densely populated cities and towns, in order to introduce systems that will prevent harassment of the civilian population. Such systems shall be in place from D-day + 60.
6. The Parties agree to ensure the unimpeded flow of non- military goods to and from the LTTE-dominated areas with the exception of certain items as shown in Annex A. Quantities shall be determined by market demand. The GOSL shall regularly review the matter with the aim of gradually removing any remaining restrictions on non- military goods.
7. In order to facilitate the flow of goods and the movement of civilians, the Parties agree to establish checkpoints on their line of control at such locations as are specified in Annex B.
8. The Parties shall take steps to ensure that the Trincomalee-Habarana road remains open on a 24- hour basis for passenger traffic with effect from D-day + 10.
9. The Parties shall facilitate the extension of the rail service on the Batticaloa-line to Welikanda. Repairs and maintenance shall be carried out by the GOSL in order to extend the service up to Batticaloa.
10. The Parties shall open the Kandy-Jaffna road (A-9) to non-military traffic of goods and passengers. Specific modalities shall be worked out by the Parties with the assistance of the Royal Norwegian Government by D- day + 30 at the latest.

11. A gradual easing of the fishing restrictions shall take place starting from D-day. As of D-day + 90, all restrictions on day and night fishing shall be removed, subject to the following exceptions: (i) fishing will not be permitted. Within an area of 1 nautical mile on either side along to add above in serial 11 after the word permitted the coast and 2 nautical miles seawards from all security forces camps on the coast; (ii) fishing will not be permitted in harbours or approaches to harbours, bays and estuaries along the coast.
12. The Parties agree that search operations and arrests under the Prevention of Terrorism Act shall not take place. Arrests shall be conducted under due process of law in accordance with the Criminal Procedure Code.
13. The Parties agree to provide family members of detainees access to the detainees within D-day + 30.

Article 3: The Sri Lanka Monitoring Mission

The Parties have agreed to set up an international monitoring mission to enquire into any instance of violation of the terms and conditions of this Agreement. Both Parties shall fully cooperate to rectify any matter of conflict caused by their respective sides. The mission shall conduct international verification through on-site monitoring of the fulfilment of the commitments entered into in this Agreement as follows:

1. The name of the monitoring mission shall be the Sri Lanka Monitoring Missi on (hereinafter referred to as the SLMM).
2. Subject to acceptance by the Parties, the Royal Norwegian Government (hereinafter referred to as the RNG) shall appoint the Head of the SLMM (hereinafter referred to as the HoM), who shall be the final authority regarding interpretation of this Agreement.
3. The SLMM shall liaise with the Parties and report to the RNG.
4. The HoM shall decide the date for the commencement of the SLMM's operations.
5. The SLMM shall be composed of representatives from Nordic countries.
6. The SLMM shall establish a headquarters in such place as the HoM finds appropriate. An office shall be established in Colombo and in Vanni in order to liaise with the GOSL and the LTTE, respectively. The SLMM will maintain a presence in the districts of Jaffna, Mannar, Vavuniya, Trincomalee, Batticaloa and Amparai.

7. A local monitoring committee shall be established in Jaffna, Mannar, Vavuniya, Trincomalee, Batticaloa and Amparai. Each committee shall consist of five members, two appointed by the GOSL, two by the LTTE and one international monitor appointed by the HoM. The international monitor shall chair the committee. The GOSL and the LTTE appointees may be selected from among retired judges, public servants, religious leaders or similar leading citizens.
8. The committees shall serve the SLMM in an advisory capacity and discuss issues relating to the implementation of this Agreement in their respective districts, with a view to establishing a common understanding of such issues. In particular, they will seek to resolve any dispute concerning the implementation of this Agreement at the lowest possible level.
9. The Parties shall be responsible for the appropriate protection of and security arrangements for all SLMM members.
10. The Parties agree to ensure the freedom of movement of the SLMM members in performing their tasks. The members of the SLMM shall be given immediate access to areas where violations of the Agreement are alleged to have taken place. The Parties also agree to facilitate the widest possible access to such areas for the local members of the six above-mentioned committees, cf. Article 3.7.
11. It shall be the responsibility of the SLMM to take immediate action on any complaints made by either Party to the Agreement, and to enquire into and assist the Parties in the settlement of any dispute that might arise in connection with such complaints.
12. With the aim of resolving disputes at the lowest possible level, communication shall be established between commanders of the GOSL armed forces and the LTTE area leaders to enable them to resolve problems in the conflict zones.
13. Guidelines for the operations of the SLMM shall be established in a separate document.

Article 4: Entry into force, amendments and termination of the Agreement

1. Each Party shall notify its consent to be bound by this Agreement through a letter to the Norwegian Minister of Foreign Affairs signed by Prime Minister Ranil Wickremesinghe on behalf of the

GOSL and by leader Velupillai Prabakaran on behalf of the LTTE, respectively. The Agreement shall be initialled by each Party and enclosed in the above-mentioned letter.

2. The Agreement shall enter into force on such date as is notified by the Norwegian Minister of Foreign Affairs.
3. This Agreement may be amended and modified by mutual agreement of both Parties. Such amendments shall be notified in writing to the RNG.
4. This Agreement shall remain in force until notice of termination is given by either Party to the RNG. Such notice shall be given fourteen (14) days in advance of the effective date of termination.

Velupillai Prabakaran
Supreme Leader on behalf
of the LTTE

Ranil Wickremesinghe
The Prime Minister on
behalf of the Government
of Sri Lanka

SELECT BIBLIOGRAPHY

Documents

A Ministry of State Publication, *Sri Lanka : Who Wants a Separate State?* (Sri Lanka Government Press, 1983).

A Ministry of State Publication, *Tamil Eelam Terrorists Murder Again : Time Bomb Kill 30 at Madras Airport* (Sri Lanka Government Press, 1984).

Betrayal of Buddhism, *Report of the Unofficial Buddhist Committee of Inquiry* (Balangoda, 1955).

Census of Ceylon (1891).

Ceylon Administration Report for 1931 – *Report of the Controller of Labour* (1931).

Correspondence relating to the *Citizenship Status of Indians in Ceylon* (November 1948).

Department of Information, *Peace for all, Prosperity for all and envy towards none* (Sri Lanka : Department of Government Printing).

Government of Ceylon : *Administrative Report of the Commission for the Registration of Indian and Pakistani Residents for 1951 to 1961-62.*

Government of Ceylon : *Administrative Reports of the Commissioner of Labour for 1950 to 1961-62.*

Interim *Report of the Commission of Higher education in national languages,* Sessional Paper XXI (1954).

Interim *Report of the National Education Commission* under the Chairmanship of J.E. Jayasuriya (1961).

Ministry of State, *The Thimpu Talks : The Stand taken by the Sri Lankan Government* (Sri Lanka : A Ministry of State Publication).

Ministry of External Affairs : *Brief on India-Sri Lanka Relations* 26 February 2007 (New Delhi : 2007).

Political Committee, *LTTE, Liberation Tigers and Tamil Eelam Freedom Struggle* (Madras : 1983).

Proposals *Relating to Persons of Indian Origin in Ceylon* framed by the Prime Minister of Ceylon and India in New Delhi (18 January 1954), Treaty Series No. 1 of 1954.

Proposals *Relating to Persons of Indian Origin in Sri Lanka* framed by the Prime Minister of Ceylon and India in New Delhi (30th October 1964), Treaty Series No. 1 of 1964.

Report of Agent T.L.R. Chandran (1934).

Reports, *Annual of the Asian Development Bank.*

Report of the Ceylon – Indian Congress, *for 1952-53,* submitted to the Thirteenth Annual Session (17 & 18 April 1953).

Report of the Ceylon-Democratic Congress Committee *for 1954-55,* submitted to the Fifteenth Annual Session (13 May 1953, Colombo : 1955).

Report of the *Commissioners appointed to enquire into the subject of Cooly Immigration,* Sessional Paper No. XXVII (1877).

Report of the *Presidential Commission of Enquiry into the Incidents which took place between 13th August and 15th September 1977* (Colombo; Government of Sri Lanka, July 1980).

Report of *the Sixth Parliamentary General Elections in Ceylon 22nd March 1965* (Colombo, Government Publications Bureau, 1966).

Report by S.M. Burrows on the question of *The education of the Children of Indian labourers* employed on estates in Ceylon, Sessional Paper No. IV (1905).

Sinhalese and Tamil as Official Languages – Report of the *Select Committee of the State Council* Sessional Paper No. XXII, December 1946).

S.Ranganathan's *Annual Report for 1923.*

Sri Lanka : The Ethnic Conflict - A Collection of Writings edited by Committee for Rational Development (New Delhi, 1984).

The Kotahena Riots, Sessional Paper IV of 1983.

The Text of Rajapaksa's Interview given to CNN – IBN in Colombo, April 2009 (Colombo : 2009).

Books

Allen, Douglas (ed.), *Religion and Political Conflict in South Asia* (New Delhi : Oxford University Press, 1993).

Arasaratnam, S. *Ceylon* (New Jersey : Englewood Cliffs, 1964).

Azar, Edward E. and **Chung-In Moon** (eds.), *National Security in the Third World : Management of Internal and External Threats* (Aldershot : Edward Elgar Publishing, 1988).

Bandaranaike, S.W.R.D. (ed.), *The Hand Book of the Ceylon National Congress 1919-1928* (Colombo : 1928).

Bindra, S.S. *India and Her Neighbours – A Study of Political, Economic and Cultural Relations and Interactions* (New Delhi : Deep and Deep Publications, 1989).

Bhaduri, Shankar and **Afsir Karim**, *The Sri Lankan Crisis* (New Delhi : Lancer International, 1990).

Bose, Sugata and **Ayesha Jalal**, South Asia – History, Culture, Political Economy (New Delhi : Oxford University Press, 2004).

Brown, W. Norman (ed.), *India, Pakistan, Ceylon* (Philadelphia : 1961).

Chakravarti, S.R., Swaroop Rani Dubey, P.C. Mathur and **Virendra Narain** (Authors), *Turmoil and Political Change in South Asia, Bangladesh, Sri Lanka, India and Pakistan* (Jaipur : Aalekh Publishers, 1978).

Chari, P.R., *The IPKF Experience in Sri Lanka ACDIS Occasional Paper* (Urbana : University of Illinois, 1995).

Chattopadhyaya, H.P., *Indians in Sri Lanka* (Calcutta : OPS Publishers, 1979).

De, Jatis Chandra, *Sinhala in the Kalkipurana.*

De, S.C., *History of Ramayana and the Indo-Aryan Society in India and Ceylon.*

De Silva, K.M. (ed.), *Sri Lanka : A Survey* (London : 1963).

Dutta, V.P., *India's Foreign Policy* (New Delhi : Vikas Publishing House, 1984).

————, *India's Foreign Policy in a Changing World* (New Delhi : Vikas Publishing House, 2003).

Ellawala, Hema, *Social History of Early Ceylon.*

Farmer, B.H., *Ceylon : A Divided Nation* (Delhi : 1963).

Geiger, Wilhelm, *Culture of Ceylon in Medieval Times* (Wiesbaden, 1960).

Ghosh, S. Partha, *Cooperation and Conflict in South Asia* (New Delhi : Manohar, 1989).

Gupta, Babu Lal, *Political and Civil Status of Indians in Ceylon* (Agra : 1963).

Jacob, Lucy, M., *Sri Lanka from Dominion to Republic* (Delhi : 1973).

James Manor (ed.), *Sri Lanka in Change and Crisis* (London : Croom Helm, 1984).

Jayasuriya, Laksiri, *Labour Problems in the Economic and Social Development of Ceylon* (Colombo : 1971).

Jeyaratnam, Wilson, A., *Politics in Sri Lanka – 1947-1979* (London : Macmillan Press, 1979).

Kaul, T.N., *Diplomacy in Peace and War : Recollections and Reflections* (New Delhi : Vikas Publishing House, 1979).

————, *Communalism and Language in the Politics of Ceylon* (Durham : 1967).

Kodikara, S.U., *Indo-Ceylon Relations Since Independence* (Colombo : 1965).

————, *Foreign Policy of Sri Lanka : A Third World Perspective* (Delhi : 1982).

————, (ed.), *South Asian Strategic Issues, Sri Lankan Perspective* (New Delhi : Sage Publications, 1990).

————, (ed.), *External Compulsions of South Asian Politics* (New Delhi : Sage Publications, 1993).

Kotelawala, Sir John, *An Asian Prime Minister's Story* (London : George Harrap & Co., 1956).

Kumar, Dharam, *Land and Caste in South India* (Cambridge : 1965).

Kumar, Lalit, *India and Sri Lanka : Sirimavo-Shastri Pact* (Delhi : 1977).

Kumaraswamy, P.R. (ed.), *Security Beyond Survival* (New Delhi : Sage Publications, 2004).

Law, Bimala Churn, *Some Ancient Kings of Ceylon.*

Ludowyk, E.F.C., *The Story of Ceylon* (London : 1962).

Mason, Phillip (ed.), *India and Ceylon : Unity and Diversity : A Symposium* (London : 1967).

Mendis, G.C., *The Early History of Ceylon* (Calcutta, 1947).

————, *Ceylon Under the British*, (2nd edition, 1946).

Mukherjee, Sadhan, *Ceylon, Island that Changed* (Delhi : 1971).

Muni, S.D., *Pangs of Proximity : India and Sri Lanka's Ethnic Crisis* (New Delhi : Sage Publications, 1993).

Myrdal, Gunner, *Asian Drama – An Enquiry into the Poverty of Nations* (London : 1968).

Narayan Swamy, M.R., *The Tiger Vanquished – LTTE's Story* (New Delhi : Sage Publications, 2010).

Navarathnam, C.S., *Tamil's and Ceylon* (Jaffna : 1971).

Nehru, Jawaharlal, *Glimpses of World History* (Bombay : Asia Publishing House, 1962).

Nicholas, S.E.N., *Estate Labourer and Legal Guide* (Colombo : 1927).

Pandian, T.B., *The Cooly Life in Ceylon* (Palamcottah, 1917).

Paranavitana, S. (ed.), *History of Ceylon*, Vol. 1, Part I (University of Ceylon, 1959).

Parkar Henry, *Ancient Ceylon.*

Patel, S.K., *Indians in Sri Lanka* (Bombay : 1977).

Phadnis, Urmila, *Religion and Politics in Sri Lanka* (New Delhi: 1976).

————, *Ethnicity and Nation Building in South Asia* (New Delhi : Sage Publications, 1989).

Pillay, K.K., *South India and Ceylon* (University of Madras, 1963).

Prasad, D.M., *Ceylon's Foreign Policy Under Bandaranaike's 1956-1965 : A Political Analysis* (Delhi : 1972).

Raghavan, M.D., *Indian in Ceylonese History, Society and Culture* (Bombay : 1964).

Rao, P.R., *India and Ceylon : A Study* (Bombay : Orient Longmans, 1954).

Rosen, Stephen Peter, *Societies and Military Power : India and Its Armies* (Delhi : Oxford University Press, 1996).

Roy Chaudhury, P.C., *Sri Lanka –Lands and Peoples of the World* (New Delhi : Sterling Publishers, 1985).

Sardeshpande, Lt. Gen. S.C., *Assignment Jaffna* (New Delhi : Lancer, 1992).

Sarkar, N.K., *The Demography of Ceylon* (Ceylon Government Press, 1957).

Sen Gupta Bhabani (ed.), *Regional Cooperation and Development in South Asia* (New Delhi : South Asia Publishers, 1986).

Shenoy, B.R. *Ceylon Currency and Banking* (London : Longmans Green and Co., 1941).

Silva, K.M. de, *Social Policy and Missionary Organisation in Ceylon* (London : Longmans Green and Co., 1965).

Singh, Rajkumar, *India-South Asia Minus Congress Regimes* (Patna : Novelty & Co., 2000).

————, *India's Foreign Policy – The First Study in Continuity and Change* (New Delhi : Samiksha Prakashan, 2001).

————, *Relations of NDA & UPA with Neighbours* (New Delhi : Gyan Publishing House, 2010).

Thomas, Raju, G.C., *Indian Security Policy* (Princeton : Princeton University Press, 1986).

Tinker, Hugh, *A New System of Slavery – The Export of Indian Labour Overseas, 1830-1920* (London : OUP, 1974).

Victor Cecil, *India : The Security Dilemma* (New Delhi : Patriot Publishers, 1990).

Vishnu, Prajapati (ed.), *South Asia –Political Priorities and Economic Imperatives* (New Delhi : Commonwealth, 2003).

Vohra, Dewan, C., *India's Aid Diplomacy in the Third World* (New Delhi : Vikas Publishing House, 1980).

Wegener, Alfred, *The Origin of Continents and Oceans* (London : Translated Version, 1966).

Wesson, Robert G., *Foreign Policy for a New Age* (Boston, London : Houghton Miffliu Company, 1977).

Wilcox, Wayne, Leo E. Rose, Gavin Boyd, (eds.), *Asia and the International System* (Massachusetts : Winthrop Publishers, 1972).

Williams, Harry, *Ceylon, Pearl of the East* (London : 1955).

Wriggins, W.N., *Ceylon : Dilemmas of a New Nation* (Delhi : 1980).

Articles

Ali Khan, Ahsan, 'The Tamil Question in Historical Perspective : Its Impact on Indo - Sri Lanka Relations,' *Pakistan Horizon Quarterly*, Vol. 2.

Aziz, A., 'Problems of Stateless Workers in Ceylon', *Blitz*, 30 October 1982.

Bains, J.S., 'India's International Disputes,' *Indian Journal of Politics* Vol. 2, No. 1 (Aligarh : January-June 1968).

Balachanddran, P.K., 'TULF Seeks LTTE's Permission to Function', *The Hindustan Times*, 6 January 1999.

Balasundaram, C.K., 'Indian in Ceylon', *Eastern World*, Vol. 12 No. 7 (July 1958).

Bali, Arti, 'Enforcing Military Solutions to Ethnic Conflict', *South Asia Politics*, Vol. 7, No. 2 (New Delhi : June 2008).

Basham, A.L., 'Prince Vijaya and the Aryanization of Ceylon', *Ceylon Historical Journal*, Vol. 1, No. 3, (January 1952).

Bastiampillai Bertram, E.S.J., 'Ethnic Conflicts in South Asia, and Inter-state Relations Especially in Relation to Sri Lanka' in Shelton U. Kodikara (ed.), *South Asian Strategic Issues : Sri Lankan Perspectives* (New Delhi : Sage Publications, 1990).

Choudhary, Sukhbir, 'Problems of Citizenship Rights for People of Indian Origin in Ceylon in the Background and the Issues,' *Foreign Affairs Reports*, Vol. 5, No. 11 (November 1956).

Deendayal Upadhaya, A Nation of the Refugees', *Organiser*, 9 November 1964.

Dieter Bram, 'Changes in South Asia Intra-regional and External Relationship', *The World Today*, Vol. 34 (London : October 1978).

Desilva Colvin, R., The Employment of Ceylonese on Estates Bill', *Young Socialist* Vol. 2.

Desilva, K.M. 'Indian Emmigration to Ceylon – The First Phase, 1840 – 1855', *Ceylon Journal of Historical and Social Studies*, Vol. 1, No. 2 (July-December 1961).

Dutta, Vijay and **Ninan Servanti**, 'The Route of Discontent', *India Today*, 16-31 July (New Delhi : Living Media, 1978).

Dutt, Amita, 'An Economic Study of Indo-Ceylon, Labour Migration 1920-38, A Critique', *Economic Development and Cultural Change*, Vol. 21, No. 1 (October 1972).

Farrell, Tom, 'For him no Sacrifice was too Great for the Objective of Eelam', *The Hindu* (Madras), 20 May 2009.

Godakumbura, C.E., 'The Dravidian Element in Sinhalese', *Bulletin of the School of Oriental and African Studies*, Vol. XI (1943-46).

Gooneratne Tilak, 'The Present Situation in Sri Lanka', *Asian Affairs*, Part I (London : February 1986).

Guha Seema, 'The Lankan Tug of War', *The Times of India*, 28 July 1997.

Hagerty, D.T., 'India's Regional Security Doctrine', *Asian Survey*, Vol. 31, No. 4, (New Delhi : April 1991).

Hariharan, R., 'Militancy and Small Arms Proliferation', *The Hindu*, 20 April 2007.

————, 'The Discarded Accord and the Unwanted War', 7 August 2007.

————, 'The Moment of Truth for the LTTE,' 5 February 2009.

————, Succession Squabble', *Frontline*, Vol. 26, No. 12, 6-9 June (Chennai : 2009).

————, 'Sri Lanka : Need to Restore Trust', *The Hindu*, 18 May 2010.

Hassan, Shaukat, 'Problems of Internal Stability in South Asia', in Shelton U. Kodikara (ed.), *External Compulsions of South Asian Politics* (New Delhi : Sage Publications, 1993).

Heine, Jorge, 'Misapplying Responsibility to Protect in Sri Lanka', *The Hindu*, 27 June 2009.

Jain, B.K., 'The Problem of Citizenship Rights for Persons of Indian Origin in Ceylon', *Indian Journal of Political Science*, Vol. 24, No. 1, (January, March 1963).

Jacob, Lucy M., 'Regionalism in Sri Lanka', in Ramakant (ed.), *Regionalism in South Asia* (Jaipur : Aalekh Publishers, 1983).

Jagunnathan, N.S., 'The End of a Misadventure', *The Indian Express,* 2 April 1990.

Jayasuriya D.L., 'Developments in University Education : The Growth of the University of Ceylon – 1942-1965', *University of Ceylon Review*, Vol. XXIII, No. 1, and 2 (April – October 1965).

Jayatilleka, Dayan, 'A Sri Lankan Analysis – Dixit's Testament : A Critical Review, *Mainstream*, Annual (1977).

Jayewardene, J.R., 'D.S. Senanayake : A Study of His Foreign Policy', *The Ceylon Historical Journal,* Vol. 5, Nos. 1 to 4 (July – October 1955 and January-April, 1956).

Jennings, Sir Ivor, 'Politics in Ceylon Since 1952', *Pacific Affairs,* Vol. XXVII, No. 4, December 1954).

Jeyaraj, D.B.S., 'A Resounding But Fractured Verdict', *The Hindu*, 29 January 2010.

Jha, N.N., 'India – Sri Lanka Relations', *India Quarterly*, Vol. L, Nos. 1 and 2 (New Delhi : January – June 1994, Indian Council of World Affairs).

Karunaratne, Victor, Tamil Federalist in Ceylon', *Eastern World*, Vol. XVI (September 1962).

Kearney, Robert, N., 'The New Political Crisis in Ceylon', *Asian Survey*, Vol. 11, No. 6, (June 1962).

————, 'Language and the Rise of Tamil Separation in Sri Lanka, '*Asian Survey*, Vol. XVIII, No. 5 (May 1978).

Khobragade, Vinod F., 'Re-Thinking Power Devolution in Sri Lanka', *South Asia Politics*, Vol. 6, No. 1 (New Delhi : May 2007).

————, 'Sri Lankan Tamil Question –India's Paroxism', Vol. 7, No. 8 (New Delhi : December 2008).

————, 'Ethnic Politics in Sri Lanka – Political Solution to Tamil Cause and Military Solution to LTTE, Vol. 7, No. 11 (New Delhi : March 2009).

Kodikara, Shelton U. 'Persons of Indian Origin in Ceylon', *Foreign Affairs*, Vol. XIII, No. 2 (February 1964).

————, 'Communalism and Political Modernisation in Ceylon', *Modern Ceylon Studies*, Vol. 1, No. 1 (1970).

————, 'War and Peace Options for the LTTE', *The Sunday Observer*, 1 July 1990.

————, 'The Indo-Sri Lanka Agreement of July 1987 : Retrospect', in *South Asian Strategic Issues – Sri Lankan perspectives* (New Delhi : Sage Publications, 1990).

————, 'Internal Politics and Foreign Policy : Prospects for Indo-Sri Lanka Relations in the Nineties in *External Compulsions of South Asian Politics* (New Delhi : Sage Publications, 1993).

Krishna Shetty, K.P., 'Ceylon's Foreign Policy : Emerging Patterns of Non-Alignment', *South Asian Studies*, Vol. 1, No. 1, (April 1966).

Mahadevan, Iravatham, 'An Epigraphic Perspective on the Antiquity of Tamil', *The Hindu*, 24 June 2010.

Mathews Bruce, 'The Situation in Jaffna', *The Round Table,* No. 290 (April 1984).

Meyer, Eric, 'Seeking the Roots of the Tragedy in James Manor (ed.), *Sri Lanka in Change and Crisis* (London : Croom Helm, 1984).

Mitra, N., 'Sri Lanka's Visitor ?' *Strategic Analysis*, Vol. V, No. 7, 15 January (1981).

Mohan Jag, 'The Ceylon Indian Problem – A Resume', *The Indian Express*, 15 January 1954.

Mukherji, K.P., 'Parties and Politics in Ceylon', *Foreign Affairs Report*, Vol. II, (October – November 1953).

Murngensa, Mudalia, N., 'Indo-Sri Lanka Friendship', *Indian Review*, Vol. 74, No. 8 (November 1978).

Muthiah, S., 'Legacy of a Dream', *The Hindu*, 24 January 2010.

Narayanan, V.N., 'Between the Devil and Deep Blue Sea', *The Hindustan Times*, 8 August 1998.

————, 'Separating Tamils from the LTTE', 9 August 1998.

Navaratne, G., 'Nehru – Bandaranaike Discussions', *Eastern World*, Vol. XI, No. 2 (July 1957).

Oberst, Robert, 'Proportional Representation and Electoral System Change in Sri Lanka in James Manor (ed.), *Sri Lanka in Change and Crisis* (London : Croom Helm, 1984).

Obeyesekere, Gananath, 'The Origins and Institutionalisation of Political Violence' in James Manor (ed.).

Perera, A.B., 'Plantation Economy and Colonial Policy in Ceylon', *Ceylon Historical Journal*, Vol. 1, No. 1 (July 1951).

Phadnis, Urmila, 'Ceylon and the Sino-Indian Border Conflict : An Appraisal', *United Asia*, Vol. XV (November 1963).

————, 'The Problem of the People of Indian Origin in Ceylon : Issues and Possible Solutions *International Studies*, Vol. V, No. 1, (April 1964).

————, '1964 Indo-Ceylonese Pact and Stateless Persons in Ceylon', *India Quarterly*, Vol. XIII, No. 4 (October-December 1967).

————, 'Emerging Patterns of Indo-Ceylonese Relations, *India and Foreign Review*, Vol. VII, No. 13, 15 April (1970).

————, 'Indo-Ceylonese Ties After Senanayake's Visit', *Economic and Political Weekly*, Vol. VII, No. 2, (August 1972).

Phadnis Urmila and **Lucy M. Jacob**, 'The New Constitution of Sri Lanka, '*India Quarterly* (October-December 1972).

Radhakrishnan, N. 'The Stateless in Ceylon', *The Indian Year Book of International Affairs*, Vol. XII (1963).

Rao Ramchandra, P.R., 'Citizenship Rights for Ceylon Indians,' *Hindustan Review*, Vol. LXXXV (July 1949).

Ray, Himanshu Prabha, 'Western Indian Ocean and the Early Maritime Links of the Indian Subcontinent', *Indian Economic and Social History Review*, Vol. 31, No. 1 (January-March 1994).

Reddy, Muralidhar B., 'The JVP Makes its Move', *The Hindu*, 25 July 2006.

————, 'War Clouds Darken the Outlook for Peace', 2 August 2006.

————, 'Not a Good Time for Advocates of Peace in Sri Lanka', 12 September 2006.

————, 'In Sri Lanka a Ceasefire Under Siege', 16 March 2007.

————, 'Sri Lanka's Muslims : Out in the Cold', 31 July 2007.

————, 'Full Implement of 13th Amendment Recommended', 24 January 2008.

————, 'Fight Against LTTE and Move Towards Political Solution Should Go Hand in Hand', 26 November 2008.

————, 'The War is Over', *Frontline*, Vol. 26, No. 12, 6-9 June (Chennai : 2009).

Rose, Leo E., 'Nepal, Burma and Ceylon', in Wayne Wilcox, Leo E. Rose and Gavin Boyd (eds.), *Asia and the International System* (Massachusetts : Winthrop Publishers, 1972).

Sahadevan, P., 'Negotiating Peace in Ethnic Wars', *International Studies*, Vol. 43, No. 3 (New Delhi : July – September 2006).

Sekhar, Chandra, 'Indo-Ceylon Relations : A Survey', *Indian and Foreign Review*, Vol. 1 (December 1963).

Sengupta, Bhabani, 'Waiting for India : India's Role as a Regional Power', *Journal of international Affairs* (Newyork), Vol. 29, No. 2 (1975).

Shah, Manbendra, 'Citizenship Problem in Ceylon', *Indian Foreign Affairs*, Vol. XII, No. 5 (May 1964).

Singh, Harnam, 'The Indo-Ceylon Agreement of 1964 : The Question of Separate Electoral Register, *The Indian Journal of International Law*, Vol. V (January 1966).

Sivarajah, A., 'Indo-Sri Lanka Relations and Sri Lanka's Ethnic Crisis : The Tamil Nadu Factor in Shelton U. Kodikara (ed.), *South Asian Strategic Issues - Sri Lankan Perspectives* (New Delhi : Sage Publications, 1990).

Stirrat, R.L. 'The Riots and the Roman Catholic Church in Historical Perspective', in James Manor (ed.), *Sri Lanka in Change and Crisis* (London : Croom Helm, 1984).

Suryanarayan, V., 'Explaining Prabakaran's Persistence Defiance, *The Hindu*, 21 December 2007.

Swamy, Subramanian, 'Sri Lanka Crisis and India's Options', *The Hindu*, 29 November 2006.

Swaminathan, M.S. 'Sri Lanka :Task of Livelihood Rehabilitation, *The Hindu,* 16 June 2009.

Thoudaman, S., 'Ceylon : An Emerging Nation', *United Asia*, Vol. XV, No. 2 (February 1963)

Venkarta Rao, 'Ceylonese Stateless and India', *Swarajya*, Vol. IX, 28 November 1964.

Vishwanathan, V.N., 'Indo-Sri Lanka Relations', *India Quarterly*, Vol. XLVI, No. 1 (New Delhi : Indian Journal of World Affairs, January-March 1990).

Wickremesinghe, Ranil, 'The Way to Resolve Sri Lanka's Political Crisis', *The Hindu*, 6 April 2007.

Wilson, Jeyaratnam, A., 'The Tamil Federal Party in Ceylon Politics', *Journal of Commonwealth Political Studies*, Vol. IV, No. 2.

————, 'Race, Religion, Language and Caste in the Subnationalism of Sri Lanka', in Michael Roberts (ed.), *Collective Identities, Nationalism and Protest in Modern Sri Lanka* (Colombo : Marga Institute, 1979).

Newspapers

Amrit Bazar Patrika (Calcutta).
The Ceylon Daily News (Ceylon).
Daily News (Colombo).
The Financial Times (London).
The Hindu (Madras).
The Hindustan Times (New Delhi).
The Indian Express (Delhi).
The National Herald (New Delhi).
The Newyork Times (Newyork).
The Patriot (New Delhi).
The Statesman (Delhi).
The Times of India (New Delhi).
The Tribune (Chandigarh).

Periodicals

American Political Science Review (Newyork).
Asian Survey (New Delhi).
Eastern Economists (Bombay).
Economic and Political Weekly (Bombay).
Foreign Affairs (Newyork).
Foreign Policy Report (New Delhi).
Frontline (Chennai).
India Today (New Delhi).
Indian Journal of Political Science (Hyderabad).
International Studies (New Delhi).
Journal of Commonwealth Political Studies.
Political Science Quarterly (Newyork).
South Asia Politics (New Delhi).
Tamil Times (London).
World Today (London).

INDEX

V

W

Y